Advance Praise for *The Fighter Within*

"Christopher Olech revels in the success of a life fully improved by hard work, commitment, risk and sacrifice—a life improved by martial arts."
—Elias Cepeda, MMA & boxing writer for Yahoo! Sports

"Olech strips away the cameras, fame, money and fans and takes us on a journey through the explosive sport of MMA." —Jason Chambers, actor, mixed martial artist, fight commentator for One Championship, UFC Fight Pass commentator and star of *Human Weapon*

"Christopher Olech reminds us that—regardless of background—the study and pursuit of martial arts can move mountains in your personal and business life."
—Bobby Razak, producer, director and founder of TapouT Films

"Christopher Olech put his heart and soul into this project—it's a book not to be missed." —Tony Reid, owner of Rattling the Cage, contributor to *Fighters Only*, host of ESPN 92.3 WVSL

"Olech brings the average reader into the world of Mixed Martial Arts that few, outside of the realm of its elite participants, will ever experience. A truly uplifting memoir, with a brawler's backbone." —Conner Cordova, MMA journalist

"This book should be on the shortlist of reading material for all MMA fans."
—Mookie Alexander, staff writer for BloodyElbow.com

"Christopher Olech shares an amazingly personal and heroic journey in martial arts and in life, and his action-packed competitive journey to Grapplers Quest."
—Brian Cimins, founder of Grapplers Quest

"Olech left his job, hit the road, and ventured into the savage world of MMA. Fortunately, he came back alive to tell of everything he saw and learned in this book. Read it cover to cover." —Marcelo Dunlop, editor of *GracieMag*

"This book helps people understand the new game of martial arts."
—Grandmaster Toddy, UFC trainer and coach on Oxygen's *Fight Girls* reality television show

"Martial arts has been my passion since I was 13 years old. I always enjoy exploring other journeys and perspectives, a ...   s a unique look into the sport." —Mark H   teran

"Just like any great fighter, this book is all about heart."
—Phoenix Carnevale, producer of everything martial arts, fight commentator, wise-cracking nerd

"The Fighter Within is a wonderful collection of essays on the personal journeys of several world class athletes and inspiring individuals. A must-read for any serious MMA fan."
—Brian J D'Souza, author of Pound for Pound: The Modern Gladiators of Mixed Martial Arts

"This is a knockout book for everyone looking to succeed in business, life and fighting."
—Tom DeBlass, UFC veteran, Bellator fighter and BJJ black belt

"A great book for MMA/UFC fans and also for martial artists!"
—Mike Smith ("Blacksmith"), Kyokushin Karate black belt and world-class boxing trainer

"As a martial-artist-turned-MMA-media-member, Christopher Olech views the sport from both sides of the cage. While telling the tales of the titans of the sport, he inevitably penned a tome with a moral."
—Jason Kelly, co-host of Rear Naked Choke Radio, staff writer for Combat Press

"This book gives an insider's look at the world of MMA. Christopher Olech does a fantastic job showcasing what it truly means to be a mixed martial artist."
—Chris Horodecki, veteran of WEC, Bellator and IFL

"Christopher Olech is able to take you deep within the world of MMA to see what it really takes to be a fighter. If you are a fan of MMA, you will be a fan of this book."
—Adam Guillen Jr., writer for mmamania.com

"Christopher takes you deep into the heart of MMA. This is a great read."
—Jeff Phillips, owner of Beardo Wear

"Christopher Olech provides an entertaining glimpse into a mixed martial artist's heart, soul and psyche."
—Bear Frazer, lifestyle editor of Fight! magazine

"Christopher Olech's great new book has a really nice foreword, written by a very good-looking guy; Bas Rutten! It's an enjoyable read about a guy whose inner search leads him to MMA and martial arts in general, and he meets a lot of wonderful people along the way."
—Bas Rutten, UFC heavyweight champion, MMA legend, actor, author and television personality

THE FIGHTER WITHIN

EVERYONE HAS A FIGHT

Insights into the minds
and souls of true champions

CHRISTOPHER OLECH

Foreword by **BAS RUTTEN**

TUTTLE Publishing

Tokyo | Rutland, Vermont | Singapore

Please note that the publisher and author of this book are NOT RESPONSIBLE in any manner whatsoever for any injury that may result from practicing the techniques described within. Martial arts training can be dangerous—both to you and to others—if not practiced safely. If you're in doubt as to how to proceed or whether your practice is safe, consult with a trained martial arts teacher before beginning. Since the physical activities described herein may be too strenuous in nature for some readers, it is also essential that a physician be consulted prior to training.

Published by Tuttle Publishing, an imprint of Periplus Editions (HK) Ltd.

www.tuttlepublishing.com

Copyright © 2016 Christopher Olech
Front cover photography by Ryan Loco
Back cover photography by Hector Quintero

Library of Congress cataloging in process
ISBN 978-0-8048-4595-3

Distributed by

North America, Latin America & Europe
Tuttle Publishing
364 Innovation Drive
North Clarendon,
VT 05759-9436 U.S.A.
Tel: (802) 773-8930; Fax: (802) 773-6993
info@tuttlepublishing.com
www.tuttlepublishing.com

Asia Pacific
Berkeley Books Pte. Ltd.
61 Tai Seng Avenue #02-12
Singapore 534167
Tel: (65) 6280-1330; Fax: (65) 6280-6290
inquiries@periplus.com.sg; www.periplus.com

Japan
Tuttle Publishing
Yaekari Building, 3rd Floor
5-4-12 Osaki, Shinagawa-ku
Tokyo 141 0032
Tel: (81) 3 5437-0171; Fax: (81) 3 5437-0755
sales@tuttle.co.jp; www.tuttle.co.jp

Indonesia
PT Java Books Indonesia
Jl. Rawa Gelam IV No. 9
Kawasan Industri Pulogadung
Jakarta 13930
Tel: (62) 21 4682-1088; Fax: (62) 21 461-0206
crm@periplus.co.id; www.periplus.com

First edition
20 19 18 17 16   5 4 3 2 1   1510MP
Printed in Singapore

TUTTLE PUBLISHING® is a registered trademark of Tuttle Publishing, a division of Periplus Editions (HK) Ltd.

TABLE OF CONTENTS

Foreword

Chris Olech comes from a middle-class Polish family who settled in Toronto, Canada looking for a better life.

He enjoyed a normal childhood, delivering newspapers, helping out at his parents' deli and playing soccer in high school, much like my own life.

He would meet the love of his life, Beata, when she was hired to work at the deli in the wake of his parents' divorce.

Chris' introduction to martial arts would come as a result of one of his friends' tales from his many trips to Thailand. Chris was especially captivated with his buddy's stories about Thailand's national sport, Muay Thai, the "King of All Martial Arts." It's also known as "The Science of 8 Limbs" due to the fact you can use your hands, elbows, knees & feet as weapons. It is one of the most brutal forms of martial arts.

Inspired by the stories he'd heard about the "Mecca of Muay Thai," Chris signed up for lessons at a local gym. Weeks later he signed up for a seminar put on by UFC Hall of Famer Matt Hughes and thus began his love affair with all things martial arts!

He took an MMA instructor's course (where he learned he can vomit from exhaustion), he mined Gold in his division at a Grapplers Quest tourney in Canada (submission grappling), and he even competed in Thai Boxing to find out how it would "feel" to fight!

All of his experiences peaked his curiosity. "What makes a fighter tick?" "Why did you start fighting?" "Where does your love of coaching come from?" He wanted to delve into the mental aspects & the evolution of training methodology as it pertains to martial arts and thus began the journey that led to the publishing of this book. For many of my peers & myself, the spiritual godfather of mixed martial arts, Bruce Lee, inspired us, but what/who inspired the younger generation?

I had the pleasure of meeting Chris a few years ago at a Paradise Warrior retreat seminar where I was one of the guest trainers. Chris has an affable personality, and his curious nature allows him to ask great questions.

So, this book is all about martial artists, kickboxers, mixed martial artists, BJJ practitioners, boxers, and, of course, their coaches.

From A-damek (a champion boxer) to Z-ahabi (acclaimed MMA trainer), and many others in between, he has interviewed them all!

Great work, Chris!

Godspeed
Bas Rutten

• Three times undefeated King of Pancrase World Champion
• Undefeated UFC Heavyweight Champion
• UFC Hall of Fame inductee
• Fifth-degree Kyokushin Karate
• Second-degree Tae Kwon Do
• Second-degree Shin Tai Karate
• Commentator / Actor

Chapter One

THE MEAT GRINDER

"It's not the size of the dog in the fight, it's the size of the fight in the dog."
—Mark Twain

The bell rang, and the sound of cheers faded deep into my psyche as I raised the sixteen-ounce gloves up to my chin, taking in the smell of used leather and sweat. My breath steadied and my eyes focused until I absorbed a hard right hook and thunderous leg kick that elevated my lead leg clean off the mat. The stark realization hit me like a speeding freight train; a mix of emotions comprised of fear, anxiety, delight, and pride swirled in the upper tier of my stomach, eating at my throat. I was in a fight!

My opponent, seasoned and much stronger, pressured me as I tapped him with weak combinations, either out of fear or from the extreme adrenaline infusion I had just endured. My endorphins were shooting from synapse to synapse, and my six months of training in Muay Thai had not prepared me for the stresses or accumulation of adrenaline before the fight, let alone the effects of depleting that adrenaline, which left me feeling drained of energy and hopeless.

I faintly heard my corner yelling in the background, through my barotrauma, better known as ear popping. My heart rate was vividly audible through my muffed hearing as it raced like a machine gun spraying bullets at the range, my skin wet and clammy with sweat, and my mind pulled in a multitude of directions. I thought to myself, "What are they saying?"

My corner yelled again, "Hit him harder, Chris! Hit him harder!"

I started throwing faster combinations, landing a few hard shots, but my opponent, at least twenty pounds heavier than I, was experienced and thus able to cut the ring much better than me. He ended his combinations with hard-hitting kicks. I was not fast enough to check them, so I absorbed each shot from his sculpted, tree-trunk legs.

The bell rang to signify the end of the round; "Could it have been that quick?" Moments felt like an eternity in the fight, but once the round ended, it felt like we had just started exchanging. It was an eerie feeling; I had lost all track of time and place. If not for the sixteen-ounce pillows on my hands, I would have pinched myself just to check if this was all part of a surreal dream.

My corner men attempted to encourage me between rounds, but in all honesty, they were just as green as I was. They were my training partners; my coaches were nowhere to be found. It dawned on me at that moment: they had already held the amateur bouts. That explained why I was fighting a guy that looked like the bodybuilder version of Rob Zombie with seven years of experience in the fight game. Our match was jammed between the pro fights—the promoter decided to pull a fast one on me, and I was the sacrificial lamb for everyone's entertainment. I was thrown into this predicament as my first hoorah—my very first fight.

I glared across the ring at my opponent who sported dreadlocks and a thick goatee that touched his barrel chest, his face emblazoned with a menacing stare. I wiped my mind clear of the flooding self-doubt. I tried to take deep breaths, feeling my lungs experience difficulty in doing what they had done for my entire life. The harsh gasping for air was expanding my chest, pressing my ribs against my skin as it became more and more difficult to relax. I thought to myself "I'm better than this. This guy has nothing on me!" Almost getting disgusted with myself, I was getting myself amped up.

We went out to the center of the ring and rhythmically danced the oldest, most savage tango known to humans, bringing our basic instincts to the surface. I tried to add speed to my combinations, and he veered backward each time I connected; it must have been doing the trick. When we tied up, he grabbed me in the plum clinch, pulling the back of my head toward his chest while trapping my head between his elbows, and diligently proceeded to bombard my torso with a barrage of knees. I ate a couple to the face, and he received a stern warning from the referee, as it was against the rules to knee the face during this smoker of an event.

I only knew of one way out of the plum clinch at that point, and that was to put my glove on his face and muscle my way out of it. He must have determined that this would be my undoing, so he proceeded to tie me up again. Yet again, I ate a knee to the face, becoming furious at that point. I caught his leg, placed my other fist in his face, and forcefully threw him over to put his knees to the mat.

The momentum swung my way, and I felt great—but only for that split second, as the lactic acid had engulfed my body with a sharp pain. I was exhausted. My mind was processing what needed to be done, but my body could not carry out the acts. That was another feeling I had never felt before; it took two rounds to finally get loosened up, only to be met by a physical wall that my body could not surmount. The round was called to an end, and I thanked God that my opponent was just as drained as I was.

The beginning of the third round was painfully slow; both of us heavyweights had expelled all of our stamina. We circled a lot, both hesitant to start something our bodies could not commit to. When we did exchange, there was no power or speed. I learned a hard lesson that day, which was to never let my guard down. He twisted his lead foot and torqued his hips. My mind predicted that a whopping right hook would be coming my way, so I decided to weave beneath it. As I tried to duck toward my left, I lowered my glove from my cheek because of fatigue, and to my surprise I ducked directly into his oncoming torpedo shin. My face did a superb job of absorbing all of his force, and all that was missing were those cartoon birds flying around my head as the final cherry on top.

My left ear buzzed for a split second, but I straightened out and got out of harm's way as fast as possible by virtue of pure instinct. I learned another fact that day: I had a granite chin, as I was perfectly fine after absorbing a colossal tree trunk to the jaw and ear. I quickly glanced through the ropes, bypassing everyone in the crowd and focusing on my wife; I gave her a quick look to show her, "Hey, it's all good!"

With the adrenaline coursing through my veins, I really did not feel much pain in the bout. My brain was registering the impacts but not communicating the information to my nervous system in the form of the sensation of pain. We clinched a lot in the third and final round, and I ate another knee to the face for which the referee deducted a point from my opponent. We ended the match swinging at each other. When the bell rang, I had a cleansing feeling of accomplishment. Frankly speaking, I got my butt kicked, but I lasted all three rounds with an experienced fighter. The referee raised both of our hands in the air in the showing of a draw as I clenched my fist and thanked God for the opportunity. I was surfing the heavens as my heart fluttered an extra beat; I was forever hooked on the fight game.

Chapter Two

LOVE ME OR HATE ME

"The pain you feel today is the strength you feel tomorrow. For every challenge encountered, there is opportunity for growth."　　**—Unknown**

I was born on a day that showcased Mother Nature's power, as a massive snowstorm blanketed Toronto to the point that a large number of roads were closed. That was the day I decided to join the myriad of others on this sphere we call Earth, and I like to think that I've been carrying positive chaos with me ever since.

My parents are middle-class immigrants from Poland who nearly nested in Austria as they sought a better future for me. My dad, Stan Olech, came from a small town in Poland called Godziszow, where farming was everything. He learned the importance of hard work very early, tending to the animals and fields every day. My grandfather was always out in the fields and was very well-known in the small town. His functional strength working on the farm was built over a lifetime; he was known to have abnormal strength, although he never picked up a barbell in his entire life.

My mom, Elizabeth Olech, was born into a large family with three other siblings, so the house was always buzzing. Her father was a police officer, as was my great-grandfather, who was a police chief. In those days, there was a big problem with the Ukrainian mafia and their rampant criminality, from petty robberies to killing innocent victims. My great-grandfather was a dedicated family man and a police chief attempting to better the community, making safety a priority.

One cold night, when he was doing paperwork at the station, some Ukrainian bandits loaded with heavy machine guns tried to take over the police station only to be met with hard resistance from the police officers in the building. What ensued for less than ten minutes was a bloodbath of horror movie proportions that took the lives of many great police officers, leaving behind a trail of pain for their wives, husbands, parents, and children.

One of the brave officers who lost their lives that night was my great-grandfather who had died doing what he believed—protecting and serving his community and doing what he thought was right. The meaningless tragedy is remembered today with a monument bearing all of the officers' names who lost their lives that night.

When my parents married and decided to have a baby, they formulated an action plan: Escape from the daily grind of a communist regime in hopes of giving me a better life with more possibilities. They decided to settle in Toronto, where a large part of my family had already been living for years. It was the 1980s, a time during which the worker had a voice in the company, pay was high, and new businesses were opening around every corner. My dad was employed as a woodworker, making great money; we lived as a cohesive, loving family with my pit bull, Spotty, as my "brother."

From an early age, my parents instilled qualities in me that I am grateful to have today. They taught me the honor of hard work and that a good work ethic will get you places. They also taught me that the values of love, compassion, and respect come from the heart, as well as to always "be yourself," regardless of your situation or location, and to be guided by virtue. At the same time, I received the "no-bullshit gene"; to put it simply, there are a lot of people in this world, and not all of them have my best interests at heart, so if I have to let the "other side" out to protect my family, I don't think twice about it.

My childhood was perfect; I played sports, had all the toys in the world, and lived in a stable home. I loved to read, and I listened to music all the time. I would draw and be creative, in order to unleash my over-worked imagination, as I lived in my own world half of the time. I was a typical kid who idolized Batman, Superman, Jean Claude Van Damme, and, of course, Arnold Schwarzenegger, and I loved my share of horror movies, including *A Nightmare on Elm Street*, featuring Freddy Krueger. I will not go into detail regarding the "wannabe Spiderman on the roof" fiasco. I also played a lot of soccer, as we always had a park or fields near each house in which we lived. I also loved professional wrestling, had the headbands, and would pump iron with my dad; of course, I used little plastic weights.

The first time I got into a situation involving physical confrontation was actually the year we moved to Poland, when I was in kindergarten. The teacher's son, who was in her class, was feared by the other students for two reasons: he was big and his mom was our teacher. If there was ever a conflict, we assumed that we would be the ones to get in trouble, regardless of who was at fault. He was obnoxious and would break toys that belonged to other kids for his own amusement.

One day during recess (I honestly cannot remember for what reason, but there were a million), we were nose-to-nose, yelling at each other as a crowd manifested around us. I remember pushing him down as I lunged and proceeded with some ground and pound, looping my arms as he assumed the turtle position. I then felt my ear being pulled with force by one of the teachers on duty as I was yanked to the office. I remember the feeling of accomplishment that day; I felt like the king of the hill up until the point I got in trouble. I was sure there would be additional repercussions at home, but I was met with acceptance from my parents.

Occasionally, other kids would mistake my kindness for weakness, but when necessary I would let my voice be heard. I would let a lot slide before resorting to my vast vocabulary to defuse a situation, especially in the diverse city of Toronto. The city is a melting pot of all cultures and personalities, and the elementary school I attended was rough, with gangs and even drugs. It was a Catholic elementary school with some great teachers, but the lack of staff, the old facilities, and the location combined to form a breeding ground of tough situations.

In eighth grade, my best friend's parents decided to move to London, Ontario, which is approximately two hours away from Toronto. We had the idea of convincing my parents to move to London, too. My parents helped my best friend's parents with their move, and when they saw the "forest city," a smaller city of approximately 300,000 people and plenty of greenery, they decided that family life would be better here. Just like that, my parents were making plans to move to London, Ontario.

Since the age of thirteen years I was working in one way or another, from delivering papers to helping my parents at their European deli. I would do everything from taking orders, stocking, cutting meat, cleaning, and, of course, serving our customers. The first years, I really enjoyed working there, but when my parents would fight I dreaded it, especially when I was busy playing soccer, doing homework, attending Polish school, or working in the deli; I was stretched thin. I was now the co-captain of the school soccer team, which meant more responsibility.

After finishing after-school soccer practice, I would walk three and a half miles to the deli and work until around 9:00 p.m. At home, I would do homework and watch television, then sleep to prepare for the next full day. On Saturdays after Polish school, I worked in the deli until closing time, pulling six days per week on this schedule.

Now a senior in high school, I needed cash. I got a job washing dishes at the golf club across the street from the school. Three of my good friends were already working there, and the pay was fairly good. I added the job to my already full plate, and I'm glad I did. On busy nights, we worked hard, but it was fun in a way, especially when my friends were working with me. As kitchen staff, we assisted in food preparation and closing duties. As a reward for my hard work, I was always assigned to the Sunday shift. This shift was the best, as I would get all the leftover buffet food, and trust me—it was well worth it. All the other dishwashers wanted to work the Sunday shift, but I was the one getting it.

All of the hours spent working kept me insulated to some degree from the degenerating politics in my parents' relationship. Yet I went through a lot of stuff that I pray no one else ever goes through. A lot was said and done, preying on my soul and pushing me to the depths of a dark world. It was even more difficult because I looked up to my parents, and their values are instilled in me even today. Suddenly, my entire world had been turned upside down with what seemed like the snap of a finger.

I remember sitting on the couch at the country club, waiting for my shift to start, and thinking, "What did I do in life to deserve this? Why me, God? Why?" The kids at school had money and easy lives, while I had to completely run on overdrive for most of my life with my family dynamics in ruins. I had to fight to get everything—I had to fight just to exist—so why was it that others had so much handed to them? I sat on the couch where millionaires came to relax and thought to myself, "I am smart, athletic, and, most importantly, good-hearted. I put the needs of others in front of my own and yet I have to struggle with my family life and finances. This just sucks!"

As the months went by, I was working out every day and putting on some serious weight. I started training when I was sixteen, adding forty pounds onto my frame. I worked out for an hour and a half a day, even after work, I took vitamins, ate like a mule, and drank protein shakes religiously after every workout. As a senior, I was a chubby 245 pounds; I had gone from the scrawny guy to the big guy. I was strong and benched over 280 pounds, shoulder pressed ninety-pound dumbbells, but I had a round face and a bit of a gut. I told everyone that I'd be a monster once I lost fifteen to twenty pounds. However, cardio was not my strong suit back then, and I did not lose the excess weight.

I think the weight was a subconscious symbol of pain in life, seeing my parents' marriage fail and my mom battle with her personal demons. My grades slipped to the point where I was barely attending classes, showing up only to ace the tests so that I wouldn't fail the class. I chose fun over responsibilities, and even when my entire world was crumbling, I was still somehow slowly pushing through. Some days, I immersed myself in movies and books to escape.

Whatever obstacles presented themselves, I lived through more drama in my first twenty years of life than most people do their entire lives. Somehow, it made me stronger, and maybe wiser to some extent. My mom battled with alcoholism. The bottle consumed her every thought and stole her from me. To make matters worse, my dad left her when she was at her lowest point, leaving me to attempt to save my mom on my own when I was sixteen years old.

My dad moved on and started a new family. I wasn't sure how to approach this situation. Needless to say, we've had a hot-cold relationship ever since. He even left the business to my mom and began working at a factory, cutting all ties with her.

I tried helping as much as I could at the deli, but it wasn't enough, and we needed more help. My mom could not work every day, as her health was in decline. At my high school graduation, no one from my family attended as I received my diploma, and I cannot lie: it hurt.

My mom then hired a gorgeous girl to help us out at the deli on a part-time basis. Beata was a smart, good-looking, brown-eyed girl. I remember her coming to the store with her parents on occasion, but now that she was working here, it made work a lot of fun! Her long, dark hair and tanned, smooth skin was more than eye candy for me! Finally, a curve in the road of life to be thankful for, although being older than me I figured she was way out of my league. I thought I didn't stand a chance. We talked for hours about anything and everything. She was so down-to-earth and knowledgeable; it was a breath of fresh air. I found myself having fun for the first time in a long time.

There were times when the deli was really prospering, as Beata and I were outgoing and had good rapport with the customers. Our products were from select distributors known to be of high quality, even though we had to drive 250 miles each week for the items. We tried desperately to get rid of the vultures picking away at the business. My mother's drinking buddies brought her alcohol and then took three times the value in products, free of charge. They were supposed to be friends, and this angered me. We had to deal with many kinds of people. Being 240 pounds helped to get the message across to various people to stay away.

I also started my college education with the Human Services Foundation to learn the art of dealing with people in service fields. I excelled in psychology but did not much care for school. With a distraction like Beata working alongside me, I skipped more than a few classes. After months of working together, we finally started dating.

That period of time was life-changing for me, as I had more fun than I could re-member and my confidence began to soar again. We frequently traveled to Toronto and Niagara Falls just to get out of the city. To me, that was more than I needed, to see and experience the world with the prettiest girl in the world. It's funny that most good things in my life have happened when I wasn't searching for them—case in point with Beata. She really is my angel from heaven.

My dad was working at a factory making good money, and because I was looking for work after college to start my own life, it was a quick fix. The factory was hiring summer students for $7.00 less per hour than they paid regular workers, which was still a lot. I accepted the job in a heartbeat and got to work. The conditions were terrible. It was hot, smoky, hazy, polluted, and it entailed hard manual labor with some power-tripping supervisors added to the mix.

A month into the job, I was more than acclimated and a productive employee, so much so that they offered me a full-time regular employee position. I could not com-plain about the job, as it paid well, but the beginning was hard, as with any new begin-ning. I woke up in the middle of the night to cramping forearms and hands, and every day I blew from my nose black sludge mixed with blood.

Beata and I had a plan: work for about a year, bank the money, and I would become a police officer. For a number of reasons it never happened. It was easy to get sucked into the thought of big money even though I had much bigger plans for myself. I got used to working the three-shift rotation, meaning each week we switched from working mornings (my favorite) to afternoons (my least favorite) and nights. After a year, I started working on the newer automotive line, which was easier and involved less lifting and welding. The months quickly turned into years.

As my relationship with Beata blossomed, my family life was still in the toilet. I was still trying to help as much as I could with my mom and the deli, but things were quickly declining. My mom's health was getting worse, and even her doctors weren't doing much to help the root cause: alcoholism. I wish I would have done more, maybe by taking her to Alcoholics Anonymous if she would have agreed, but she likely would not have. I had dozens of heartfelt conversations with my mom where I begged her to stop drinking for her sake, as well as for my sake. It was always the same, we would break down, my true mom would come through, and then a day later she would be reaching for the bottle again. It was becoming the norm for her to be in and out of the hospital at that point.

My dad and I were constantly at each other's necks, figuratively speaking. He gave me yelling lectures and went on rants that made no sense, offering no real insight or help. I think he was taking out his anxieties and regrets on me, and I was done taking it, as I had for too long. I was my own man now, and I still showed respect, but also stood up for what I thought was right.

It was a windy November day in 2003 when I received a phone call from the hospital while I was getting ready for my afternoon shift at the factory. The nurse on the other end said "I'm not sure how to say this, but I really think you should be here with your mom. She's not doing so well, and we had to take her to the intensive care unit." I remember a million thoughts racing through my mind, but I knew my mom was the strongest person I had ever known, so it could not be so bad, could it?

At the hospital, I was told that my mom had lost eight pints of blood and that they continued pumping more into her. She was losing blood at an alarming rate. A medical device was her one last hope. I was a complete mess; it all seemed like the worst nightmare in the world, and it honestly felt unreal.

My dad and aunts, accompanied by cousins from Mississauga, came to the hospital. Of course, Beata was by my side from the beginning. I spoke to my mom on the hospital table for as long as I could, thinking that maybe she could hear me. The doctors asked if they could switch off the machines that were keeping her alive. Nothing had helped, and it was only a matter of time. I would never agree to it and thought that maybe she would still wake up; maybe by a miracle everything would be fine, just maybe. I clung to the hope with every part of my being as I prayed for her. After all we had gone through, the mother who had given me life and taught me all that is good could not leave like this… no way.

No matter how badly we want something, God often has other plans. The electro-cardiographic heart monitor showed that she had flatlined; Elizabeth Olech had passed away from this Earth to the next. I lost my mom. I thought I knew sadness, defeat, anguish, and pain before that point, but I quickly learned that what I felt previously was nothing compared to this. As if by calling, it had been raining that day, and I believe that it was a sign of a great human being, a messenger, and soldier of God leaving our human existence. I knew that angels were crying over her departure that day.

The strangest thing about it all was that I felt an emotional boost for some reason. I think it was my mom's way of giving me strength. I took time to grieve and organize my mom's townhouse and funeral. I had been calling work to let them know I would be out, but through the grapevine I heard that even though I was a hard worker, they were thinking of letting me go, as I had being calling in for over a week. I was supposed to fill out a bereavement form, but no one had told me that. I was nineteen and not well-versed in labor laws. I was learning that when a person is at their most vulnerable and down, people tend to take free shots and kick them. I filled out the form and proceeded forward through this entire mess that had ravaged my life.

Hundreds of people attended the funeral to pay their respects, and it made me feel good that she had affected so many people. My cousin approached me afterward and told me that my mom was in a better place and that her time on Earth had a bigger meaning, which was me. She also told me that I was destined for something big and that everyone saw it. I thanked her and started thinking differently; maybe there was something good I could do in her name.

Years later, as I write this, I believe that my mom is in a better place, where she cannot feel pain or hurt. I think she watches over me and gives me the strength needed here on Earth. I cherish all the good moments we had together. I try to make her proud of me through my everyday actions, using all of the lessons she taught me.

I began volunteering a lot more, taking on many activities to help people and animals whenever I could. I was not only a board member for a few organizations, but also helped out with many volunteer days whenever my calendar allowed it.

Every one of the events I went through in my life, good or bad, shaped and molded me. My good nature, respectful approach toward people, mental strength, and never-say-die attitude are all attributable to my upbringing and milestones in life. We all have a story; we all have a battle to fight and goals that we are striving for in the rat race of life. I had many forces pulling me to martial arts and pushing me to uncover the mixed martial arts (MMA) world as I set out in search for the truth.

Why do we do this? What is it that draws us to something that can hurt us? Why do we deliberately put ourselves in the path of danger? What makes us different from so many others? I believe that this is rooted in the many layers of both the psyche and the heart. The same questions can be posed to great soldiers that volunteer to participate in wars around the world, fighting for our freedom. From the adrenaline junkie to the deep camaraderie built within your team, you give time, sweat, and blood for the mats. There is respect and a bond with your opponent, regardless of whether you win or lose. They too had a path that led them to stare at you once the buzzer or bell rings; you will both leave it all in the fight to see who is better that day. The feeling of getting that win and of having all those bumps and aching muscles pays off. Finally reaching the top of the mountain makes it all worthwhile.

So, I ask you: what is your fight? What is your place in life? Truly ponder this question; use it and the humility of martial arts to create a better you, whether it be with your family, your friends, your work, or anything else. Let it take over your thoughts and use it to set those goals that you can systematically achieve over time. By the time you reach the final chapter of this book, you will see that these processes hold true for some of the best in the world. I've traveled the world to train in many areas of mixed martial arts with some of the world's greatest names and champions. Their stories are shared here.

This is a journey that, as a fan, makes me giddy with excitement. I have done my best to shed light on these people that we idolize on television, along with detailing who they actually are, how they train, why they train, and what they do to be the best. Peer into them as individuals as well as martial artists. I sought the answers to the questions posed above and attempted to uncover the information that every fan wants to know. I also trained myself as I prepared for fights and competitions, rolling and sparring with the best, changing cities, even countries in search of the best fighters, coaches, and gyms the world has to offer. I invite you to take this journey with me. I am prepared to fight—no one has said that life is a bed of roses, right?

Chapter Three

THE DOG DAYS OF SUFFERING

"If you have built castles in the air, your work need not be lost; that is where they should be. Now put foundations under them." **—Henry David Thoreau**

There I stood, hunched over the dirty yellow railing, hypnotized through the smoke by the automated movements of expensive welding robots. Despite the treacherous locale, I was mesmerized by the solitude of my thoughts when I was ripped back into reality. "Hey, Chris. Let's go." It was my close friend Jeff Phillips, keeping an eye on me so that I would not get reprimanded by the lazy supervisors if they happened to leave their air conditioned bear cave offices, as they did once in a blue moon. "Here we go," I motioned as I turned back to the production line. Looking at the truck frame that this robotic pulley line fed us from a seemingly never-ending supply, I had the duty of inspecting and patching up all holes, imperfections, and/or deficiencies in the frame.

No customer wanted to buy an award-winning heavy-duty truck only to have the part of the truck that needed to be the strongest fail due to human error. Picking up the weld gun in heat in excess of 100°F (40°C), wearing my mandatory long-sleeved uniform, work boots, heavy gloves, and a welding helmet, I welded 380 to 450 frames in one shift. I took a deep breath and thought to myself, "Man, there's got to be more to life than this crap!" Given the forty-five-minute drive to and from work and the dreaded midnight shift that I was privileged to work, I was like a zombie living in a hell on Earth.

I thanked Jeff, palmed the button to let the frame proceed down the never-ending line, and went back to the railing, which, sadly, was my safety zone where I could talk to Jeff; this was one aspect that helped make work better. Jeff was 5' 11" with dirty-brown hair, and he did well with the ladies. A world of knowledge was hidden within his eyes, and a very friendly demeanor made him the popular guy. He was one of my best friends, and was a self-made man to say the least. When he had an idea, he dreamed big and went for it, regardless the thousands of miles or obstacles he had to surpass in order to accomplish his goals.

He had traveled the world, and I do not mean that he stayed at five-star hotels, but in the jungles of Thailand riding on elephants and the wild rainforests of Costa Rica for months on end. He, too, viewed our current employer in the same light; it was great for a lot of people, and we could not complain about the wages or benefits. When it came right down to it, that's what kept us there, but we felt like wild birds that needed to soar and capture prey to feed our innate animal instincts. Instead, we were completely locked in a cage in which we could not even stretch our wings.

There I was, standing in a factory, not pleased with the work or safety of the place, and I would learn that things could operate better. I read about a massive union, called LIUNA, that encompassed over 500,000 members in North America and ran like a well-oiled machine, covering the construction and waste management sectors. I had learned that they actually cared for their members, as business manager for local 1059 Jim MacKinnon would later tell this author, "We listen carefully to our members' needs, our representatives have direct connections to the many new Canadians that form our union. We are very pragmatic and work closely with our signatory employers for the health, wellness, financial remuneration, pensions, and benefits that our members need."

They ran a tight ship, in contrast to what I was used to, and safety was paramount. While we received our training for welding at the factory out of a barn (yes a barn!), LIUNA on the other hand had state-of-the-art buildings to train their members. They also would give back to the community, as Jim added, "Ontario locals give between one and two million dollars per year to charitable organizations and also perform work with their members for charities." There was contrast in safety, unions, and production, but I did not know any better.

Jeff told me that he had been planning a big, three-month endeavor to Thailand. He read books about Buddhism and travel during lulls while we waited for the next frame to arrive. He told me about the culture, land, people, and scenery, and about Muay Thai. I was mesmerized by a world so different from the one we were used to, which consisted of work, my beautiful wife (fiancée-to-be at the time, who kept me sane), television, and the incessant day-in, day-out cycle. Here was something new and revitalizing, something that captured my imagination, and I ran with it a mile a minute. He told me about his plans for a trip into the jungle where he would ride elephants, ride down the river on floats constructed of bamboo, and reach an Indian village that 99.9% of the outside world had never ventured to.

He then started to tell me about Muay Thai, the art of eight limbs, where you may box or kick box, and if that is not enough, you can use your sharp elbows and knees to release a melee of strikes on your opponent. He told me that Muay Thai originated in

Thailand and that kids, bred to be fighters, could have over 100 fights already under their belt by the age of fifteen!

I knew a little bit about the sport, as I had been watching the Ultimate Fighting Championship (UFC) since the first event when Royce Gracie did the unthinkable by winning a tournament in no-holds-barred fighting when he was the skinniest competitor, representing the art of Brazilian jiu-jitsu against many other forms of martial arts and against some bigger, more muscular guys. I remember being young, still living in Toronto and watching the first UFC fight, glued to the TV. Being a fan of professional wrestling since I was able to watch television, it was natural to transition into a fan of mixed martial arts in which any martial art was fair game in competition, including Muay Thai.

I vividly remember driving home that morning from work, not being able to get the art of Muay Thai out of my head. Once home, I couldn't sleep, I jumped onto the Internet, searched for Muay Thai, and was bombarded by millions of pages worth of info and videos. I kept coming across a legendary kickboxer by the name of Rob Kaman. As fate would have it, both Jeff and I would be in his company for days on end, years later.

I was continuing to work through the same tedious cycle of life, getting five-minute heat breaks when the smoke-filled factory reached over 113°F (45°C), creating a sauna-like setting. All I could think about was my escape: Muay Thai. The days seemed to flow together like water as the dog days of summer weighed heavily on my shoulders. I needed an "out," some kind of yin to the yang that I was living, something of import to supplement my great family life and to counter-balance the tedious hard labor I was accustomed to. Close to the end of summer, I picked up the local newspaper; little did I know, it would change my life forever.

I read about a local mixed martial arts club that was putting on a big seminar for a local women's charity with Matt Hughes, who at the time was the reigning welterweight champion of the UFC. Matt Hughes was a force within the UFC, a devastating wrestler who was known for his vicious slams, crafty ground game, and sheer power. He was a farmboy who had taken that farm strength and mentality and really imposed it on his craft of MMA. He had beaten some notables such as Georges St-Pierre, Royce Gracie, and Carlos Newton, among many other great warriors. I knew of Matt from television, but I figured that it would be quite an honor to meet him and train with him in my hometown of London, Ontario.

Beata, who had become my loving wife, agreed that it would be great for me to take another healthy step forward in joining the MMA gym that was bringing the champ down to London. The wheels in my mind were spinning; it was a great idea, as I had yearned for something physical and as I was getting chubby, my health deteriorating with each passing day. There was 243 pounds on my 6' 3" frame, which was mainly composed of fat cells. Not only did I aesthetically not look great, but also I felt sluggish to the point that I was sleepy all of the time. A very bad diet coupled with stress from work and strange sleeping patterns contributed to a round, soft version of myself staring back at me in the mirror each morning. Given all of the variables, I came to the realization that the astute decision was to stop thinking about it and just sign up!

The next day, I called the gym and spoke with the owner. He had a very calm demeanor and asked me to come in to check the place out. Beata and I ventured up the narrow steps to Suffer System, which was a newer club making a name for itself with a lot of up-and-comers on the MMA scene. The doors at the top were closed with fight posters showing upcoming club fighters posing against their opponents. Before entering, all we could hear were shrieks and grunts behind the door. As I pushed the door open my eyes scanned the entire gym, observing my new-found love: mixed martial arts.

The first thing that hit us was the heat and humidity accompanied by the strong odor of sweat and old leather, which I would later learn was a staple scent at any good training facility. The gym was narrow and long with a huge octagon crammed right at the front. There were mats starting at the cage and proceeding all the way to the end of the room. I can honestly say that this gym looked like it came right out of the Rocky movies, with heavy bags lining the walls around the mats, ending at a small kiosk counter stocked with gym wear from the club. A narrow hallway led to the washrooms/changing rooms. It was "old school," and that is exactly what I liked and needed.

There were at least forty practitioners present in a room that likely should not have exceeded thirty. They were holding and hitting pads with their partners in boxing style, working jabs, uppercuts, hooks, and overhands, making fierce "wahhh" and "psssss" sounds immediately before each impact with the pads. The sounds they were making actually had meaning; it was more than just a psychological war shriek, but it actually helped get air out of their lungs faster to keep them fresh. The fact that everyone present sported sweat-soaked shirts looking as if they just took a dip in a pool meant they were training hard. It is a sport in which the other guy is looking to take your head off or submit you with the thousands of moves available to him or her; you'd better be training smart and hard.

Milton began to talk about the gym, then he asked me if I was looking to do this for fitness or to actually compete. I quickly looked at Beata and then back at Milton with a smile. "Definitely compete." I've always felt something deeply rooted within me: the drive, the ambition, and the fight, and this was my way of nurturing it. Milton said that once I was ready, he would put me into competition that was appropriate for my skill level and that he would never use one of his team members as a lamb to feed a lion fight. On the other hand, if I wanted to participate in higher competitions at some point in the future, he could also set that up.

Milton is a short, stocky guy, with broad shoulders and a square face accompanied by a granite jaw. He looks like a typical wrestler, but he has trained in many forms of martial arts. He was a straight shooter, and I respected that. The way I looked at it was this: if you're looking for a lemon car for $400 and want your ego stroked by a Las Vegas-style car dealer, you know what you're getting yourself into. But, when you are looking to compete in boxing, kickboxing, jiu-jitsu, and MMA, where your bodily organs are at stake, I would rather go with the "no B.S. approach." Milton has a very calming presence, which definitely came from years of training. He is a nice guy but you wouldn't want to get on his bad side, as he could do some real damage.

I began attending as many classes as I could, each one focusing on different components of the fight game, usually with different instructors. There were a bunch of jiu-jitsu instructors, a judo instructor, boxers, and kickboxers. We always started with warm-ups and then proceeded to the technical aspects of the game, to rolling (ground grappling) or sparring to finish off the hour or two. I loved rolling, which essentially meant practice grappling while trying to submit your partner. We took each other down to work on our wrestling skills. Then, we would go in for the kill with some form of submission, a joint manipulation or choke to make the partner tap or nap. Although we never went hard enough to hurt each other, we would push enough to know that we could have done some damage if we wanted to.

It was an exhilarating feeling, a primitive awakening that could occur in any of us in one way or another. The technical aspects were fun, too, as I was soaking up knowledge like a sponge. It was back to school for me, except this time in a fun way, in the school of hard knocks.

On the Tuesday of my second week, I was contemplating not going to class, as I was sore from training and tired from work. I mustered up some energy and dragged myself to class. I had learned an entire four jiu-jitsu moves by then; in this fifth class, I learned the rear naked choke. As we practiced on each other, I seemed to get the hang of this move quickly, unlike some of the other moves that were a little too advanced for me at the time.

In the class, we rolled for five-minute rounds with the goal of getting verbal or physical taps. After the five minutes, we received a quick minute of rest before changing partners.

I was partnered with a 6' 6"-tall cop who had been training on and off for a year, and I was amazed at how quickly I could get his back, and "boom," I clamped the rear naked choke and he quickly tapped out. I thought that he must have been taking it easy on me. We regrouped and just as quickly I found myself on his back with my hooks in, and seconds later I got another tap! Two taps within one minute, I was ecstatic, while he was not. He slammed his fist on the mat as his face turned red. I figured he was just being hard on himself with no disrespect aimed at me.

We regrouped again, but this time he was really putting some pressure on me in side mount, which meant that while I was on my back, he was situated sideways with his chest on mine, pinning me down. It was definitely not where I wanted to be. With a grunt, he had the Kimura on me, a shoulder lock that can shred the deltoid muscles if one does not tap. My reaction was to straighten my arm straight above my head; little did I know, it was one of the better escape methods to get out of the Kimura lock. With an explosive thrust of my hips, I jolted him into the air and scrambled, taking his back and submitting him once more. He was livid at this point. He stood up and left for the change room. I looked at the clock and noticed there were two minutes left to go, so I took a break before the next partner came up. That day really left an impression on me. This sport takes humility, self-control, honor, and a willingness to evolve and overcome obstacles to truly reach one's potential.

As the weeks went by, I got used to getting choked and tapped out, but worst of all hit, and hit hard. I dreaded sparring sessions, as I would enter the cage with many training partners ranging from novices to pros. Some guys were lenient toward my lack of knowledge, while others saw a great opportunity to use me as a punching bag. I would get bloody noses regularly, but never black eyes for some reason. I quickly learned that the toughest opponents were small, quick guys who seemed to have a never-ending gas tank. Guys over 200 pounds were better to face off with, as they were slower and I seemed to find rest opportunities in the rounds, giving me time to better formulate my attacks.

Some days, we had "king of the mats rolling," which meant that we were split into two groups in a tournament-style set up. If you lost against any opponent, you were disqualified and did not proceed. Winning let you proceed to the next round until one man stood out as the king. I regularly did well but never won. My day came; I won the first round with a guillotine, which is a type of head lock submission that puts strain on the neck and chokes you at the same time. My second opponent was a big guy, about 250 pounds, and he was strong! He slammed me on my back. I guess he wanted to win just as badly as I did, and I knew I was in for a hard round.

I had him in my guard, which meant that while on my back I had my legs wrapped around his torso. It's not the worst place to be, but also not the best, and we both knew it. He was trying hard to pass the guard and lock me in a submission to gain the advantage. But the beauty of jiu-jitsu, literally translated from Japan as "the gentle art," is that technique will always conquer strength in the grappling realm. I went for an arm bar, swinging my leg across his face while holding his arm, which put tremendous pressure on his elbow joint and forearm.

He lifted me off the mats and slammed me down in a last effort to save his place in the tournament, and it worked. The intense slam made me loosen my grip on his arm and he took the opportunity to pull his arm out. Within the scramble, I got my guard back and kept him close as I sucked in his head to my chest to catch a breath. From there, I saw the perfect opening to my favorite move. I reached around his arm and pushed it across his face with my left hand as I sucked in his head with my right hand to lock it in, known as the "head & arm triangle." From this point, there was a lot of pressure on his neck, choking him out, but I took it a step forward to gain more leverage. I popped my hips and twisted to the left to roll him on his back to reverse our positioning so that I was on top, keeping a lock on the head & arm triangle. I simply proceeded to the side mount, where I went to the same side of the choke to apply extra pressure, and I knew he was done. About two seconds later, he tapped. I immediately let go of the choke and he took a big breath of air deep into his lungs. I just made my place in the finals.

In the finals, my opponent was a really athletic guy that I knew would be a handful. He was boney and technical, my nightmare. I kept my mind on track; I wanted this win too much to let him get in my head. We circled for a good twenty-five seconds before I went in for the shot, a single-leg takedown, where I lunged in on him with one knee on the mats with the rear leg following to the front while I grabbed his front leg, placing me in a squat-like position. This kept the momentum moving to his side, which made him lose his balance and fall.

"Wow," I thought in revelation. "I took this guy down." It gave me a huge boost of confidence. I knew that if I could use my strength to offset his speed, I could finish this. I used my elbows to put pressure on his inner thighs to the point that he opened up his guard, just what I needed to pass. Once I was in his side mount, I was having difficulty keeping him down. He had squirmy hips, which meant he was not half bad on the ground. I had to work twice as hard to keep my position. I was breathing really hard while he stayed composed. The lactic acid was really starting to set in at this point, my muscles were burning and I was having difficulties getting a good breath in. But, one thing I was beginning to learn through all of my MMA training was that I had heart. My arm could have stopped working from all of the lactic acid built up in my shoulders, but I would still keep going with one arm. There was no way in hell, in my mind, that I was not going win.

I tried going for a key lock, but he got out of it quickly. From there, I transitioned to trapping his arm with my leg, getting him in the crucifix position. Now I had his arm and head pinned so I could use two hands to submit him, or so I thought. I was trying to transition, looking for a Kimura, but he almost actually threw me off of him. I managed to maintain position in the side mount. He was trying to push my head with his inner hand against my jaw, and I figured that maybe I could get an arm bar; but, before I could collect my thoughts, my instincts took over and I put his hand across his face, placed my weight on it, clasped my hands around his trapped hand and head, and squeezed. I had him in the head & arm triangle. I squeezed as hard as my weakened muscles could and with only one minute left in the five-minute round, he tapped. I felt a surge of emotions, followed by complete fatigue, coupled with happiness. I had finally done it, and against some tough seasoned competition.

The next morning, I made my way to the Carling Heights Community Centre with a sense of anxiety of what was to come. Once in the building, which was a newer, modern center for almost any sport imaginable, there was a long line waiting to enter the gymnasium for a seminar. Over 200 spectators and practitioners filled the over-sized area, with mats in the center and large bleacher-style seats surrounding the area. I bought a Suffer System long-sleeve shirt from the merchandise table, as did most people there, and awaited the champ. Matt Hughes walked in from a side room, with a half-smile and wearing a Suffer System shirt himself. He walked with confidence, his stocky image mirroring what I was used to seeing on television.

We started with warmups, running around the mats, changing directions, and in-corporating jumps and stretches; nothing too taxing, but enough to get the muscles warmed up and the heart pumping. Next, we got paired up and the seminar started with Matt Hughes showing us some of the techniques that helped him attain—and keep for an impressive period—the UFC belt. I learned how to properly perform a single-leg takedown, how to stuff one, different variations of takedowns, punches, and jiu-jitsu moves. To be honest, I cannot remember most of them now, as seminars tend to be that way. You are bombarded with so many moves and detailed descriptions that by the next day you only really retain ten to twenty percent. It was a long seminar, so we had a lunch break, during which we could get pictures and autographs with Matt, or we could opt to wait until the end of the seminar. The line was short, so I decided to meet the real-life UFC champ for the first time ever.

As I waited in line, I had no idea what to expect. I thought it was a cool experience. When I was fourth in line, a guy in his mid-twenties was amped as he spoke to Matt and asked him if his picture could be of Matt choking him out. Matt seemed laid back, but at the same time a complex guy. He menacingly smiled and said "Sure, let's do it." As Matt put his hand around this guy, you could tell there was a mismatch between a kid off the streets with a small belly and this machine of a man—a world champion. Everyone in line was laughing, and just as my first calculated thought processed, the guy went to sleep; he got choked out by Matt Hughes. To be honest, Matt did not actually try to choke him out, and he seemed perplexed as he prevented this guy from slamming to the floor and slowly laid him on the gym floor. Seconds later, he came to, smiled as he got up, and asked his buddy if he got the picture. His friend was put on-the-spot and turned red, and said "Man, I don't know how to use your camera." It was like a comedy sketch done live, absolutely everyone in line started laughing and clapping. You just cannot make this stuff up.

It was finally my turn to have my picture with Matt, I shook his hand firmly and asked if I could get a picture with him, to which he replied " I don't know, can you?" I just smiled and stood there while he laughed out loud to himself, and then a weird silence ensued. I honestly did not know what to say or even if I should say anything to that as he just stood there. But I got my picture with Matt, thanked him for coming to our city, and wished him luck in his upcoming fight. I did get to hold the UFC belt that he brought with him for the pictures, which to my surprise was much heavier than I had imagined and quite shiny, too. My first meeting with a UFC champ was a bit lackluster. Maybe I just built up the day more than I should have.

The second half of the seminar was faster paced. Milton and the guys did a great job organizing the event. Matt was a really good instructor, as he was very detailed and knew how to put things together to make us understand the moves and techniques.

Then, just like that, it was over. I guess the old adage is right; "time flies when you're having fun." The training was over, but we still had a question & answer period with Matt. He was more outspoken than on television and opened up about his training, diet, and thoughts about the UFC and other organizations. It was really refreshing. I tried to take everything in, from his runs he did every morning at 6:00 a.m. to the whey proteins he took after training. He spoke to us about his amateur wrestling career and that it was a natural transition to MMA fighting. He was a true farmboy, and that was evident as he could not leave that subject out, speaking about how he still farmed on a daily basis and how his father instilled that hard-working mentality in him as a young boy, which easily translated to his MMA training. He was even contemplating buying more farm acreage at the time, which I believe he ended up doing.

It seemed easier to go to the club each day to train after that, as I felt my game getting better, especially the jiu-jitsu portion. When it came to striking, my leg kicks were accelerating at a steady rate. They had good power and snap. I was starting to contemplate competition, but there was a lot that needed work, from my non-existent conditioning to technique and speed, but I was definitely getting the itch to compete. One of the trainers, Rob Haynes, was doing well in his MMA fights. He was a monster of a man, standing 6' 3" with a muscular build as a successful heavyweight. He had a European face, lanky hair, and a world of experience as a judo and jiu-jitsu champion. I would also learn the hard way that he had very heavy hands. I was lucky that in a sense he took me under his wing when we trained at the same times. He pushed me to my limits, and I have always been thankful for that.

He had the warrior mentality in the gym. "Train hard, wear your heart on your sleeve, and never give up." This was beginning to be the only way I knew how to train, thanks to guys like Rob. Every time I came home after training with Rob, I knew I had just come back from war, which was really toughening me up mentally and physically. I guess the grind from work coupled with the rigorous training was good for my mind.

Mentally, I felt good, but as for my conditioning, I honestly did not know what to expect. With some of the other amateurs I felt I could hold my own, while with some of the more experienced fighters I would get dazed and roughed up. I spoke to Milton, and he said that I might as well give competition a try, and just as casually as that, I had a fight to prepare for against an unknown opponent at a card that would take place in Grand Bend, Ontario, forty-five minutes from London, and a hotspot in the summer because of its beautiful beaches. I remember going home that day and thinking "What the hell did I get myself into?" I figured that everyone starts somewhere just like this, and then I started visualizing the fight in my head, and it felt great. My partner ended up dropping out due to a back injury, which I later learned was a common occurrence in the fight business; to have cards change at the drop of a dime.

I would get my chance a short time later, and yet again I had no idea what I was doing when preparing or what I was getting myself into. I did the same thing leading up to the fights, only by now I had lost some weight, and I was feeling good at 216 pounds as a heavyweight. This time, my fight would be at the MAS Thai Boxing gym, and it would be unsanctioned, unlike the previous event where my bout was canceled. There would be a referee, but they just dubbed it as "hard-sparring." Some of the coaches were showing me moves that I was trying to integrate into my technique so that they would become natural reflexes instead of having to think so much during the fight.

Some of the coaches were not always around, and we had a rotation of some new trainers in the gym. They all had different styles and techniques, and I did not notice that I was beginning to get overloaded with all of the information. So, instead of working and building my fundamentals, I was good at nothing and working on everything. I still felt confident; I thought that I was unbreakable, and all I needed was that opening in a fight and I would get my knockout through my natural power. I was still a little inconsistent with my training due to my work schedule and could not believe how quickly time had drawn me closer to fight day.

The morning of the fight I was experiencing a mild level of anxiety, so I did not eat a big breakfast that morning and stuck to drinking only water. I was really hoping Milton would be able to make it. He was a great coach, and I was used to hearing him in my corner.

We arrived at our destination. It was still morning and we managed to park across the street in a grocery store parking lot. We were early, and the gym was already busy, but the yellow, rundown building gave off an eerie feel, making us all the more anxious. MAS Thai Boxing was located on the top floor of an older industrial-style building. We proceeded up the rundown dingy stairs, and they squeaked in protest as we climbed each step slowly. Once upstairs, we removed our shoes and were led through the large doorway into the official gym of my first Muay Thai fight, which turned into a war.

As I turned the corner into the gym, that familiar leather and sweat smell hit me. The walls were old industrial brick, which gave it a nice old boxing gym feel. Right away, I noticed the ring situated on the left side at the end of the room and the metal folding chairs set up to the left and right of the room for the spectators. There was a wall dividing the gym in half. As I walked in, I went up to a guy holding a clipboard who was weighing all of the fighters. "I'm Chris from Suffer System." He glanced at me momentarily, then flipped through his pages and replied, "Yup, I got you here, just step onto the scale, please."

I put my gym bag down and stepped onto the medical-style scale, "216 pounds, thank you. You can get changed in the room at the right." As I proceeded to a changing room, I remember my mind racing, thinking that all of this was happening very quickly and nonchalantly, making my emotions swirl a bit deeper. I vividly remembered that even though it was not cold outside, the gym seemed to have a chill to it. I changed quickly and started doing what all the other fighters were doing, stretching and getting to know each other.

People were really filling the seats at this point, and there were sixty to seventy people there. My coaches were at the doorway and seemed pretty agitated for some reason. My heart sunk when I saw that they were leaving. I went out to the hallway to see what was going on, as curiosity got the better of me. They informed me that coaches had to pay the ten-dollar fee to get into the show regardless of whether they were cornering a fighter and that they had refused to pay the bill. So, there I was, at my first Muay Thai fight, unprepared and without a single coach to help me in my corner.

We were called to a separate room for a fighters' meeting, and the club owner went over the rules, which included knees, kicks, and punches but excluded knees to the face, elbows, and spinning back fists/kicks for the amateurs that were fighting, including me. He told us that this was not sanctioned and that we should not try to completely kill ourselves but that we should have fun with it, just like sparring. "Yeah, right!" I figured, any time I was going into a fight that was not in my own gym and hometown, it would be a war regardless. I have heard stories from Thailand where they loved to beat down foreigners to prove they're the best, and this would be no different.

Our names were written on a board with our designated opponents along with the fight order. I noticed that my club comrades were all in the lower portion of the fight club where the amateurs had been situated, while my match was closer to the end, sandwiched between the pro fights. I initially wrote it off as a mistake and that I would find my match as one of the first ones.

Then came yet another obstacle: my opponent, walking through the door fashionably late. Standing about 5'11", he sported dreadlocks reaching past his shoulders, a thick Viking beard, a barrel chest, and a stocky build. He weighed in at around 242 pounds and seemed relaxed for an amateur as he strolled into the gym with ease. One of the club's fighters came over and smirked as he confirmed that the newcomer was to be my opponent. I just shrugged and said "Lets do it," but in my psyche I was starting to panic more than a bit. I managed to stay positive as much as I could and recalled why I was there, while I maintained my train of thought that I would knock this guy out!

I went to the Suffer System corner, where the other guys from my gym were sitting with Beata. One of the guys turned to us and said, "Oh shit, look at that guy!" as he pointed to my opponent. I rolled my eyes and told them he was my opponent, as they all laughed in a stressful manner, probably fearing for my safety. I wouldn't let him get in my head any longer, and I sat there trying to conserve my energy taking deep breaths. They then made the official announcements for the start of the fights. Just like that, the first match was over, and I had no idea when it even started. My opponent had these big bamboo-style drums that he would bang on instead of the traditional Thai music. "Great, the guy not only looks like Rob Zombie on steroids but he's also some Amazonian," I chuckled to the guys. But, I was hoping that he was wasting needed energy for the fight and that it would work in my favor as he beat the drums mercilessly.

The third fight showcased my novice friends. As our coaches were not present, the leftover Suffer System guys went to the corner. I helped get the gloves on him and reiterated "Stay calm and kick ass bro; it's all you," as he pumped himself up in his corner. The fight started, and they went at each other like wild animals. Both being lightweights at 150 pounds, they had plenty of energy to burn. It seemed as if all technique went out the window and all that remained were wild round hooks and overhands. It was an old style barn-burner to say the least, and once the first three-minute round had concluded, both practitioners were drained of energy.

When he came to the corner we gave him water, asked if he was all right, and tried giving him a strategy as best as we could. I was telling him to circle right, away from the power hand as he got tagged hard a couple times. My other training partner was telling him to throw more kicks and so on. Again, I told him, "Remember, it's all you in there," in a stern voice to get him to focus.

The second round started wild and fast, as our teammate landed a nice "superman" punch that I had been the recipient of the week before in sparring. In that split second, I started yelling "Superman! Do the superman, it works!" And a second later, he landed a perfect superman punch, rocking his opponent.

The third round seemed to mirror the second, and our corner was sure he had the win. It was up to the judges now, and there was no way that the combatants could sway it the other way. I was right; our club got the first win that day, and it was a great feeling, especially having been in his corner.

The fights came and went, and the pro fights had already started; I was still waiting. I made my way over to the jiu-jitsu room to stretch and get my head ready for what was to come. I was warmed up, so, doing some stretches, I went over scenarios in my mind—visualizing the entire fight. According to the board, my turn was next, so I put my mp3 player on with my usual song list to get pumped. To my surprise, they did not call us up, but instead called the demo fight that was supposed to be after us. They had their two best guys, who were champions, demonstrate an MMA demo match for the crowd.

They finished with everyone clapping, and through my mp3 player I could hear my name called, saying that I was from some club other than Suffer System, an error on their part, I guessed. So, I made my way to the ring with my hands already wrapped up, I bounced back and forth on my toes as I proceeded to the ring, amazed at the ovation I received. To tell you the truth, it was quite nice, and it helped get the adrenaline pumping.

I maneuvered my way into the ring and my teammates put on my gloves which were disgusting in the sense that they had been the same gloves used by everyone else before me in the red corner. By the time I had them on, they had a foul odor and were drenched with everyone's sweat. My opponent was already in the ring too, and he was all ready to go as the referee called us into the middle of the square ring.

Something wasn't right, but I could not put my finger on it. I glanced at my opponent and saw that he was wearing his headgear, while I was not. No one gave my corner the headgear, and to add to that, my inexperienced corner thought nothing of it! It was a disaster, and at least the referee called for the headgear as I saw a couple guys at the edge of the gym scramble for it. I had a good three to four minutes of waiting, which worked against me since my mental edge was slowly dissipating while I stood in the corner waiting. My muscles were slowly cooling down, so I started bouncing around, wasting more energy. They finally got the headgear into the ring, my corner helped put it on, and it was time to touch gloves and go to war.

I do not remember my corner saying anything during the beginning of the fight, as I was so focused on what was happening inside the ring, but toward the end of the round as I loosened up, things seemed to be right. The rest is history as you already know, (see Chapter 1), and I have been asked on numerous occasions if I would have changed anything even though I was put there as a lamb for the slaughter. No, I wouldn't, and I think I learned a lot about fighting that day—but more so about myself.

After the fight, when both of our hands were raised in a draw, my corner made me feel better. I had finally done it. Regardless of the outcome, I had gone into a rough sport, and held my own, in a way. I did not get hurt, used some of the things I practiced so many times, and showed my heart. I had established a base from which now I could build upon, to which I could better myself and be better prepared for the other times to come. It is pleasurable to prove who is the better man and to experience the primitive instincts in the ring or cage, with the only the basic tools that we are given—our "eight limbs." In the back of his mind, the winner knows that, if this had been a dark alleyway, he could have ended the other.

Once the emotions were settled after the fight, which included happiness, nervousness, relief, and a sense of accomplishment all rolled up into a tight ball, I was on the outside of the ring where Beata was wiping the sweat off my face and body. Walking around the club to gather myself, I saw one of the club champions that did the fight demo. He shook my hand and congratulated me on the fight. "Thanks, but I could have done better, and may I add that he kicks like a mule." I chuckled, but he quickly remarked "No, no, you did really well, you showed heart kid, I know Jason [my opponent] has crazy power in his kicks, he makes the big Thai bags sway!" I looked with open eyes thinking to myself, either he's trying to make me feel better or maybe he saw something, but either way my heart swelled, and it was just what I needed.

I was sore for a couple of days, but nothing serious. I was walking perfectly fine, I had no bumps or bruises, and I gained a lot of experience. Most of all, I realized that this game is tough and you have to really work hard and put your heart, sweat, and tears into training if you want results. I learned that I have heart, that no matter how hard I get hit, how hard it gets to breath, that I do not quit, that the four-letter word does not exist in my vocabulary.

As the weeks passed, I had less time and will to practice, and rumors were circulating that Milton was looking to sell the gym. With the factory life taking its toll on me and just taking more time to be with Beata, I had months on end of no training, except for some strength and conditioning in my garage.

I had picked up a squat rack with an Olympic bar for a good price, to add to my punching bag, free weights, and pulley system. The truth is that I was doing routines better suited for bodybuilders—not conditioned MMA athletes. Doing signature curls, benching, and squats for the typical six to eight reps with long rest times made me feel good but was not doing very much for my MMA conditioning, particularly because I always had a hard time with cardio training. I came to understand that there was a big gap I had to fill when it came to my strength and conditioning program. Little did I know that it would fall into my lap in the near future.

I would later learn from famous IFBB pro bodybuilder Scott Milne—owner of Pump'd Supplements London Ontario, and a complete hulk of a man who competed at the peak, weighing 302 lbs shredded—that my nutrition knowledge was lacking as well. He empowered me with some great advice years later that I wish I could have absorbed much earlier, rather than running my body and immune system into the ground due to lack of proper replenishment.

In regards to recovery and performance, he taught me that "the big thing is making sure your protein levels are high—without protein you cannot repair. What a lot of people—especially for MMA guys—forget about is all of their amino acids. They could really stand to take certain aminos before they train, such as creatine hydrochloride for increasing strength and athletic performance, and beta-alanine, which buffers lactic acid so you can train longer and harder without getting fatigued. Also, arginine, which dilates your blood vessels so you transport more oxygen and nutrients to get a better pump. Afterwards is the recovery portion, requiring loads of amino acids; glutamine is the main one for muscle recovery and repair. All of those aminos can help one perform longer and harder, and to recover in order to train again sooner. Without that you will stress your immune system and get sick."

Milton sold the gym months after my fight, and I was definitely feeling an itch to get back to some good old-fashioned training. I was also starting to take a look at the Team Tompkins gym, which was the biggest and most popular gym in London, for a change of scenery. But before I did, my friend and an acquaintance convinced me to train at Suffer System in the mornings, as I was working the night shift at the factory. This way, we had the octagon ring to ourselves, and it was great for me at that point in time, as we would work on all the things I needed to address.

That was the first time I learned the Brazilian jiu-jitsu technique known as "the teepee," which is an alternative to the triangle where your feet shoot straight into the air once the opponent's head is squeezed between the thighs, without the traditional trapped arm. You lock it up by hugging the legs and trapped head with your arms until your hands clasp together, then squeeze with your thighs and arms, and "voila," the opponent has so much pressure projected on his neck that he will either tap from pain or fall asleep from the lack of oxygen going to the brain. This move is not commonly used or even known and is quite easy to implement for someone like me with long legs and arms. It would prove to come in handy throughout my training sessions.

We had a lot of fun pumping our loud metal, rap, and techno music as we pushed ourselves to the limits. Given that no one wanted to stop before anyone else, we sometimes ran into three-hour training sessions. One day, my acquaintance had an idea. He had finished watching the Sean Sherk and Brock Lesnar training session on the UFC All Access show on Spike TV, which gave fans a glimpse into the training regimen of a top fighter before a big fight. They had aired a marathon and showed how Sean Sherk, who would become UFC champion, was steam-rolling through countless reps and exercises of some the most abstract and MMA-oriented strength and conditioning programs that anyone had ever seen, at a gym called API—Athletic Performance Inc., located in Minnesota.

They also aired the heavyweight monster Brock Lesnar's training regimen. He was once a pro wrestler and had quite a fan base, which he brought over to MMA. They showed him doing similar exercises and unbelievable circuits that were exhausting just to watch, also at the famed API gym. Our acquaintance suggested that we take a trip to train in Minnesota at the API gym and at the Minnesota Martial Arts Academy, which was located right next door.

The idea more than intrigued me, as the timing could not have been any more perfect. My career at the factory was coming to an abrupt halt as the economy had hit its bottom and all of North America was in the grip of recession, especially the automotive industry. There were rumors circulating around the factory for months until we finally received our letters that the factory was officially closing and that we should look for employment elsewhere.

I was beginning to get used to layoffs, as within my five years at the factory, I had been laid off four times, ranging from a week to months, but this was different. I knew I was not coming back this time. As scary as it was, on the flip side it was a blessing, as I could move on in my life and career, away from the factory. I only meant to work at the factory for one year, but I got sucked in, and the months flew by because the checks were enticing, so one year turned into five and easily could have ended up to be a lifetime. However, now there was no excuse for not stretching my wings and soaring out into the world.

Beata saw going to Minnesota as a great opportunity because with more research, we found out that API was certifying instructors and that class would start the day after my last shift at the factory. Fate could not spell it out any clearer for me; this was definitely something I had to do, but more importantly, something I wanted to do more than anything else. Just like that, I packed my locker, said my farewells, and was ready for the drive down to Minnesota, where once again I had no idea what to expect—all with a big smile on my face.

Chapter Four

GOT CAVEMAN TRAINING?

"'Shit…Fuck'…is my barometer for when I have reached the perfect level of strength and conditioning for groups…. I also like, 'I'd cheer for you but I can't breathe!'"
—Matt Olson API Owner/Instructor

At the border, we chatted about MMA with the border cop, which was a clear indicator of the quick rise in popularity of MMA. Once in the United States, we were met with many toll plazas, which to us Canadians was a new experience given our pay highways are express highways that can be taken by choice. For the direction we were headed, Wisconsin and then Minnesota, we took the toll routes for some reason. Illinois had over a dozen tolls, and after we paid the first two, we figured it would be fun to just blow through them. That's exactly what we did, and every time we drove through one without paying, we made comical faces toward the cameras like seven-year-olds. It was fresh and fun to act like goofballs, especially after escaping the drudgery of life's responsibilities back in Canada.

The trip was tiring for all of us, as we had barely slept the day before. The entire trip was 830 miles, which took us just over fourteen hours to travel. Along the way, we stocked up on energy drinks to help us keep our eyes on the prize.

Once we arrived in Wisconsin, the flat plains consisted of farmland as far as the eye could see. Unfortunately, it was the only thing we could see. It was really dull to watch, so we discussed MMA as the testosterone level increased in the car, helping us stay alert. Once in Minnesota, we were reinvigorated; we knew we were almost there. Had we known then what was lurking for us, I'm not sure we would have been so giddy.

Our hotel was literally minutes from the famed Athletic Performance Inc. (API) Training Center and the Minnesota Martial Arts Academy, which are next door to each other. As we approached the building, the huge, and I mean gigantic, industrial complex loomed in front of us. The buildings were connected, looked very new, and were at least forty feet tall. The area was very well-maintained and honestly did not look like your typical gym. It was an honor to pass through the doors into such an elite fitness gym.

API was established by Scott Ramsdell and Matt Olson. Scott is the one you see sporting the long goatee in the UFC All Access shows yelling to motivate Sean Sherk and Brock Lesnar. It is one of the premier strength and conditioning gyms in the world, catering to the best athletes in several different sports. They are known for their "pain is weakness leaving the body" attitude and pushing their athletes into the red zone.

API includes 150 to 300 students/practitioners depending on the time of the year. Including high school programs, classes, specialized specific groups, fighters, and personal training clients, there are about 200 members at the Minnesota location. As for schools affiliated around the world, Matt Olson put it best when he said that "We have a shit ton! A metric shit ton." [laughing] "I think by the time this comes to print, we will have over twenty API affiliates worldwide!"

Their caveman routines are tough, with exercises hand-picked for maximum results and that make the practitioners stronger, faster and more agile, like well-oiled machines that do not let up! With specimens like Sean Sherk and Brock Lesnar to tout in their company profile, it says a lot. Matt Hughes was known to frequent the gym as well. The routines are endless and are constructed with specific goals to achieve faster and better results. Caveman training came from the philosophy of going back to the basics with clean natural food and functional training that can be transmitted directly into the cage. The concepts are derived from the actions of cavemen, such as throwing, picking up, and flipping rocks.

The second benefit to training with API is the brotherhood formed from working with such intensity, similar to that in the military. The mind gets tougher, too, as you work through many points of exhaustion and fatigue; you want to stop, but you keep going, with everyone helping to motivate you. Once you step into the ring or cage to fight, you know you did all that you could to prepare. The fight would probably be easier than the grueling training, and that edge alone could prove to be the deciding factor between getting a Win or Loss on a fighter's record.

API's Matt Olson grew up in Hopkins, Minnesota after being adopted from South Korea along with his two older sisters. He also has a younger brother from his adoptive parents, regarding whom Matt added, "Poor Adam; he grew up thinking he was Korean until he started the first grade." Matt had the typical upbringing playing many different sports, but it was weightlifting that always played an important role in his life. He was also actively involved in the Catholic Church and the Boy Scouts of America.

Matt's wife, Candice, keeps him in check and in line with both API and the Minnesota Police Department. They have four dogs that help round out their loving family.

Matt was a silent investor in an already established mobile business that Scott began in 2004. They became coworkers while working for the Police Department before becoming partners on the Community Response Team, a plain-clothes vice unit. Matt wanted to invest some money he made from a home sale into a long-term business that would eventually allow him a second career or a long-term investment. They conversed more about the prospect of API while arresting drug dealers and raiding drug homes.

Scott eventually told Matt his business plan. Matt put his money down, and the two decided to go into business together to centralize the mobile training business into an actual training center. Their timing could not have been better, and the location was a good fit with the Minnesota Martial Arts Academy. "I remember busting my ass for two weeks straight to get the gym up and running because the UFC All Access show was coming to film Sean Sherk's workouts."

Things haven't always been peachy, as Matt laughingly explained: "When I first met Scott thirteen years ago and after transferring to the CRT team, I hated Scott. I thought he was brash, arrogant, blunt, and irritating. I came to realize that he was going to become one of my best friends—that he was going to push me past my limitations to become involved with something that brings me a sense of joy and satisfaction. But I still hate him!" Having seen them in action, they are like two feuding brothers with A-type personalities. They make fun of each other and beat each other up, but they would go to war at the drop of a hat for one another; they truly are family.

API is the most edgy and gut-wrenching strength and conditioning program around, and Matt gave me his thoughts on how they made their program distinct from others. "What people are experiencing is the methodology and training style of Scott Ramsdell and the emotion, the kind of 'chip on the shoulder' attitude we both bring into the way we live, especially in our profession and the way I live life. Scott is definitely the 'good cop' to my 'bad cop.' I think this analogy aptly illustrates the differing views Scott and I bring to API and to MMA strength and conditioning in general. I will always defer to Scott for the technical and professional aspect of fitness because he has the experience and education. I bring the outsider's viewpoint, the person who sees things 'outside' the fitness box and the traditional way of thinking."

Matt explained their approach, "The basics must be established before an athlete can progress to advanced levels. You would be amazed at how many pro athletes have so many basic physical issues. In my experience, MMA fighters have the worst agility and hand strength issues when weights don't come with handles. Even high school athletes to college athletes have some of the worst forms in the most basic of lifts, including squats, cleans, dead lifts, etc. The basics establish the API method regarding every athlete prior to increasing speed and weight."

An average Joe should do Caveman training about three to four days a week at most and incorporate both cardio and strength days. That means that the average Joe would be in a beginner's or intermediate class and could pull off doing that many training sessions per week.

Pro fighters should be doing a periodical schedule of at least two days per week. And, more importantly, they should listen to the strength and conditioning instructor when it comes to tapering and stopping rather than listening to their technical coaches. Matt elaborated: "That is one of the sore spots that Scott and I have had to deal with—technical coaches overriding a periodical schedule for professional fights. I can't think of us going to an MMA or grappling class and telling the athlete, 'you don't have to work on your strikes because we'll take it from here up to your fight.' Are you fucking kidding me! It's a passionate topic that is still pretty raw to both Scott and I."

Their slogan adorned the walls inside the famed institution, reading "Commit... No Excuses." It was a simple slogan, but direct and to the point. It came to fruition when both Matt and Scott were training a group while chatting about part-time clients and athletes who had been asking them to train. They kept saying that they would come in but never did, just bullshitting and talking a good game. Matt recollected, "We were both fed up with it, and Scott said, 'Matt, I want to paint "Commit... No Excuses!" on the wall because I'm tired of these pussies telling us what they were gonna do. Either you commit to it or don't. The other slogan that we've been thinking of and that we like to use a lot is, 'Don't fucking tell me what you're gonna do.... Show me.' Scott was always the more diplomatic one. But that slogan is the epitome of how Scott and I have looked at training and how to approach all aspects of life. You can talk a big fucking game, but talk is cheap. Run your mouth somewhere else. We don't care about shit that you may or may not wanna do."

Scott and Matt came from an inherently dangerous profession. The attacks and ever-changing world of vice, drug dealers, duplicitous informants, bullshit administrative backstabbing, and the pressures that go with it required a real, solid approach toward how to live and how to do a job. How does this translate to training? They go in, set a goal they want to achieve, and they get it done. This is how they want all of their athletes to look at training, a great principle that their students can take with them to their professions and the real world.

API is known to be hard on their athletes, and for good reason, as I asked Matt whether they would baby their athletes. I received the expected response: "Hell no. Life is hard. Training is hard. Sometimes you will get shit on, sometimes you will fail or embarrass yourself, but if you can have the right frame of mind in place from the very beginning, from the very first time you step into API, anywhere around the world, then you are already ahead of the game. When that cage door closes behind you, the only person you can rely on is the man in the mirror. Your coaches and teammates can yell all they want, but the person who either survives or attacks is up to you. Train like the way you fight. Train your brain to push past all that bullshit."

It takes a really different type of human to make a career out of fighting, and the prima donnas need not apply. People need to be able to push past their perceived limitations to mentally step on the accelerator when everyone else presses the brake; that's what it took to be the best, and that is the type of athlete Matt was looking for.

"I have personally kicked paying clients out of our Training Center and gave them directions to Crossfit because they don't have the heart. If you don't have the competitive juices to push yourself or don't want to learn, then go somewhere else because I do not want to be held responsible when you quit on yourself."

Another drastic approach API uses is that if you attend advanced classes and you quit a routine, you leave and do not come back. This seems harsh but it's proactive, instilling team loyalty in all of their athletes. They did not push people past their physical limitations to the extent that it appeared. All API certified instructors would taper weights for students, and Matt put it best: "Yes, you will suck ass, you will look like shit the first time, but if you quit, then you really don't want to get better. I would rather have an athlete who sucks ass and chokes but keeps pushing forward than a top athlete who quits because they don't feel it. It's pretty simple, it goes back to Scott and I being work partners. We bang down a door on a narcotics search warrant and I'm going through that door first, Scott is right over my right shoulder. We are not going to quit in the middle of the breach; lives are at stake! It's the same here at API. Your life of being better, your commitment to yourself is at stake. You wanted to come to Advanced? Then prove to us you belong here. Or keep working at Intermediate or Basic. If you commit, there's no going back."

Sean Sherk, who was known as one of the hardest training athletes in the world, only had positive things to say about Matt and Scott. "I love those guys. You know I'm really good friends with both those guys. So I think that Scott brought something really great to the table for me, and when he did I grabbed onto it and we both ran with it, you know? I mean, anyone who has seen my UFC All Access, you know.... So you know I think they've helped me immensely."

We had no idea what we were getting ourselves into as we drove up to the monstrous complex and became giddy as we saw the API sign above the doors. We had finally made it, buzzing off junk food and energy drinks, not knowing what was in store for us past those doors.

Once inside, we were greeted at the front desk by Dan Piper, one of the head instructors, and we were then taken on a tour of the facility. We marched through the corridor with rooms on both sides as we were introduced to the massive facility. The inside of the building was just as impressive as the exterior, with a 2,000-square-foot multi-purpose area and 1,000 square feet of strength and conditioning gear. All together, with the adjoined Minnesota Martial Arts Academy, there was a combined 11,000 square feet of fun.

Once I walked into the open area, I quickly noticed tires probably weighing in excess of 300 pounds, the different sizes of sledge hammers, bars hanging off the walls, ropes off the ceiling and on the walls, dumbbells, machines, gas masks, Airdyne bikes, and wheelbarrows, all creating the space known only as "API." I whispered to my pals, "Wow, definitely not your typical weight room" as we slowly made our way in. I immediately felt a surge of adrenaline as my eyes widened even though we had not slept all night.

A familiar face approached us with a kind smile and a firm handshake. "Hey guys, I'm Scott. I hear you came down all the way from Canada?" I recognized him from the Sean Sherk and Brock Lesnar UFC All Access show, although now he was missing the crazy goatee. He had a warm face and stocky frame with slightly rounded cheeks, with a darkness I could not put my finger on. He was very friendly with a bright demeanor, which was quite the opposite of his image, as he looked like a very tough guy, rugged with a helping of "I will kick your ass!"

There were others present for class who were more punctual than we were, but I noticed that there were no tables at which to sit, and stations were set up along the gym. It started to dawn on me that we had a hell of a night in store for us, and we weren't going to be burying our noses in the books that night!

During the warm-up, we did dynamic stretches and a little cardio to get the heart pumping, but the truth was that all eight of us were working hard and dripping with sweat, with our hard breathing indicating as much. After a good twenty-minute warm-up, the instructors started preparing the circuit. While we waited, we learned about proper warm-ups and that training cold was a recipe for disaster that could lead to muscle cramps, strains, or worse, injuries. Even small injuries meant time away from the gym, preventing you from reaching your goals in a major way. We were also shown the puke buckets and their locations in case we would need them; we thought it was more for show than anything else.

As we saw the gauntlet of pain set up for us, I felt sluggish from the lack of sleep and sitting in one position in the car for so long, but I was stubborn by nature and pushed on. We had to do the activities at each station for one minute straight, working as quickly as possible. There were three exercises per station followed by a one-minute break before proceeding to the next station.

The entire routine was a Muscle Power Cardio Power circuit.

- Jump Push-Ups on Twelve-Inch Steps
- Jump Clap Push-Ups
- Airdyne Bike with Hands Only

****

- Push-Ups on the Ball
- Push-Ups Side-to-Side Over the Ball
- Push Tractor Tire Across Gym

****

- Throw Ball on Wall and Sprawl
- Sit-Ups with Medicine Ball
- Run on Incline Treadmill

****

- One-Legged Squat with Olympic Bar
- Squat Jumps with Olympic Bar
- Bike

****

- Switch Lunges with Olympic Bar
- Thirty-Pound Ball Jump Over Punching Bag
- Skipping

Now, when I write this, I have the same feeling as most of you probably do, it really seems easier than it is. Believe me, or give it a try for yourself, after speaking with your health physician of course, working as hard as possible over and over is anything but easy. At first, I was doing very well, and I even grunted a few times as I was exerting my muscular system to the max. It felt good! I was training where the pros trained with the best instructors in the world, and I was going to give it my all.

Halfway through the routine after I blew through the stations, I made it to the inclined treadmill. After positioning my fee on either side of the deck, I jumped onto the belt and into a full-out run, and it was going so fast that it was a little tricky for me to stay on the treadmill; I was pumping my hands and legs for dear life. It took a lot out of me, and I felt my insides ready to come out, as I started getting the vomit burps. It was a good thing that afterward, I had a minute of rest until the next circuit.

I started the one-legged squat with the Olympic bar, and I felt worse and worse from the inside out. I was having difficulty containing my insides, until my body finally had enough. I ran toward the designated puke bucket, remembering the flight attendant-sounding instructions that had been given earlier, grabbing the bucket for dear life and running out the door for fresh air. My head was spinning; I really did not want to be the one to throw up. With an effort, I forced back down most of what had attempted come up; don't ask me why, but I was not thinking right at the moment, and I was running with the bucket instead of stopping to spit into it. I think my mind was so fatigued and set on the goal of getting outside that the rest was not computing.

Once outside, the smell hit me, and I realized I should have just thrown up into the bucket without reservation; that's what it was for! I knelt down outside to catch my breath and just spit into the bucket to get the taste out of my mouth. I needed that cool breeze on my face, something that a millionaire would give their fortune for at that point. After a good thirty seconds, I heard Scott inside asking "Where's Chris? Did anyone see Chris?" followed by muffled sounds.

Seconds later, Scott came out to check on me. I told him I threw up a little but was coming right back in. Just like triage, once he comprehended that I was okay, he then asked, "Let me see it" and I met him with a bewildered look, "See what?" "The puke; let's see it. How much did you puke?" It took me a few seconds to realize he was serious, and I explained what had happened, and he chuckled and told me to take my time.

I ran in almost right after him to my next station which involved squat jumps with the Olympic bar. I found my groove again and went hard at it, surprisingly almost fully charged to keep going. I put the vomiting incident out of my mind and figured that I had some making up to do.

All of us were breathing hard with our mouths open, slowing down tremendously toward the end. But we all had the fight in us to keep going, even though none of us were used to this pace in our workouts. I think the fact that we were all here for the same reason and that we were all motivating each other and training at a premier gym made us work much harder than usual.

We had all done it, soaked in our sweat, with small chips on our shoulders; we had completed a notorious Caveman routine! We were like explorers that had just reached the top of the mountain, pushing past adversity, the bitter cold breath of mountain air being no match for us. Matt quickly brought us back down to Earth. "Alright, so tomorrow we have a lot more training and many exercises that we have to do for perfect form!"

I must admit that I was very happy being there that afternoon, so far away from my comfort zone. Life brings many opportunities, and when it works, it works. I believed that I was meant to be there at that point in my life and that I had a lot to experience, learn, and grow with, as a person.

As we all clutched our knees while trying to get our heart rates down, Scott mentioned, "Not sure if everyone saw, but Chris did use the puke bucket, but then quickly came back in and went right back at it, and that is exactly the attitude we are looking for."

I was feeling good before this, but I was floating on clouds after a compliment from Scott. Life is funny that way, too! I would not want to be anywhere else in the world at that point. All that was missing was Beata, my second half, and I wished she could be there to see me.

We chatted a bit with everyone, got changed, and made our way back to the hotel room to our beds as we were practically sleepwalking at that point. We first stopped off at the gas station and bought over twenty vitamin-infused waters to keep us hydrated and then crashed for the night. I could not remember when I had slept so well; I started snoring the minute my head hit the pillow.

In the morning, we were all aching and sore to the point that it was hard to walk straight, as the lactic acid invaded our muscles. Our legs were as stiff as wood as we tried to bend them to walk. We learned another lesson about what most of us take for granted: simply walking! One of the guys decided not to go for breakfast in order to remain in bed, but I was hungry and I knew my body needed fuel for another day, only this time it was going to be an entire day of fun that awaited us.

At the gym we found that everyone else was hurting too, even the tough muscle guys. Day two started off with anatomy work, which was good, as I had not brushed up on my anatomy knowledge since my school years. We learned about the skeletal system, tendons, ligaments, articular cartilage, and articular fibrocartilage and their functions. We then moved on to neurological anatomy and the nervous system, which was more up my alley. I could shine at this, as I had studied it extensively for my Abnormal Psychology Degree and the other classes I had taken in college. It really is fascinating how our bodies are built and how every aspect of the body is linked to everything else. Have you ever asked yourself how is it that your body tells you that your joint is bent in a way it shouldn't be? Well, that would be your kinesthetic receptors in the joint capsules, which respond to mechanical forces such as pressure or overextension, letting you know where your limbs are. So, next time you are tapping in class due to an arm bar, you can thank your kinesthetic receptors for letting you know to tap before you end up with a broken arm to nurse.

To keep us on our toes after learning some theory, we did some physical training and took breaks. I thought it was brilliant since it made the day move by faster and was more exciting. We proceeded to our dead lifts and their variations in the weights section of the gym. I never knew there were so many different variations of doing squats. We meticulously went over proper technique to prevent injury and learned what we should look out for in others while watching over them. Scott hammered into us that "Perfect form and perfect training makes for perfect results."

I had seen the sumo squat before but never tried it, and it ended up being my favorite type of squat. It is similar to a regular squat but your stance is not shoulder width apart; it is much wider, making you look like a sumo wrestler when squatting. The second difference is that you have the dumbbell or kettle bell in-between your legs rather than above on your shoulders.

For the shoulders, there was a lot to cover, as they house so many strands of muscles and as their organization makes it a very complex part of the body. We learned that on the bench press and shoulder press, maintaining a narrow grip will help build the cuff and make you stronger in the wrestling "shrimp" defensive maneuver.

We then received exercise instruction in "cleans." I only knew the regular power cleans before my API experience, but yet again we covered many variations. I enjoyed the cleans from the lap, as that way only my upper body was working twice as hard, instead of receiving help from my legs.

That day, Scott and Matt actually took us all out for lunch, which I thought was a really generous gesture. After lunch, we moved onto the physiology of training, which really intrigued me. We went over the motor units and muscle fiber types: slow twitch and fast twitch. We went into great detail, and I must admit a lot of what we learned was directly applicable to my workout routines. I really took to heart that it is possible to use lactic acid for energy more efficiently when the body adapts to resistance and cardiovascular training. This was important to me, as I was known to have unbelievable lactic acid build-ups that brought agony to my muscles and anguish to my brain.

I even learned why I threw up the day before, which had never happened to me before. The lactic acid is toxic, so if it accumulates, the body gets rid of it. Hard training can increase the lactic acid threshold, meaning less pain and higher capabilities. We finished the lesson by learning about biomechanics such as force, torque, weight, mass, inertia, acceleration, center of gravity, strength, power, and endurance.

It was again time for the exercise instruction portion, and we learned about the "snatch." I had seen Sean Sherk doing this on television and thought it was great, as it uses your entire body to explode with power. The weight, whether it be a dumbbell or a kettle bell, starts on the floor and gets shot up straight into the air above your head. I really liked this as it taxed me after the first couple of repetitions and I was feeling my legs and shoulders pumping blood as I exploded each rep.

The nutrition portion was next, and I followed it closely as we dove into short and long chains of glucose, simple sugars, complex carbs, glycogen, and what to look out for. For your information, stay away from high-fructose corn syrup, *trans* fats, and alcohol!

We also covered vitamins, of which athletes need a surplus to sustain good health and optimum performance. The best sources are brightly colored fruits and vegetables accompanied by a good multi-vitamin supplement. Vitamin B and C are water-soluble, meaning that if you take in too much, the body will excrete the excess in your urine. The fad now is for exotic berries that have antioxidants such as acai ("asaee") and goji berries. They are really healthy and pumped full of goodness, but finding them is a little harder than looking in your local grocery store since they are usually shipped from Brazil. Green vegetables should be the staple in everyone's diet.

The need for water is no big secret, but many athletes neglect the fact that they need a lot of it each day. Our body is comprised of sixty-five to seventy-five percent water, while our muscles are compromised of seventy percent water, bones twenty-five to thirty percent, and blood at ninety percent. We lose water through sweat, urination, and breathing, but as an athlete we lose a *lot* through sweat. So what does this mean to you as an athlete? If dehydration exceeds two percent body weight, physical performance is limited, which has been evident in many UFC fights to date. The last one I can remember was Jake Shields against Martin Kampann, as even though Jake Shields won that fight, he really slowed down throughout the fight and later admitted that the weight cut and water deprivation affected his performance.

Going back to antioxidants, an important note is that through emotional stress, environmental stress, and training, we produce free radicals that attack our muscles. Our antioxidants eliminate them, which is a good thing. So, the more we train, the more free radicals we produce, and thus the more antioxidants we need to stay healthy.

We learned about the digestive system and meal planning. Eating balanced foods and eating a variety of foods that offer amino acids, vitamins, etc., is key. Our metabolism is like a fire, and if we dump a lot of food at once and then wait six hours to eat again, it responds like a rollercoaster. By eating six to eight smaller portions each day, metabolism burns on a straight line, and, under the right circumstances, your body can burn fat without you doing anything—a win-win situation.

The time had finally come; we had to take a written exam covering a lot of what we had learned, followed by the notorious circuit test during which we would be pushed to our physical limits, which would conclude the test. No one from class knew what to expect, and that was enough to bring butterflies to our stomachs. I did not bother asking Scott or Matt about what they called the "final test circuit," as it would add to the nerves. I was sure it was something along the lines of "The Death Gauntlet" or "Dungeon of Doom." You get the idea—the less I knew the better. All I could do was to prepare my body with an adequate night's sleep and mentally get myself into the zone, and I did just that.

The written test went well; I've trained my mind to relax during tests through a lifetime of testing in schools. It was easier to absorb the information, as it was fun and actually useful to learn about body mechanics, anatomy, and exercises; it was a passion. After the exam, we found that the API gym had been fully transformed into a super-circuit with pro fighters at some stations to determine whether we had proper form; each station had a set amount of either time or repetitions; if a rep was done incorrectly, it did not count. My jaw dropped as I noticed that there were so many stations for us, ranging from heavy weights to body exercises to cardio. And, yes, the inclined treadmill was on the list, the same station that treated me so well the first night. But things were different now. I was stronger, faster, and mentally stronger, thanks to everyone at API, and I was going to make them proud. I psyched myself up before we started. I told myself that I was doing this for Beata and everyone at API.

The API facility was a buzzing nest of giddy students as we walked through the stations, guided by Scott. As he explained each station, it seemed that each one was progressively harder than the next, and it was intense. When we had progressed around the gym, Scott walked us outside and said "Then you will run out," he paused with a menacing smile, "and run around the entire complex where you will conclude the test right back here!" My jaw not only lowered, but my eyes must have popped out like Homer Simpson's, as it was a really large complex. It was a killer long run that we had to do after the biggest, baddest circuit we had yet to be put through.

At that moment, I had mixed emotions, as I knew I had a tough road ahead of me, but I was going to go all-out to prove to everyone that I had it in me and most of all to prove myself that I was indeed a warrior. I was paired with a U.S. military soldier who was built like Arnold Schwarzenegger, which is why we had nicknamed him "Arny." He was one of the most conditioned in our class, aside from an ex-navy seal. I thought it was great that I would pace myself with him, as we would bring the best out in each other. We were paired together because some of the exercises such as dead lifts were determined based on our body weight, and because we were the two heaviest guys in the class, we were paired together to lift the heaviest weights … lucky us!

The time had finally arrived for us to dig deep, block out any pain, and go to war. Throughout the long circuit, I was pacing myself at a high rate. I knew I had to maintain that rate throughout and all would be good. I remember blasting through the pull-ups with ease, as each station had an instructor or pro fighter counting our reps. I blanked everything out, I just kept pushing and pushing without a distracting thought, which helped.

My muscles were aching and my lungs felt like they would pop, but I took no notice. Arny and I were neck-and-neck throughout the circuit; it was a see-saw battle of wills. I would get a small lead at one station, then he would get the same at another. The last station before the run consisted of twenty squat jumps, and I was behind, my body staggered to the station as I wiped the sweat out of my eyes, to see Arny slowing down. Some weird jolt of energy came over me as I popped off twenty consecutive squat jumps like it was a walk in the park, then to run out first through the API doors, only to be assailed by the scorching sun on my face.

I must have looked like Big Bird running at that point, because my legs were behaving like Jell-O as I heaved to raise my knees with each step, but at least I was jogging fairly quickly. My hips wobbled side-to-side and my ears kept popping, so I experienced a weird muffled sensation in which the sound of my heartbeat was pronounced. Every time my sneakers hit the hard pavement, I could hear the impact from my joints through the muffled noise, which was an eerie sensation.

I think I had an epiphany shortly after, a realization of something bigger. It was my life I had just re-enacted, every part of my body at that point was telling me to start walking, take a small break at least, that I was not a machine and had just put myself through twenty hard minutes straight of taxing myself. My life has thrown me curve balls on a regular basis, but no matter how beat up I got I had to dig deep, have heart, and trudge forward. The prize was within my grasp, and in my typical self-talk I started with, "If I were to simply stop…." But, in mid-thought, I said "Fuck that!" I instantaneously got mad, thinking "If this shit doesn't kill me, I am going to make it, and I will make it in life, damn it!"

I looked back and saw that my friend Arny was a long way back and that I was actually catching up to another pair in front of us. I closed my eyes as my zombie-like movements propelled me forward, saying to myself over and over, "I am never going back to the factory. I will succeed. I am never going back to the factory. I will succeed!" I turned the last corner as the distance to Scott, who was holding the stop watch, shortened. I tried to sprint the last few yards but my body honestly could not do it, and it was a strange feeling as I passed the finish line with a stagger. I made it, I did not stop once. I was hurting from my toes to the top of my head, and I could barely get my breath, but I was in sheer ecstasy. Life is fucked up that way isn't it? True happiness comes through adversity, pain, and accomplishment, and as I learned, a lot of hurting muscles.

I owe a lot to Matt and Scott. They are excellent at what they do, but more importantly, they are amazing human beings who bring out the best in others. I really like their hardass persona, and they will kill me for writing this, but they are like big teddy bears once you break that wall down. They are good, genuine, hard-working people who look out for their families and friends. The best part was that everyone at API is family. Recently, they changed the name of the gym to Fitness Solutions, but it boasts the same atmosphere as before.

We stayed an extra couple of days after finishing the classes, as Matt and Scott had extended some extra routines for us on which they had been meticulously working. We were not going to deny the invite and would have been crazy not to stay.

We did some really fun routines that took us back to being in the great outdoors. We were running with heavy wheelbarrows, sprinting with parachutes, and pushing/pulling Scott's pickup truck like strongman competitors with some of the newly inducted instructors and pro fighters. It was a blast, and I was still surprised at how strong I was. I never really realized it until I started doing the functional exercises. We took a full arsenal of knowledge with us, but we learned more than that while there; we took kernels of life experience and new building blocks to become better versions of ourselves in all aspects of our lives.

We also went next door to Minnesota Martial Arts Academy, which was the MMA home base for Brock Lesnar and Sean Sherk. The training center was part of the industrial complex and seemed to be even bigger than API. It had all the necessities of a world-class gym, the grappling mats, punching bags of various sizes, pads, gloves, contraptions, and a lot of eager students. Nick "The Goat" Thompson was preparing for his mid-day training session when Sean "The Muscle Shark" Sherk walked in. The two were about to start their training session when I asked for a picture and introduced myself. Sean was really personable, and I got the impression that he was genuinely a good guy.

I had to watch as Sean trained with Thompson and as they started grappling after some warm-ups. I was amazed at how quick and explosive he was in real-time. I managed to train a little while down there and picked up a great takedown technique. The double leg with a small variation added to it, when you shoot in bring your back leg in once you grab the back of the knees and explode through them to take down your opponent. GSP used it in his fights, as it adds an explosive element to the takedown.

By then, my body was taking such a hard beating that it started to feel good. Not sure how that worked, but I think my body was adjusting to the heavy workload. It's amazing how our bodies work, isn't it? I was like a kid in a candy store between API (Fitness Solutions) and the Minnesota Martial Arts Academy.

I must admit, lying on the benches at the famed MMA institution, similarly to how Sean Sherk and Brock Lesnar spent their downtime, made me feel great. Living the life of a fighter for those few days was enough to make my blood flow faster. At the same time, I could see how unrewarding and stagnant that lifestyle could get for some. You put your body through hell day in and day out, you become mentally and physically exhausted, and then you wait until your body recuperates just enough before the next session to do it all over again, getting punched in the face while doing it. There are no cheerleaders or people applauding you along the way, and it is all done for such a minuscule amount of time in the spotlight: the cage.

Similarly to how Olympians feel after training for so long, for only a short amount of time on the world stage, if they had an off day at the event it seemed as if all of that tedious work was for nothing. As documented throughout history, a fighter's life can get lonesome at times, yet for a young pup like me in the sport every little training session was a godsend in my eyes.

Life was good at that point. I was out of a job, far away from home, with not many future prospects in the career department, and with a mortgage and bills to pay, but none of that mattered. Life was good, just lying there with a sense of pride, being the newest inductee into the API family. Time seemed to stand still as I lay grounded and at peace for the first time in a long time....

Chapter Five

THE MUSCLE SHARK

"Do not pray for an easy life, pray for the strength to endure a difficult one."
—**Bruce Lee**

Sean Sherk grew up in a big family with six kids and a plethora of relatives and other kids around. That made for a lot of excitement in itself, but coupled with growing up in a family of wrestlers, the fight game flowed through his veins from the start and kept him busy. His dad, uncles, cousins, and brother were all immersed in the sport. Naturally, he was thrown into the wrestling scene at an early age.

As a youth, he spent a lot of time training, wrestling, and playing sports such as baseball and football. But wrestling was where he excelled, and as Sean put it, "(wrestling) was more of an individual sport, I was less of a team sport kind of person." Sean's brother, who was eight years older, mentored him in wrestling. While in college, he taught Sean the techniques and training of college athletes. This was how Sean got ahead of the game early on.

Wrestling competitively for thirteen years during his youth garnered him 400-plus amateur wrestling matches. He watched his first UFC event in 1993 and started UFC-style training shortly thereafter. Within a few months, he started training at a judo school, as that was all he could find in the immediate area, but wanted to train in the various styles being utilized in MMA.

Sean's road to success and the coveted title was not an easy one to say the least. He spent some time as a plumber, as his family is full of plumbers, including his dad and his brother, who own their own businesses.

Sean recounted, "There were a lot of plumbers in my family, so of course, you know, I have the plumbers' rite of passage, you know you got to plumb. So I plumbed for a little while.... I wasn't much of a plumber, I was more of a digger, you know, digging holes. So that didn't pan out too well for me. I did a lot of construction growing up, built walk-in coolers at one point in time, eventually that moved on to factory work."

Similarly to my path in life, Sean did heavy labor jobs and found himself swallowed up by the abominable confines of factory life. He worked for a total of three years in a union factory, during which time he began fighting professionally.

I began fight training with Suffer System while working at the factory, which was the best thing about working there. The experience gave me, and likely Sean, the ammunition to get the hell out of there! It was funny how our scenarios paralleled so closely. A high school friend of Sean's convinced him to start training full time sometime around 1997, making him a full-time warrior.

I shifted gears to ask him about his epic triumph over Kenny Florian at UFC 64 when he won the Lightweight UFC Championship belt. Sean had lost to Matt Hughes back in UFC 42 for the Welterweight Championship, and while working his way back up, the UFC offered him the title fight at 155 pounds. First, they asked him if he could make weight, he said that he could, and that's when they told him it would be for the world title.

Sean understood the opportunity placed in front of him, so while training hard to prepare he actually tore his shoulder only a week before the fight. His shoulder rotated and tore 100%, preventing him from moving his right arm. He had been training for eleven hard weeks and was in great shape mentally and physically, aside from the shoulder tear. Canceling the fight was not an option in Sean's mind; he had already fought for the belt once.

"How many times do you get to fight for two world titles in your life? I mean, how many times do you get to fight for one world title in your life? Not very often," Sean added.

Winning the title was euphoria, "I mean, to feel that belt wrapped around your waist… I got goose bumps, you know? As soon as I wrapped that belt around my waist, it was something I wanted to feel my entire career, coming up through the amateur and pro ranks, then against Kenny—that was my thirty-fifth or thirty-sixth fight."

Sean received no charity or handouts on his road to the most prestigious belt in the MMA world. The long, winding road was arduous, but through hard work, determination, and perseverance, he achieved his goals.

Interestingly, Sean had many opportunities to fight for other organizations' championships but always turned them down. "I always told people, I said 'that first belt I ever want to win is going to be a UFC belt because I never want to feel a belt wrapped around my waist unless it's a UFC belt.' That was by choice." Winning the UFC championship, not to mention with a torn shoulder, was the highlight of Sean's career up to that point.

As Sean had mentioned Matt Hughes, I figured I would ask him about his epic match and being cut by the UFC, having to work his way back to the big show and how he was impacted by these events. When Sean fought Matt Hughes, Matt was the

Number one pound-for-pound fighter in the world. He was considered by many to be unbeatable. Sean acknowledged that he was a huge underdog in the fight, with odds of around six to one. "So I wasn't expected to do anything in that fight. Went up fighting five rounds you know? We went to war, and I won one or two of those rounds."

After the fight, both warriors knew that they had gone to battle with one of the best in the world. A sense of camaraderie was born, and Sean figured that he had just cemented his place on the biggest stage in the world. Two weeks later, Sean received a phone call from his manager informing him that he was let go from the UFC. Sean needed his manager to repeat the news several times just so the reality could sink in. He had just gone five full rounds with the best in the world, and was then released by the organization.

Sean explained the gravity of the situation: "So, we were the main event in there. Going from being the main event of the UFC, fighting the number one guy in the world, to fighting my next fight in, like, it was like in a barn somewhere in my hometown."

Life has a funny way of twisting and turning, and I could definitely relate on a different level regarding a million different experiences. Nevertheless, all you can do is shake your head and persevere. Before perseverance though, anger typically manifests, and I bet Sean was confused and riled up after dropping so hard and so far from the clouds. Sean pointed out, "So it was like… to go from fighting in the main event of the UFC to fighting in a god damn barn, you know?"

Sean was doing whatever he could to be the number one guy in the world, but he kept hitting bumps in the road, and this one was a big one. He fought in small shows for little money, barely enough to pay the bills. He experienced the financial hardship faced by most of us at one point or another.

He had a small stint in the Pride Fighting Championships and experienced similar results. He fought the Rings Champion, which was a big event over in Pride at that time. He mopped the floor with the Rings Champion for fifteen minutes, demolished him, and won the fight.

They thanked Sean for the performance but let him go from that organization as well. As Sean's troubles mounted, it seemed that no matter what he did, life was always an uphill battle.

"So, like, okay, well, there is another kick in the butt. So, it's like that happened twice within a year's time; I got let go by the UFC, I got let go by Pride, and I'm stuck fighting in these small venues."

Most people would have crumbled under such pressure and circumstances, as nothing bruises the ego more than when hard work does not pay off. To add to his responsibilities, after ten fights outside of the UFC, his baby arrived. He made the tough choice to do what was right for his family. He retired from fighting and juggled two jobs. He couldn't cover the bills *and* be a fighter. He started his own business installing hardwood floors, and worked in the shipping & receiving department at a factory. The humbling reality of the situation was that while Sean was ranked number two in the world in his division, he was stuck working at a factory.

Working full-time was a huge adjustment for Sean, as he had not done so in about four years. He had been laid off from a job he had years ago after his fifteenth fight. As Sean spoke, I could not believe how similar our paths were; I, too, laid down hardwood floors and lived the factory life. The hardest part for me to bear was to know that I had a set of skills that could be utilized for something much greater. The dampening of the soul, the layoff adding to the unremitting stress, and late bill payments adding their own frustration…I knew exactly where Sean was coming from.

"I had one loss in my career, I was like thirty—I was like thirty-two wins and one loss… you know? Making fifteen bucks an hour, you know it's… I mean, like I said, I was willing to do whatever it took and that's the path that I followed and I did it." Sean accepted the cards he was dealt and did what was best for his family. But he also persevered, put his nose to the grindstone, and battled through the obstacles, knowing that someday it would be worth it.

So, Sean worked long days, five to seven days a week, weekends, holidays—whatever it took to pay the bills. He had been working for six months at both jobs when the Ultimate Fighter Season was announced. The show was widely successful, the Forrest Griffin fight with Stephan Bonner was legendary, and the show along with the fights attracted millions of new and faithful fans.

Shortly after the show aired, the UFC began announcing extra shows, fifteen shows a year to be exact. Before the addition, the UFC would put on a show once every few months. Sean realized that the need for fighters would also increase. Sean then made a life-changing phone call to his manager. "So you want to try giving the UFC a call and see if they are interested?"

Trying to open doors only to find them locked can get discouraging, but that 100th door might actually open, unveiling a new path before you. That is exactly what happened to Sean when the UFC gave him a nice four-fight contract.

Sean did not like working at the factory. His hot-head boss was nineteen years old and liked ordering everyone around, including Sean. Sean couldn't handle it, but really who could? The job sucked even without having a punk there.

Sean was on his phone talking to his manager; a four-fight deal, the pay and date being decided, giving Sean twelve weeks to prepare, and the kicker was that it was not going to be a tune-up or warm-up fight. Sean was ranked about number five at that point, and he would face a hungry, young contender ranked number two; Georges St-Pierre. Rather than second-guessing himself, Sean was pumped and ready to go to war.

As Sean discussed his future plans on the phone, sitting on the dingy factory floor, his boss was staring like an eagle from his desk, as it wasn't break time yet and Sean was on the phone. "I could see him pacing back and forth… Watching me talking on the phone. As soon as I got off the phone, I just walked over to him and said 'I quit, so, well, see you, I'm done.' I said 'I'm a fighter, dude, I'm out of here.'" As easy as that, Sean had wiped the smirk off his boss's face, told the place to fuck itself in a figurative manner, and proceeded to fulfill his life plan all in a matter of minutes. He was back on track—thanks to his patience, perseverance, strong conviction, and faith in himself and his abilities.

Sean lost to GSP, but then beat Nick Diaz and won the UFC world title, which he also successfully defended. Sean had made the right decision, and the psychological war between responsibility and risk must have been hard for him, but he believed that he would reach the top. To top it off, he beat some of the best fighters in the world.

I chimed in to let Sean know that, speaking for all of his fans, we were very happy he decided to pursue this path despite all of the hardships. His actions revealed a great deal about the strength of his character.

His eyes widened as he explained his philosophy on quitting and the toughness of the sport. "You know, you're going to find yourself in a lot of different situations in this industry, not only in the industry but in the cage. I mean, you're going to be in a lot of bad situations that you've got to fight back from. So your demeanor and your personality is what's going to help you win fights regardless of whether it's inside the cage or outside the cage."

I shifted the focus of the conversation to his nickname, the mystery of its origin had been burning in my mind. The "Muscle Shark" was a bad-ass nickname. He enlightened me, saying that the name had come from Japanese fans when he fought in Pride. The "Muscle" part is self-explanatory; I mean, Sean looks like he should be winning bodybuilding competitions, as new muscle appears to grow on top of existing muscle. As for "Shark," it written in Japanese *kanji* characters and refers to the shark-like ferocity of his attacks and takedowns.

Sean didn't know about the nickname when he went over to fight in Pride FC. He didn't have a nickname and didn't think he was a nickname kind of guy. Sean fought at Pride Bushido 2 in front of a crowd of 22,000. However, Japanese fans are different from North American fans in the sense that they don't make noise during the fight except for some "oohs and ahhhs" and that they clap when a fighter makes a transition or lands a move or punch.

As Sean was battling it out, he could practically hear a pin drop in the ring. He heard the commentators discussing the fight. "Which was a trip, you know, because I can hear Bas Rutten, who's sitting front and center commentating the fight, and he keeps talking about 'The Muscle Shark… The Muscle Shark' and I'm actually thinking to myself who the hell is this Muscle Shark guy? I'm putting on a pretty good fight… Bas keeps talking about this Muscle Shark and I'm thinking to myself, 'Man, why he is talking about the Muscle Shark dude?' I'm fighting, you know? I'm getting a little frustrated now. He's talking about the damn Muscle Shark, and I resolved to address this after the fight.

Afterwards, Bas comes over and says 'Hey what do you think about your new nickname, "The Muscle Shark?"' I'm like, ah, you were talking about me...."

Sean had obviously reached this level through hard work, which included strength and conditioning training at API. Sean had been training with the Minnesota Martial Arts Academy for a long time. Scott Ramsdell, one of the owners of API, originally wanted to work with fighters at the Minnesota Martial Arts Academy. Sean recounted the first time he was put through a Caveman routine with Brock Larson and Nick Thompson. It was only a fifteen-minute workout and Sean was in good shape; he was training for Kenny Florian at the time. Sean was sore for two days after the fifteen-minute routine!

"So, that was the wake-up call for me. It's like, look, I'm in great shape, but obviously there's more I can do, you know, because there is always more. There's something missing here if I'm getting sore from the workout that he just put me through. I shouldn't be getting sore."

Sean began working with the API guys on a regular basis, and (as detailed in Chapter Four) they eventually opened a facility right next door to the Minnesota Martial Arts Academy, making it very convenient for the fighters.

During our interview, Sean told me that he worked with API twice a week. But, when he was fighting at 170 pounds (welterweight division), he would still pursue free-weight training six days a week. While in the 155-pound division (lightweight category), he lifted weights four days a week.

His free-weight training had been reduced as a result of so much API functional strength training. "Functional training overplays, overpowers free weights any day... How many times am I going to need this motion in a fight? [Demonstrating the shoulder pressing motion.] Not too often."

Sean really enjoyed functional strength exercises, such as flipping tires, sprints, cable work, sledge hammers, and climbing ropes that used various muscle groups for the strength conditioning portion, but he also enjoyed the cardiovascular system for full mobility. He maintains weight training using heavier weights to gain some extra power. However, weight training is no longer his primary focus.

He spoke about UFC All Access, which generated significant interest in this new style of training. API was pioneering the training field in this regard, and Sean had the definite edge, thanks to the API trainers. He credited Scott for the training, as showcased on the widely popular show that highlighted how these athletes prepared for their fights.

As for his six-day per week training with the Minnesota Martial Arts Academy, he would do some type of striking, wrestling, and grappling training every day. The routines changed constantly—it would not be hard and intense every day, nor would it be the same workout every day.

Some days he did pad work while others he jumped into live sparring. Some days he wrestled from the feet, while others from the clinch. When it came to jiu-jitsu, he started on the ground some days, while other days he drilled with submissions. He switched things up to keep it fresh and new, but his rule was that he would do something on the feet as well as on the ground every day.

As for the mental game, I pried into the deeper recesses of his mind, regarding what he felt and thought during his fights. He did compare fighting to an emotional roller-coaster ride. Spending twelve weeks engulfed in training and preparing for one day; the fight day. "Everything comes down to this fifteen-minute time period of your life, you know? You've got to depend on all your hundreds of hours of training and video, and breaking down your opponents and all your conditioning and your mental and physical preparation, all the physical preparation is complete come fight day. Now, from that point on, it just becomes mental."

I had opened Pandora's Box as he proceeded: "There are so many different emotions going on, you know, nerves obviously, excitement, anxiety. You just want to get in there, you want to get it done, you're excited to show everyone what you can do, you're excited to fight for your fans and your friends and your family and everything like that. So it's a pretty damn emotional day; it's an exciting day. You know, that's the day I most dread—fight day… And that's the day I most look forward to. So there's a kind of a double-edged sword involved there."

We also spoke about injuries, as he had been out of action for a while. He battled injuries for some time until deciding that he would not fight injured anymore, as it was not worth the risk at that point in his career. With injuries, he'd gone into training camps, unable to train at full capacity, then into cage fighting at about eighty percent of his ability. He did add that, when he returned, he wanted to fight top contenders, as he had fought only top contenders in the last five years of his career. It has been five years since he fought someone outside the top ten in the world. That was the momentum he needed, and he couldn't see himself deviating from that.

Sean is always focused on goals; thus, he trains and diets hard, second to none. He does everything he has to in order to keep focused on pursuing his goals, remaining strict with no excuses.

I figured that all the focus, travel, time, and commitment must have been hard on his family life. Sean was very frank with me: "It probably is, you know, but there is going to be some kind of a give and take somewhere. Either my family life is going to suffer a little bit or my career is going to suffer. Either way, someone is going to suffer.…"

Sean has a wonderful family, an amazing wife and two kids, and they actually live in the same town he grew up in. He saw no reason to move away or do anything different after his climb to success. He literally lives three miles away from the high school he attended.

He did admit that at this point, his career was very important to him and he wanted to focus on it as much as possible. When training for fights, Sean would be home more often, but when not training for fights, he would be gone three to four days a week doing seminar circuits in different states and countries. While in training camp, he would be home every day.

Sean spends about eight to ten hours a day at the gym, not training every minute of that time, of course, but he would stay at the gym all day, even between training sessions. He naps or eats during breaks; he brings his own food so that he doesn't have to leave the gym. Sean goes home around seven in the evening, similarly to when working a regular nine-to-five job.

His diet at the time of the interview was 80:20, meaning that he was eating very clean for eighty percent of his diet, while the remaining twenty percent was not so clean. When in training mode, Sean is in 100% strict eating mode, mainly eating fish, chicken, raw fruits, and vegetables while trying to keep his sodium intake very low. He would eat about 3,500 calories a day, with any more making him feel run-down. He stated: "I look at my body as a machine and it will perform better if I put better fuel in it."

During our second interview, I asked Sean to break down a typical day while in training mode. He would wake up, eat, take his vitamins, and drink his fruit shake. He would gather all of his stuff and prepare a meal or two to take with him because he lived forty miles from the gym. On the way to the gym, he would have something small to eat; he mentioned that he always had raw oatmeal, almonds, and baby food in the truck. He would then work out and make a protein shake in his own blender he kept at the gym. He would make sure to add a banana for the potassium, so that he would not get cramps from the extreme duress he was putting his body through. He would have lunch and then chill out for an hour or two while surfing the Internet. Sean would then try to fit in two training sessions in a row in an attempt to get home earlier. Typically, he would get to the gym at around 10:30 a.m. and get home at around 7:00–7:30 p.m.

Changing our conversation to a question I thought he would have to think about, I asked him who would be his dream match, and his eyes lit up. He stated that there had been a minor feud between Dana White and boxing bad boy Floyd Mayweather during which Floyd stated that he could knock out any UFC fighter. Dana was quick to retaliate, asking Floyd to fight his lightweight champion, which happened to be Sean Sherk.

Sean answered my question before I could even ask him whether he would fight, "I would have; fuck, yeah, I mean, you know what I would do to that dude, do you have any idea what would happen?"

Sean, Dana, and Lorenzo Fertitta decided to attend the Floyd Mayweather vs. Oscar De La Hoya fight to show their interest in the super fight. As soon as the boxing match was over, Dana received a text message from either Mayweather's manager or trainer stating that they were just kidding and they did not want to fight Sean Sherk. Sean was visibly disappointed at the cop out, as he clearly would have liked to get his hands on the boxing champ in an MMA match.

For aspiring athletes looking to get into the MMA scene, the veteran had some advice: "If you don't put the time in, you can't expect to get the results. I've spent the majority of my career in the gym, and the results have shown that."

Sean also finds time to help train police officers and military soldiers any chance he gets. He spoke about the fact that he would train the two professions differently, as the military had no "use of force" issues. He hoped that they would use what he passed on to them, particularly in life-threatening situations. There was one such situation that I wanted him to open up about. Sean had conducted a seminar for police officers and received a phone call from one of the officers about a month later. The officer wanted Sean to know that he was confronted while on duty by an individual with a knife. The officer used Sean's techniques and took the perpetrator down with a double-leg takedown to get him under control. It reaffirmed the way that MMA could save lives and made Sean want to help in any way he could.

Sean was also busy building up a revolutionary tool for athletes, being half owner of Training Mask. It was a gas mask used for training that had been redesigned to fit the face better. It was also much smaller and more ergonomic. He started using it to train for his fight against B.J. Penn when no one was using it. He was in really good shape at the time, and it tired him out quickly, so he figured there had to be something to it. "It simulates a high altitude atmosphere and provides resistance breathing. Simulated altitude effect means that the red blood cell count is going to increase and your conditioning is going to get better. The resisted breathing effect means that it strengthens your lungs, as you have to fight to get air in and out of your lungs… thus it promotes the ability to expand and retract, in turn, more oxygen goes to your muscles. The response has been phenomenal."

It is amazing how versatile Sean is while helping pioneer so many facets of the sport. That's why it comes as no surprise that MMA websites and forums suggest that Sean should be inducted into the UFC Hall of Fame. I asked for his thoughts on the matter, and he replied in a way that "go-getters" often do, stating that he hadn't accomplished all of the things he wanted to yet. He would like another World Title. Being a two-time UFC World Champion would put him into a entirely different class of athletes, as there are only a handful of guys that have managed to do that.

"As far as me ever being indicted into the UFC Hall of Fame, I mean that would be phenomenal, you know that's something that you can never take away; that is something that would highlight my entire career. I've had an eleven-year career, and to be inducted into the UFC Hall of Fame would be a great ending to a storybook career."

The famous host and MMA analyst for Sportsnet's *UFC Central*, Joe Ferraro, spoke to this author about his thoughts on the "Muscle Shark." "I met Sherk on numerous occasions. Sherk actually fought for me when I was working for Universal Combat

Challenge, and it was my first real glimpse at what an exceptional wrestler can do to another elite fighter. Overall, outside of the cage, he is one of the most intense guys, always smiling—just one of those super, super nice guys."

Sean has devoted his entire life to sports, be it MMA or wrestling, and both sports meant a lot to him. He lived and breathed the sport, and sacrificed a lot, but he would not have it any other way. He has experienced a lot during his rollercoaster career; there was good and bad; but he always pushed forward, regardless of the situation. Although he has found success, his innate drive will not let him stop, and his experiences will make sure he gets by unscathed. Sean parted by adding, "You know, every time I get into a situation, I can draw from previous experience, which I think is really important."

It's another life lesson that we can all use.

QUICK ROUND
What's your favorite junk food?
Pizza.

If we listened to your music playlist, what would we find?
You'd find a mix of everything. I've got rock music on there, I've got 80s music on there, I've country music on there, and I have rap music on there, and that's a lot of everything, like 600 songs.

Favorite city to fight in the world?
The places I like to fight are the places that are more low-key, you know, not so much Vegas, maybe more Chicago, Indiana was cool.

Favorite dinner dish?
Maybe lasagna. I can cook, too; a lot of people don't know that. I do cook man, I grew up wrestling and I spent half of my life dreaming about food. You know, because as wrestlers, I think wrestlers can never eat.

In your eyes, who is your favorite and most notable win?
I would have to say Tyson. That's probably my favorite fight just because I think when we were out there fighting, we were legitimately having fun. My favorite win would be when I won the belt.

What would you say is your biggest strength?
Mental toughness.

Chapter Six

CANADA'S FIRST PARADISE WARRIOR RETREAT

"Destiny is not a matter of chance, but of choice. Not something to wish for, but to attain."
—William Jennings Bryan

After the API trip, I had new and high standards for how I wanted to pass my time. One evening, an acquaintance called screaming into the phone. "IIII just thinkImight-thaveesomethingreaalyybig!" I had no idea what the hell he just said. "Hey, slow down. What are you talking about?" He took a breath, "Paradise Warrior Retreat is coming to Toronto, and we are putting it together!"

The Paradise Warrior Retreat was founded by Yoram Gazit, who resides in sunny California, and brings together the best trainers and fighters in the world for huge, multi-day workshops. Yoram was in the Israeli military, and after learning Krav Maga, took a liking to combat sports. The rest is history.

I knew that if I committed to this, it was 100% or nothing; there was no half-assing it. To put together a three-day seminar with food, hotel stays, flights, nightclubs, and plenty of negotiations for the best fighters in the world was a large undertaking. I figured it was a once-in-a-lifetime opportunity and that I had the skills to put it together, but most importantly, I brought the ultimate fan's perspective to the event.

My fan experience was a key component in how I thought the seminar should go. As a practitioner *and* a fan, I had ideas that were unheard of in typical seminars. A second important component was the quality of instruction and the quantity. Yoram always had anywhere between three to five top quality instructors at his seminars.

The uphill battle began, as months flew by while meticulous planning, negotiating, and marketing took place. Yoram and I were tracking down fighters as we spoke with managers to get the best deals. The math was against us from the start when we added seven paid fighters to our roster. I was stoked when we secured MMA legend Bas Rutten, UFC champion Matt Serra, Muay Thai legend Rob Kaman, Strikeforce Champion Renato Babalu Sobral, UFC MMA rising star Demian Maia, UFC Veteran David Loiseau, and IFL star LIUNA-sponsored Chris Horodecki. On top of that, Jeff Joslin, one of my coaches from Hamilton who fought Josh Koschek in the UFC, was attending as one of the practitioners. Eight respective champions were going to be under the same roof, projecting their knowledge onto some really lucky participants. We had all elements of Mixed Martial Arts covered, ranging from wrestling and jiu-jitsu to striking.

The next phase involved hotels, food, transportation services, and nightclubs. This was definitely not an easy endeavor, as we made painfully slow progress, and truthfully, we were stretched thin financially. The venue was chosen to be Kombat Arts, a monstrous gym off the highway in Mississauga, Ontario, whose management was used to having the best in the world present their skills within their facility. Hector, one of the owners, provided never-ending assistance.

However, such a large-scale event inevitably brings planning hiccups along the way. Initially, we had newly crowned UFC champion Antonio Nogueira and ex-UFC champion Andre Arlovski on board. But at the last minute, neither could make it. We got used to shuffling the roster.

I had made countless trips to Mississauga and Toronto to scope out hotels, the gym, and to drop off our flyers at local gyms across the Greater Toronto Area. My wife joked, "After your API caveman training, you have now taken that to heart. You are a caveman. All you do is lock yourself in the computer room and work!" Admittedly, I did have a beard growing out; I must have looked and smelled like a caveman for sure.

But I pressed forward. The months melted away the summer heat, and September came rolling faster than I could have imagined. I spent countless hours on the phone with Yoram, devising strategy, checking on ticket sales, etc. As the three-day retreat approached, I zoned out on everything, forgetting that all of these guys coming were my idols and looking at it as "business"; that was the only way I could be productive enough to pull this thing off.

Day one of the event involved organizing and checking on talent arrivals. I had recruited Jeff Phillips to help out, and without him I would have never pulled this off.

It was Thursday, a sunny September day as we drove to the airport to pick up MMA bad boy Renato Babalu Sobral, as we couldn't secure a sponsored limo that day. The flight was a bit delayed, and we weren't sure if the flight would ever arrive. Not wanting to pay for the overpriced airport parking, we had another guy circling the airport every time the parking police told him not to stand in the No Parking zones.

Renato Babalu Sobral is one of my all-time favorite fighters—he will never shy away from a fight, regardless of the circumstances. From his early days of bare-knuckle boxing on the streets of Brazil, he always had a reputation as a tough guy. I liked his all-out style in the cage, as well as his tattoos. It was Babalu with his tribal tattoo on his hand that got me thinking about getting inked. It eventually led me to three tattoos as of the writing of this book from Perfect Image Studio in London, Waterloo, Grand Bend and other locations across Canada. I decided to go with the best shop and the best tattoo artist Jesse Smith, as his style and attention to detail were second to none. Renato had his symbols and warrior pride etched across his "canvas," and it convinced me to do the same eventually. We chatted to the techno beats of Scooter playing in the background of our car, and he mentioned liking it as he bobbed his head to the beat. I couldn't believe that he had never before heard Scooter's mastered beats.

As the troops began slowly trickling in, I started getting that gut feeling that this was special. I quickly bonded with Demian Maia, known as the best jiu-jitsu fighter in the middleweight division and quite possibly the entire UFC. He made guys with black belts look like amateurs in his MMA matches. He was a bit shorter than me, with a very warm and friendly face. He was built like a fighter, cauliflower ears and all, but with a coat and hat on, one might never suspect him of being one of the highest-ranked fighters in the world. There was something very genuine about him that I could not grasp, an aura of goodness. I quickly learned that we had a lot in common.

As we spoke about our backgrounds, I learned that he was half-Polish in a sense. His father had the warm blood of Brazil, while his mom came from a place that used to be Poland but eventually ended up as part of Russia. Our discussions on heritage reminded me of how small this world really is.

Renato Babalu looked like he should be cast with Vin Diesel in an upcoming action movie. He had the looks that girls liked and the skills that guys wanted. He was a straight-shooter and had a great sense of humor right out of the gate.

I had trained at Adrenaline for quite a while, so I knew Chris Horodecki fairly well. He had boyish good looks and devastating kickboxing skills, thanks to his coach, Shawn Tompkins. He was unstoppable, and undefeated, in the IFL. Chris was great with the fans, and I was very happy to have him with us during the event.

We had a few beers that night at the hotel bar, just shooting the shit, while Yoram kept getting last-minute phone calls from people wanting to sign up. It was fun sitting with the best talent in the world over a cold brewski; I was privileged to be in such great company.

The next morning, we escorted another one of my favorite fighters to the limo, ex-UFC welterweight champion Matt Serra. Matt was a shorter, stocky fighter; as we greeted him at the terminal, it was hard not to notice that his neck was wider than my thighs. He had a thick New Jersey accent. "Hey bro, what's happening?" The guy had the ability to put a smile on my face every time he spoke.

In the past, I had the privilege of attending a seminar with him at Kombat Arts. He asked which moves he had done at the past seminar, so as not to duplicate them, and I jumped into my flying monkey routine, showing him all I could remember. Looking back on it now, I must have looked like a buffoon mimicking funny movements to Matt

Serra in front of the limo driver.

The entire squad, excluding Bas Rutten, had arrived at that point, and everyone was situated in their rooms. It was time to proceed to the gym. Once there, Hector of Kombat Arts had things running smoothly. We could not have done the retreat without him. Students of the game were warming up and were filled with excitement as we brought the fighters inside.

In the middle of the mats, Yoram and the fighters sat in front of the crowd and began the opening ceremonies, which were customary for Paradise Warrior Retreats. A few words regarding accomplishments were provided about each fighter, followed by some quick questions from the crowd. I was happy to see that Canadian rock star, fighter, and commentator Robin Black was one of the attendees.

The seminar proceeded with each fighter filling a slot throughout the day. It was something different to have the best fighters in the world showing the techniques that helped them become the best. While I spent a lot of time running around making sure everyone was taken care of, I jumped into the seminars any chance I got. The setup was great; we had a nutrition store handing out protein shakes so that the practitioners could re-energize during their breaks.

Surprisingly, going on coffee runs provided the most fun, thanks to Matt Serra himself. The other fighters, gym owners, and Yoram all had regular coffee requests, but Matt's were astronomical. His request looked more like separate coffees than all the others on the list combined. It had two shots of this, three shots of that, mixed with sugar, creamer, and a shot of that. The only person at the Starbucks who could put one together properly was the manager. Every time I would place the order, I bypassed the "These are all separate right?" questions by asking them to get the manager. I thought it was hilarious, but it was also a reflection of the complexity of Matt's character and sense of humor.

After the seminars, we waited for the limo to drive us to dinner. Demian Maia was the first one downstairs, with his signature UFC ballcap on. We sat on the couches in the lobby and chatted about MMA. He had just finished a workout, as he had a fight coming up in six weeks against Nate Quarry at UFC 91. Demian did go on to submit Nate with a rear naked choke. His very popular jiu-jitsu instructional DVDs really helped excel my game.

The rest of the guys slowly started arriving downstairs, but, as expected, we were running late. Once inside the limo, Rob Kaman commented that he had to go back to his room to use the washroom for a "number two." The other guys started heckling him in a playful way, but he protested that he would not go anywhere else to do his business.

Ten minutes later, we were finally on our way, and all the guys were in good spirits as we embarked on a busy night. That was the first time I had actually been in a limo, and I would not have it under any other circumstances. I felt like a movie star, with the best fighters in the world sitting beside me. We went to Shoeless Joe's for dinner, which was fun, and the food was amazing. The restaurant was packed with MMA enthusiasts, and all of the fighters were class-acts. Despite hot food in front of them, they took the time to pose for pictures and sign autographs.

After dinner, we ventured to a nightclub, where the real adventures began. We were escorted to the VIP section with an oversized bottle of Grey Goose glistening in an ice bucket. We were at one of the most popular clubs in Toronto, and the party was being thrown for us. Everyone was having fun, but I couldn't really let loose, as I had to oversee all matters throughout the night. Between pouring alcohol, making sure the guys were staying out of trouble, and getting Demian Maia his water bottles (he doesn't drink during fight prep), I was busy all night.

The VIP treatment was nice, and even with the long line at the bar to purchase alcoholic beverages, I just motioned what I needed and the bartender would stop what she was doing to fill my order, free of charge of course. The bartender killed it with the drinks, while the DJ was giving props to our visitors. The place was complete craziness, the music pumped, and alcohol flowed.

Once the time came to round everyone up to get back to the limo, I felt like a school teacher on a class trip, and I really could have used a freaking rope to tie everyone's hands together to lead them out. I led a couple of fighters out, and then one would go back in while I was rounding the next two up. It was a complete Three Stooges skit.

I thought everyone was back in the limo when, to my surprise, Demian was still inside, so I ran out for him but first I admonished everyone to behave and stay in the limo. When I came back with Demian, all hell had broken loose and the club owner was outside trying to defuse a situation in the middle of the street with some guys that got kicked out of the club. Tensions were high, and a couple of fighters ran into the circle. At that moment, my heart skipped a beat. I felt my stomach rise into my throat. My brain took a fraction of a second to grasp the potential catastrophe, and I scrambled to run after my errant fighters. Another fighter, not to be named, was there to help, so we gently guided the first fighter to the limo to avert a potential disaster.

Once inside, I was sitting on the floor of the limo because we had too many people crammed inside. We were cracking jokes as the limo, which was parked in the alley between the club and a store, started moving but then came to a screeching stop. From the corner of the limo we heard a thick Brooklyn accent, "Holy shit! It's a horse's ass!" All heads in the limo turned in unison to see an actual horse's ass pressed up against the limo window, and it was making a squeaking sound as it squashed up on the window. Matt Serra was not lying. A mounted police officer had shown up near the crowd where the pushing match had spilled into the busy downtown street.

We were all in stitches laughing; I actually had a tear in my eye from laughing so hard. The limo was buzzing with excitement as we proceeded down the street and away from the action. We were yelling at the driver to get the hell out of there.

A few stoplights later, when everyone was calming down from the excitement, Matt Serra opened the window beside him. Matt was our jester who was conjuring up another round of hilarity. Matt's thick accent echoed "Wow, it's like the exorcist!" All heads turned once again with one quick swoop to focus on Matt's corner of the car.

Matt had his head out the window as he was staring at the epitome of the college lifestyle. A kid in his early twenties was inebriated to the point that he had his head stuck out of his cab window and was throwing up between our limo and his cab. The best part was that he had his mouth open with zero gag as a steady stream of vomit was gushing out of him. It truly looked like a scene from the famous movie. His eyes were yellow, his eyelids drooped low, and he was as pale as a ghost as he emptied his guts onto the street. Yet again, we all burst out laughing, this new experience adding fun to the already memorable night.

Then I murmured something about what the kid would tell his buddies the next day, "Hey man, I was so messed up yesterday I could have sworn that Matt Serra was laughing at me as I puked!" And everyone burst out laughing again, as it would likely prove to be true.

David Loiseau was cracking jokes left and right as the night wound down, and we pulled into the entrance of our hotel. We piled out one-by-one with smiles on our faces. Once in my hotel room, I was ready to crash but had a bit of a stomach ache, either from the bad fast food I had been subjected to the past few days or from the stress from the weekend getting to me. It hit me just how much responsibility I had on my shoulders.

The next morning was another early one, and all that kept me going was my duty to put on the best seminar anyone had ever seen. We started the day off well. Everything was on track, and a lot of the practitioners were expressing their excitement to Yoram and me. It was enough to put a semi-permanent smile on my face; all of the hard work was paying off.

Jeff and I drove over to the hotel to pick up Rob Kaman, as his part of the seminar was coming up. We were slightly early and figured it would be better if the fighters had to wait a bit rather than making the paying practitioners wait. We knocked on the door and got no response. We looked at each other with panic-stricken faces. Fearing that he might still be sleeping, we banged harder on the door. The door opened and neither Jeff nor I could contain ourselves as we burst out laughing. Rob opened the door wearing only a hand towel on his waist. It was like the scene from *Starsky and Hutch* with Ben Stiller and Owen Wilson, when they wore comically small towels in the locker room. He must have been sleeping and rushed to open the door, grabbing the first towel he saw, all the while being fully cognizant of the comedic value of the situation. I really respected Rob as a fighter, but thanks to the experience with the Paradise Warrior Retreat, I began to respect and like him even more as a person.

I participated in Rob's well-attended seminar, in order to learn a few new techniques. What I noticed right away was that even the big guys were still students of the game;

Demian was enthralled with Rob Kaman's training, Matt Serra was super attentive to Demian Maia's techniques, Jeff Joslin was taking in all that Babalu was demonstrating, and so on. It was a great thing to see that they still felt they had a lot to learn, even at the elite level.

I paired with Jeff Phillips as we tested our newly learned techniques. Chris Horodecki was snapping kicks beside us as I was perfecting my switch kicks. Toward the end of the session, we lined up at the Thai bags and were tasked with throwing ten consecutive kicks on each side. Renato Babalu was in front of me, so once he was done with his kicks it was his turn to keep the ninety-pound bag from swaying too violently. As he stepped beside the bag to hold it with his palms, he seemed a bit spaced out, so I laid into my kicks as hard as I could. Being that my best weapon is my right kick, I put the heat to the side of the bag, which in turn swung and hit Babalu to the point that he took a step back. Chris Horodecki and the rest of the bunch in my line were chuckling as I seemed to bring Babalu back to us, gripping the bag tightly to his body right away, to keep it from swaying again. It felt great to show off my skills and train with these guys, I mean, I never missed any of Babalu's fights, and here we were, training and having fun together!

During Matt Serra's session, I paired with Demian Maia himself, which was an honor. We were working a bit on takedowns and takedown defense when Demian asked me to do some live drilling with him. I was to try to stop his takedowns at all costs. I pumped my arms and got into a low wrestling stance, hoping to test the UFC's best grappler. As you may have guessed, he had me down within a few seconds, over and over again. Although I had a good twenty pounds on him, it was ridiculous how easy it was for him to take me down and pass my guard. I felt like it was my first day of Brazilian jiu-jitsu training. He earned world Brazilian jiu-jitsu titles for a good reason.

The event created a lot of new friendships, including one between Renato Babalu Sobral and Rob Kaman. Because of that weekend, they began working together, as Rob Kaman helped prepare Renato Babalu for his future bouts in Strikeforce.

That night, we had a similar itinerary to the previous night, this time at Boston Pizza and then at another club where the VIP room awaited us. Boston Pizza was absolutely packed with fans as we squeezed our way inside. The guys took their pictures with the establishment owners and staff, and then we were on our way to the club.

Bas Rutten had the nicest and largest watch on, so I complimented it. His response was golden: "It adds weight to my punches to produce knockouts!" I saw another *Hangover*-style night unfolding in front of my eyes. While en route to the night club, we drove by the Rogers Centre, formerly known as the Skydome, which is the home of the Toronto Blue Jays baseball team. It is a monstrous dome with a roof that opens during good weather, and it can accommodate really large crowds.

Bas noted that he loved fighting for the Japanese organization, Pride FC, in front of 50,000-plus fans. He correctly predicted that one day there would be a UFC event held at the Rogers Centre with just as many fans as were at Pride FC events. Bas has always been known as an astute fighter, coach, commentator, actor and businessman, but now he could add seer to the list. He knew very well back then where the sport was heading, and years later, the UFC sold over 50,000 seats for their first showing in Toronto.

For a legend in the sport of MMA, Bas was very personable and warm. We engaged in small-talk together as we inched closer to our destination, but during that short time I found out a lot about him. He really is a shrewd individual, and there is a good reason why he achieved so much success in life. As we rolled to the back entrance of the bar, we piled out. Surveying the scene from the very back of the group, I mused about how wonderful it was to have eight of the best from the martial arts realm all together for one goal.

The practitioners and fans were entering the club as we bypassed the line and went in. The head of security came up to me to have a few words about the night's proceedings. He said that the bouncer in charge of us trains at Xtreme Coutures and that they would handle any situation that would arise. He pleaded with me for us not to intervene, as they really liked the club "the way it looked." I quickly thought about potential disasters as I considered the makeup of the crowd. We had eight world champions and a lot of MMA practitioners that would jump in at a drop of a hat, plus Jeff, Yoram, and me. I figured that World War III would be the worst-case scenario if someone started trouble.

The night flew by yet again as my duties kept me busy attending to the guys. I even had the opportunity to meet the owners of Round 5 Collectibles. They were the makers of some amazing collectible UFC fighter figures, and I must admit to being a "big kid," as I have a large collection of my own, including most of the fighters present there that weekend.

Once we got back to the room after the long night, I was really not feeling well. The long twenty-hour days coupled with the long months of preparation had taken its toll on me. I crashed like a baby, dreaming about a hammock and a beach.

On the last day, there was a memorable moment when one of the practitioners actually shed a few tears as he explained his dreams to his idol, Bas Rutten. The practitioner was a long-time ultimate fan of Bas Rutten's; he even religiously trained to Bas's tapes in his basement. The emotions swept him to tears as he expressed his happiness at training with and meeting his long-time idol.

The experience was second-to-none, the highs and lows of putting it together, the amazing individuals I had the opportunity to meet, from the fighters to the participants … this was something I will always cherish. I proved to myself that I was capable of doing it. In fact, doing a Paradise Warrior Retreat on such a scale was an amazing achievement and something of which I can always be proud. Would I do it again? Well, I will leave it to Yoram and attend as a participant. Sure, I earned plenty of gray hairs from the experience, but I will never forget the crazy weekend with the boys.

Chapter Seven

A PIECE OF ME IN POLAND

"Victory is reserved for those who are willing to pay its price."　　　**—Sun Tzu**

For our honeymoon trip, Beata and I decided to go to our native country of Poland. I had not been to my homeland in over fifteen years, and I was definitely chiding myself for taking so long to get back to my roots. I was not planning on training formally while there, but neither my wife nor I really believed that I could resist.

During our second week, we were touring the beauty that Poland offered, and I noticed a flyer for K-1 kickboxing with Poland's kickboxing and Savate champion, Rafał Chwałek. I quickly glanced at my wife, only to see her roll her eyes and mutter "Okay, take the flyer and let's go," pushing out the words with an effort.

A couple days later, I had my shorts and fight shirt in hand as we walked through the old fairytale-like city with a smile stretching from ear-to-ear. The European architecture was breathtaking, with charming stone carvings and decorations not found in Canada. We decided to grab a quick bite before tracking down the high school where my first class was to take place.

We ordered large glasses of beer, as we took in the sites and the warm breeze kissed our cheeks while we lingered on the cobblestone patio. I was still reworking my questions for Rafał, as after doing some research I learned that he was a bad-ass fighter with a similar style to Chuck Liddell. He was known for taking a Savate fight on short notice against the French Savate champion who came to Poland to fight. When the intended Polish opponent became injured, Rafał accepted the fight and soon realized that he did not know how different the rules were compared to kickboxing, but went into the fight anyway. Without following the rules, he managed to knock out his opponent and become the Savate champion without ever knowing what he was doing in a sport still foreign to him.

My wife gave me her unfinished beer, and I chugged it down as quickly as I could so I could get to class. That decision was not the best I've ever made, as now my knees felt a little wobbly as the alcohol robbed my head of its clarity.

The run-down high school looked like it had seen better days, with a decrepit yellow brick facade and bars on the windows, likely present for the sole purpose of holding them in place and not for keeping intruders out. It was a far cry from the beautiful European buildings surrounding it; I guess someone missed the memo when it came to renovating the building.

Once inside, we followed the long empty halls to the basement where the gymnasium was located, and I was shown to the washroom, which doubled as our changing room. I went over to the first sink to quickly wash my hands and rinse the beer stench out of my mouth, when I noticed it was not working. I proceeded to the next sink. I glanced at the toilets and noticed that they must have been put in before World War II.

I changed into my MMA gear and rushed out to meet the rest of the class as they were warming up. I also quickly checked on my loving wife, who was taping the session, and I joined the circle of participants in a run around the gym in circles. I had to pack enough clothes to last the trip; thus, I had to make the tough decision not to bring my gloves with me to Poland. Rafał Chwałek, who looked like he stepped off a hard-hitting action movie set, was instructing our movements.

Rafał had a gritty tough-guy look with a shaved head, broad shoulders, and sleeve tattoos. But when he smiled, he lit up the room. A yin-yang phenomenon was at work. He was very kind and generous, as he ran out of class to get me his gloves so that I could participate with the rest of the class. I still had the image of him being a stern, cigar-smoking type that shits bricks and eats children for breakfast, but that side of him only came out when he fought.

He was very well known for taking on the French Savate champion on last-minute notice when the Polish Savate fighter withdrew. Rafał and his coach did not know the rules of Savate, and when it dawned on him to ask his corner right before heading out to the ring, his coach yelled, "Knock his ass out!" That was exactly what he did to take the championship, without ever fully understanding the rules, which was badass in my books.

After having those two large beers prior to my arrival, I felt sluggish and sloppy as my heart raced to its own rhythm. Due to the intensity of the warm-ups, I could have sworn that I saw it protruding through my shirt. If a regular kickboxing class would run an hour in North America, it ran two hours in Poland. If regular warm-ups usually consisted of ten to fifteen minutes in North America, it felt like an eternity in Poland. Everyone in the class around me was drenched in sweat as we partnered up for the techniques portion of the class.

Rafał partnered me with one of his best students from that particular city—Rafał had molded many champions through two or three of his schools in different cities.

I noted that my partner had some experience under his belt just based on the way he swayed and moved.

We did our combinations on each other just like our instructor showed us. We did some combinations that I was not used to with a lot of switch kicks. My favorite was the left body switch kick to a harsh left sway followed by a left hook, as we had just put ourselves in an optimum position for it, then a right straight to switch high kick. It was one of those combinations that, with a little bit of work, was wonderful to use in sparring or a fight because the punches and kicks came in an unexpected sequence.

After we had spent some time perfecting four solid combinations, it was time to put them to use in the sparring portion of the class. I got a second wind at that point, as the blood was flowing more quickly through my veins. I was enjoying myself doing what I loved most with the person I loved most watching. We touched gloves and began the "oldest form of artistic dance," as my partner popped a jab first and bobbed back and forth very "Frankie Edgar"-like to sting me in the abdomen as I returned the favor to his midsection. He threw a left jab to right kick, so I threw a left, right to kick right back, tit-for-tat. He was aggressive and definitely had high proficiency, keeping me on my toes right from the start. My head movement proved to be beneficial as I swayed out of the way just enough to catch the breeze of his sixteen-ounce leather gloves, recoiling shots right back on numerous occasions.

I figured that within this chess game, I had to elevate the stakes. I aggressively rushed him in Vitor Belfort style with lefts and rights that accumulated a solid eight punch combination as he clambered and moved back. My confidence was soaring at that point; I was holding my own and even landing some nice shots of my own. I threw a lot of kicks and had to watch out for his Chuck Liddell-style overhands, which were solid. I landed a crisp Superman punch to the stomach and redirected the punch from the face midway, as I would have clipped him hard had I maintained course because he left his chin unguarded while throwing an overhand right at the same time. The moment I projected the Superman punch, it was rolling with some force, so not wanting to hurt him I quickly transitioned to the midsection. It made a snapping sound as it connected.

Only moments later, he showed me that he could also throw a solid Superman punch, as he clipped me with one. We were on the same technique level, and I thought it was great to be pushed like that. After the five-minute round, we embraced to show gratitude; I had a lot of respect for the guy. We did not let off the accelerator once during the long round.

We switched partners two more times, and my lungs burned. During my second sparring session, as we had others around us, we had to watch our immediate space, so we floated to the side of the gym. I kept stepping in a water-like substance and almost slipped once on it. It was starting to bug me, as it was a hazard on the gym floor.

My wife was waving at me as she videotaped the events. I just nodded and kept doing my thing, as I was trying to pull off some of the great combinations I learned earlier from Rafał. It was only after my last sparring session when my wife was really waving me down that I ran over to her. She was trying to tell me something important. I wish I would have been clued in much earlier.

She had noticed that one of the amateur fighters had reached his cardiovascular system's limits and had stopped midway through his sparring session. His face turned white as he put his hands on his waist, ate a hard right to the face for even daring to lower his guard, and then bend over like an accordion and went to town! The puke was very watery, and it spewed onto the old mosaic-style hardwood floor.

Beata had just clued me in on the mystery of the funky water that we were all slipping on. Only at that point did the culprit find a wet mop to clean up the mess he had made. I remembered my fond memory at the API facility when it happened to me, and I grinned. This was the outcome of pushing ourselves past our limits—it was lovely.

We had a small break and then worked the Thai bags hanging on the other side of the gym. Three minutes of smashing and bashing was unloaded onto those poor bags. I was paired up with my friend from my first spar. We pushed each other; I am sure from his eyes there was no way he would let some Polish-Canadian out-work him, and in my eyes, I would not let him out-work me. Boys will be boys, I guess. We popped long combinations as hard and fast as we could onto those Thai bags. I would usually finish with a solid kick or hook. We were both fast and quick on our feet given that we had just endured close to an hour and a half of solid hard work.

After three or four rounds, which seemed like an eternity, we grabbed some water and went back for stretches and a cool down. The stretches were mixed between static and dynamic types, and really felt great after such a demanding class. I was humbled, delighted, beat up, gasping for air, and once again in my element as we closed out the session. I really enjoyed the knowledge I took away from the class, adding more techniques to my repertoire.

Once in the locker room that doubled as a washroom, there was a line up to the showers and even the sinks; these guys were hardcore. They were also using the bathroom sinks to wash up so I figured "When in Rome…" I washed myself using the bathroom sink, thanked everyone for welcoming me to their team, and proceeded to the hallway, where my wife was waiting.

While in Poland, I knew that I had to maintain the pace I set out for myself in preparing for one of the largest grappling events in the world: Grapplers Quest. I would make it a morning ritual to go for a nice brisk run and take in the beautiful scenery. Then, I would add some sprints and shadow-boxing to the mix. I would usually knock off with some good stretches to keep me flexible. As I did not have an opportunity to grapple, I had to make the best of the situation.

My kryptonite in Poland was definitely the amazing food; meats, cheeses, desserts, ice cream, cakes, and crepes galore. My wife's grandmother prepared the best food, and given that almost all the food there is organic, I was in paradise.

I maintained a good workout schedule to keep myself in top form for the month, but the biggest change I noticed was the mental edge. My mind did not have to compute the stresses of everyday life; all it focused on was the gold medal at the event. My mind was at ease. I had the opportunity to train in many gyms with some amazing athletes, giving me confidence in my preparation.

During one of my workout sessions toward the end of my trip, I injured myself. It was ironic because, throughout the trip, I was throwing large clumps of coal using an oversized shovel. I was throwing strongman-style stones around, squatting with them in my training regimen, but it was during my light run that my back decided to give out. I was doing my normal routine, when at one point, I actually heard a pop come from the middle of my back. As I was still pumping my arms and in motion, the pain stung and spread a second later to such a degree that I had to completely stop midway through my stride. It felt like a sharp lightning bolt had hit my back. As easy as that, I was out of commission for weeks, even after returning to Canada. I was not happy to say the least.

I decided to use the down time to its fullest potential, taking advantage of the opportunity to sit out in the warm sun with a beer to be enlightened by some raw inspiration. I spoke with my wife's grandmother and grandfather on a very deep subject—something I knew I had to relay to others: their path through World War II.

In 1939, my wife's grandfather Edward was a young boy as his family attempted to flee from their native city of Bedzin due to the war, managing to reach the Russian border. As they were fleeing from the Nazis, his father had a bicycle packed with their clothes and food. They trekked more than 60 miles (100 km) on foot in approximately three days. Edward tried jumping onto the bike at one point because his feet pained him from the journey, and he ending up scraping his leg, resulting in a deep cut. The family took a detour so he could be helped by a doctor at a nearby hospital before continuing the trip. Once at the border, the Nazis had already closed all access out of the country, and everyone was being turned around, except for Polish military and anyone that caused the Nazis problems, who were detained or dealt with.

They stayed by the border for a couple weeks. While there, Edward saw the Nazis place so-called troublemakers in a straight line as they loaded their machine guns for the human firing range. However, in the nick of time, a superior officer came in, yelling at the soldiers and preventing death from occurring. After a couple of weeks, the entire family returned to their home in Bedzin, Poland, on a borrowed horse.

Edward was fortunate enough not to be taken against his will, but his world definitely changed after the Nazis took over the land and way of life his forefathers spent their entire lives building. They were able to walk the streets freely, but all adults had to work, no exceptions. The Nazi military was evident around every corner, as they patrolled with loaded weapons and heavy tanks rumbling over the loose cobblestone roads.

He lived through the war, but not without experiencing sacrifice and terror because of the invaders. The experience definitely contributed to his outlook on life in both positive and negative ways, but he was lucky to have survived such a sad and turbulent time in human history.

Years later, from 1953–1959, Edward worked as a rail police officer and really enjoyed the vocation. In 1958, as he was leaving the detachment, some hooligan blindsided him with a bottle, which connected with extreme force to his forehead and knocked him out. The bandit was trying to hit another rail officer and mistakenly hit Edward, thinking he was the target. Edward was laid up in the hospital for twenty days. Beata's mom was only four years old at the time when her father was in the hospital. Edward couldn't work for some time, as he was afflicted with constant dizzy spells due to the effects of the concussion. This prompted him to change professions, and he became the town painter until 2000, when he eventually retired. He was very busy as a painter, as the locals and business owners were put on long waiting lists for his services, meaning that he was good at what he did.

Beata's grandmother, Zofia, was placed in a Nazi camp in Lauf; her path during the war was completely different from Edward's. Her family ran with her from the Ukrainians to a local church, as Poles were being killed during the war. They were at the church for approximately one week in hiding, hoping to remain out of sight. The Nazis were retreating from the Russian military's insurgence and took all the Poles in the church with them, whether they liked it or not. The Nazis told the Poles that they were taking them somewhere within the Polish border, with a location to be decided in due time, which was a lie because they would take them straight to a German concentration camp in Lauf. The camp was surrounded by only a fence and sat within a vast forest. There, they endured oppression for nearly three grueling years.

Within the fences of the concentration camp, there was extreme poverty and complete filth, with people dying left and right. The camp's guarded entrance was gigantic, as was the walking path door, from what Zofia recalled. The showers were freezing cold without a pinch of heat, denying even the slightest measure of comfort to the captives. Life was not easy, and they all counted the days to what they thought was their impending doom.

Each room within the concentration camp contained approximately five families, and the beds were bunk bed style. Kids had to sleep with their parents, of course, in the tiny beds. The food was horrendous; for breakfast they had a small slice of bread and tea made from herbs that they picked from the surrounding forest. For lunch, they were given two potatoes with some sauce made from flour and some stray noodles—if they were fortunate enough to have a few make their way onto the plate. Dinner was the same as breakfast. Her parents would get tokens for working twelve-hour days at the factory nearby making ammunition so they could have butter and some extras to supplement their atrocious meals. The kids were stuck within the camp confines all day, under the watchful eyes of the elderly who were unfit to work.

They somehow survived while being subjected to monstrous conditions. Her father's foreman at the factory, who was a Nazi, would give him scraps from his regular meals to take back to the family as a reward for good work. But for others, it was common to see people swell up from hunger and eventually succumb. When her mother gave birth to twins, the Nazis took the opportunity to give the newborns "vitamin shots," as they called them. In reality, they were testing various harmful concoctions that caused internal damage at an alarming rate. Unfortunately, both of the twins passed away from the experiments, and Zofia would never have the opportunity to know her siblings.

She also recalled that the soap they were given was made of some unknown substance that attracted these funny bugs from the forest. The bugs added to this living hell, as they would arrive in swarms and bite in unconceivable numbers. Leading up to the end of the war, the danger of fly-over bombings by the Allies also existed. The detainees would hide in shallow dirt holes, a futile effort, because the holes couldn't provide shelter from the massive bombs being dropped nearby.

Finally, in 1945, when the Americans came to their rescue, the survivors gained something they had dreamed of for years: freedom. Zofia still remembered the taste of the American food and how good it was. They were well-cared for by the Americans for just over a month. The captives were allowed to go anywhere they wanted in the world and were encouraged to go stay with family in other counties. Her family opted to stay in Poland, as they had family-owned land they wanted to take back. However, they soon discovered that the Russians had taken over their land and surrounding areas, so it was no longer a viable option. They made do with what they had by starting from scratch in a new city within the Polish borders.

Zofia got past the horror of the war and worked for most of her life in the city of Kopalnia. She married, had two kids, and lived a wonderful, love-filled life. I was lucky to be in the presence of these two wonderful people and to call them family. They had overcome many obstacles, which only brought them closer together over the years. They had recently celebrated their sixtieth wedding anniversary—a true inspiration and model for others to follow.

I sat in amazement and awe as they told me about a world harsher than I could ever fathom. There have been many instances in life when I thought things were bad, but my problems paled in comparison to being taken against one's will and thrown into a concentration camp, not knowing when the end would come. My heart filled with compassion for my in-law grandparents as they described the hardships they had endured in life. On the other hand, they became stronger life partners and saw the world in a better light, and had relied on their perseverance and strength to guide them through their nightmares.

I knew that the fight game was harsh and an uphill struggle, but having the inner fight, drive, and tenacity to overcome anything was a key contributor to success. There would be times of hardships and peril, and times when quitting would cross my mind, but at those crossroads I could uncover the ability to overcome and reach Maslow's hierarchy of needs—the highest pinnacle of self-actualization. Maslow described the self-actualization stage as the hardest to achieve and as the ability to reach full potential. Mastering all other levels in the pyramid, which included physiological, safety, love/belonging, and esteem, is the goal. Hardships provide the opportunity to reach deep inside ourselves and gain a better understanding of our wants, needs, and true desires, as well as to build thicker skin to reach our goals.

Talking to Edward and Zofia reinforced the idea that things could always be worse and that having the right people around was the most important variable, and if I was healthy, all else would follow with smart, hard work. I started looking at life in a different light; I came to the realization that I had a lot more to fight for than I ever imagined, and that this new vitality would be key in the test of wills against other trained combatants on the mats. I was fighting for my family, my country, my roots, and myself.

Chapter Eight

PARADISE IN MONTREAL

"I hated every minute of training, but I said, 'Don't quit. Suffer now and live the rest of your life as a champion.'" **—Muhammad Ali**

My wife and I had just flown back from Poland and had a few days to recuperate before heading off to our other favorite place, Montreal, Quebec. The Paradise Warrior Retreat was returning to Canada, only this time to Montreal's Tristar gym, with famous names such as Rashad Evans, Jon Jones, Kenny Florian, Kru (now Ajarn) Phil Nurse, Firas Zahabi, Greg Jackson, and John Danaher. I would also see Professor Bruno Fernandes and his crew at the Gracie Barra Montreal location. I obviously felt like a kid in a candy store!

After arriving at the hotel and dropping our bags in the room, our stomachs rumbled with hunger, so we decided to check out restaurants in Montreal.

Although it was October, the weather was spectacular as we walked through downtown Montreal taking in the beautiful scenery and architecture reminiscent of Old World European architecture. That is one of the many draws of Montreal, especially old Montreal, the location of our hotel, which boasted beautiful pillars, carvings, and statues. It was as if each building was nicer than the previous one. There were grand entrances, terraces, and lights illuminating the buildings in the setting sun.

On the way to the restaurant, I wanted to go to the Gracie Barra Montreal gym to speak to the head instructor, Professor Bruno Fernandes, as I had only left a message on his phone regarding attending a few classes and having a chat regarding my book project. I hadn't actually spoken to him, as I had only been back in the country for three days. As we approached the Gracie Barra academy just outside of all the skyscrapers lining downtown Montreal, I breathed a sigh of relief. With smaller buildings lining the road, the academy was located inside a massive industrial building housing several offices and businesses. As we confirmed the address and approached the front door, a tall figure was leaving the building. The man was lanky with broad shoulders and longer dark hair; he looked like a surfer from the sandy beaches of California, walking in a confident manner and giving us a friendly smile. It took me a few awkward moments to recognize him, and in a flash I blurted "Bruno? Professor Fernandes?" as he greeted me with a firm handshake.

I quickly explained who I was, that I train with the Gracie Barra family out of London, Ontario, along with the purpose of my trip. He acknowledged that he had received my message and told me to come back the next day at noon, as he was heading to the airport later the next afternoon to travel to Europe and then on to Brazil. Bruno exuded a kindness as he spoke that is rarely seen these days, and I was honored to be in his presence. Bruno was a sought-after black belt coach in Brazilian jiu-jitsu who had trained many champions, including Georges St-Pierre. Our meeting was set, but the only bump in the road was that I had to figure out the scheduling because the Paradise Warrior Retreat was starting at 10 a.m. and ending at 5 p.m. I was double-booked and decided to just commute back and forth with a lot of running between subway trains.

I slept fitfully from the excitement I felt that night, and not surprisingly, had just as much running through my head the following morning. I was equipped with a hotel map and poor directions from the subway terminal to the famed Tristar gym that housed some of the best MMA champions in the world, including Georges St-Pierre, Rory MacDonald, and David Loiseau. The hotel desk told me that the nearest metro (subway) was in an adjacent building, but they did not tell me that the building was as long as three Wal-Mart shopping centers. I got lost running through the halls trying to track down the entrance, so I decided to ask for directions. That was the first of the many delays and obstacles I experienced that day.

I asked an electrician fixing the lights for directions, but he did not speak English, and my French was nonexistent; I guess I should have paid more attention in my high school French class! The scenario must have looked hilarious for whoever was walking by and saw my hand gestures in an attempt to ask where the metro was. I stayed on course and eventually found the entrance, but was running late. The subway system in Montreal is safe and immaculate, and there is only a ten-minute wait time (at most) between trains.

On the metro, I was going over the questions that I had prepared for each fighter, making sure I had all the details covered. With great speed, I reached my station and ran up the stairs. I was amazed at having to run up four very long flights of stairs to reach the top, but I figured that it was a good warm-up. I asked the attendant for help with directions, but he had no idea where Rue Ferrier was and was just as puzzled looking at the hotel directions as I was. Then he glowed "Oh yes, take this here" as he handed me a bus schedule. "Take this bus and it will take you right to the location." I thanked him, and just as fast, I said goodbye and ran out into the intersection to see that there was a bus stop on two corners. I looked at the bus schedule and could not find the bus number, and then I wondered why I needed a bus if the directions stated that it was an eight-minute walk.

I saw a woman standing next to the other bus sign, so I ran over pleading for help. It was well-past 10 a.m., and I was wasting time with absolutely no idea of where I was. She was perplexed, as she could not find the bus number; we finally located the information in very small print. She directed me to the bus stop I came from only to stop me halfway there "Excuse me, today is Saturday. That bus does not operate on the weekends." How could I not roll my eyes and laugh at this point?

I crossed the street to a large plaza housing some fast food joints; somebody had to know something, right? There was a Greyhound bus standing by the Burger King and the driver was having a smoke outside. I figured he would know in which direction to point me. Yet, the pattern of my sour morning continued. He had no clue. I thought to myself that the Burger King would be my next stop, but was met with a closed sign at the door. At that point, my subconscious kicked in as I saw a Wal-Mart in the horizon. At the location near my house, cab drivers always hang out in the parking lot, so I started running toward it. As I reached the edge of the lot, my jaw dropped as I halted and stared out into the open abyss. There was not one taxi in sight. Time for plan F or G at this point, I did not care; I just wanted to finally reach the Tristar gym. So I ran toward the Wal-Mart looking for a phone to call a taxi, but as I approached the doors I noticed one taxi at the far end of the parking lot.

He knew where the street was but had no idea where the gym was located, so he told me to hop in and that we would find it even though he was off-duty. I felt a large weight lifted from my shoulders and thought that I was finally going to reach my destination and be done with this rat-race trip to the gym. We left the parking lot, took a left and hit the second set of lights, took a right and approximately ten meters to the left, the gym was there, an entire sixty-second ride. I laughed at the insanity. I could not believe my luck, but chalked it up to the day. Looking back on it, the experience makes for a good story.

Tristar was located in a large business building, on the third floor. Once inside, I was amazed at its cleanliness and at the number of people still in line waiting to get in. There must have been at least eighty people lined up. I was waiting on the steps thinking that I was running really behind, and in an hour I would have to be back downtown to meet Professor Fernandes at Gracie Barra. The line was moving slowly and spectators were the last to enter, as the participants had to change and stretch. While in line, Firas Zahabi came in smiling and greeting everyone. Firas walked with his head up, smiling at the crowd. He had a very approachable aura, yet a mysterious element behind his dark, piercing eyes, which showed me that he had another side to him, a trait exhibited by all fighters. I saw the Incredible Hulk lurking within his soul.

I heard the crowd getting louder again, as UFC standout Jon Jones entered. I was amazed at how tall he was; he was a good head taller than me, and I stand at 6' 3" tall and am definitely not used to looking up at someone. He, too, had broad shoulders and a warm smile, taking the time to give high fives with his gangling arms and exchange words with people in line.

Tristar gym is the home of great champions such as Georges St-Pierre, Kenny Florian, and David Loiseau, and boasted regulars such as Rashad Evans, Dennis Kang, and Nate Marquart, to name just a few. It seemed very well-organized, with an area selling supplements and Xyience drinks as well as a large sports shop where you can find fighters' shirts, shorts, and equipment. A small hallway containing several pictures of fighters and magazine spreads led to the main gym area, which was 13,500 square feet of raw training facility, including two professional boxing rings, a cage, over thirty punching bags, and enough inspiration to swell the heart of any novice MMA fan. Several large windows lined the entire gym, bearing the signature three-star logo on each one, and providing plenty of light. High ceilings and newer, thick mats on the floor conveyed a world-class impression.

Once inside, the opening ceremony ensued, with Yoram Gazit introducing each coach and fighter. We had the best in the world sitting in front of us: one of the biggest standouts and fan favorites in the UFC, Jon Jones; former UFC champion and next in line to get a title shot for the light heavyweight belt from Mauricio Shogun Rua, Rashad Evans; famed coach of champions in MMA, Firas Zahabi; world Muay Thai champion and famed coach Kru (now Ajarn) Phil Nurse; and last but not least, the mastermind jiu-jitsu coach, John Danaher.

Jon Jones was up first. I was running late to meet with Professor Fernandes, but had to see at least a couple of techniques. Kru Phil Nurse started the warm-up with Jones, and everyone was intrigued as they definitely used unconventional methods for the warm-up. With partners sitting and facing each other, their legs were bent and the soles of their feet were planted on the ground. One partner put his knees on the inside of the other partner's bent legs. For thirty seconds at a time, the outside-legged partner did his best to push inward and force his partner's legs inward while the other partner used his strength to push out to open up his partner's legs. It seemed easy enough, but I was amazed at how many problems this caused for everyone, with even the well-conditioned participants sporting a tomato red tint on their faces. The exercises kept on coming, with mini-hopping squats and more until people were literally pleading for a reprieve when Kru Phil's face lit up as he exclaimed, "That's a good warm-up!"

Jones was well-spoken, and I was shocked at how light he was on his feet for a light heavyweight. He reminded me of Georges St-Pierre as he bobbed back and forth on his toes like a bouncing tennis ball. It was clear why Jones was touted as the next big thing, and by the time you read this, he will likely be considered one of the best pound-for-pound fighters in the world. Jones has a different type of style in MMA; he throws very flashy kicks and spinning elbows and has world-class wrestling skills.

I had places to be and ran for dear life to catch the next subway train, running through the streets to Gracie Barra Montreal. Unfortunately, it would turn out that I had just missed Professor Fernandes as he left for Brazil, but I knew I would be back and this was the perfect excuse to tell my wife we would need to return soon. Glen Mackenzie greeted me at the gym. I had befriended Glen at my second BJJ tournament in Toronto. He was very welcoming and asked if I wanted to stay for the upcoming class.

Although I had to get back to the seminar, this was an offer I could not refuse, but I had one minor problem: I did not pack my gi. Glen pointed out that I was about Professor Fernandes' height and offered me his gi to train in. Wearing the cloth of a world champion, I thought that maybe I would absorb the residual powers through osmosis. I changed in the professor's office and looked in the mirror; I felt a strong dominance trickle through me. I was ready to roll!

On the mats, Glen introduced me to a renowned practitioner, brown belt (now black belt) Mark Colangelo, who took me under his wing. We chatted a bit, and I learned that he had trained under Renzo Gracie in New York for a long time before moving to Montreal. He had already participated in many super-fights and made a name for himself in the BJJ community. He was a commentator at MMA events and even tried his luck at MMA. He was definitely the right guy to look to for pointers.

He was very knowledgeable and showed me some tricks and tips. Then, we got to the fun part; grappling in live action. I was holding my own only because Mark was taking it easy on me. He let me sweep him and almost gave me submissions, but when he wanted to, he would twist me into a pretzel, something I was getting used to feeling.

I hadn't had this much fun in a long time, as I was pulling off moves I never could in a live simulation. The professor's gi was either magical or the power came from my mindset, but grappling with blue belts was fun because I was actually submitting them. While this was going on, I noticed that Glen was patiently teaching the white belts in the class. Then it hit me: this was exactly why so many champions came to train at Gracie Barra Montreal. It wasn't just the venerable head professor, but everyone at the school was approachable, generous, and knowledgeable—and they could all kick butt.

Mark invited me to try his 7 a.m. class, and I murmured, "I don't even get up at 7 a.m.!" But yet again it was an offer I could not refuse and was honored to attend the next morning. The class proved very beneficial, as I really took to his teaching style.

I bounced around in the following days between Gracie Barra and Tristar gym, and was amazed at just how humble, generous, and down-to-earth the practitioners were. Their type-A personalities made them want to achieve more in their fields and life, but they also hadn't forgotten where they'd come from on their way to get to their respective positions in life. Rashad sat on the edge of the Tristar ring and gave me his undivided attention as he shared stories about his life, even after a long day. Although we had never met before, Kru Phil Nurse gave me hours of his time and knowledge. I could go down the list of examples. That struck a chord with me, and I knew that when I got home I would have to pay it forward, meaning that I would have to project that kindness onto others. If these guys, who were multitasking, busy, and probably tired from long days, could give me their time, I had no excuse for not doing the same as well. I believe that is the most important value I learned over those days, although the chokes, sweeps, and wrestling techniques would come in handy a short time later.

Chapter Nine

THE INTELLECT

"Always ask yourself: is there anything more I could be doing to make myself and the people around me happier?"
                                                                    —John Danaher

John Danaher was born in Washington D.C., but only lived there for a few short years before moving back to his parents' home country of New Zealand. His parents worked at the New Zealand Embassy during the Vietnam War, coordinating military liaisons between New Zealand's military forces and those of the United States. John lived there for twenty-three years, doing all of his schooling and early university work in New Zealand. He was raised in the northern town of Whangaparaoa, which literally means "Bay of Whales." The town was located along a beautiful beach featuring a myriad of marine life.

Before ever considering martial arts, John was interested in weightlifting. Similarly to my beginnings as a youth, he had a primitive weightlifting regimen based on body-building tradition. He continued this regimen during his time at the prestigious Columbia University in New York and got fairly big, weighing a maximum of 240 pounds.

I had to pry into how John had stumbled into the BJJ life, as he is regarded as one of the best BJJ trainers in the world as well as an astute strategist, second to none. John helped many world class champions and practitioners with their BJJ arsenal including Georges St-Pierre, Chris Weidman and Frankie Edgar, who were all UFC champions at some point in their careers. John explained that he became interested in MMA and jiu-jitsu because he worked nights as a bouncer to pay his rent and tuition when he first moved to Manhattan to earn his Columbia University master's degree in philosophy. He found that very often, altercations would go to the ground and that a lot of wrestling was involved in bar fights. He also noticed that the best people he worked with in such altercations were American wrestlers, and he quickly became impressed by their efficiency.

"I heard that there were Brazilian wrestlers who had a different style of wrestling, where, instead of winning by pin, they won by a stranglehold or arm hold. So I started to hear more and more about these people until I was shown an old VHS copy of UFC 2 and got to see it for myself, and I was massively impressed by the performance of Royce Gracie. I think everyone knows him," John stated with a smile on his face. Just like any fairytale story, he had a lot of work in front of him to reach the level of success he would achieve throughout the years.

At the time, there was a group of people teaching a rather primitive kind of jiu-jitsu in Manhattan, and John signed up. Like most people, he jumped into the sport with great enthusiasm but little technical direction. He found that his size and weightlifting routine were a hindrance to his jiu-jitsu game; he was too slow and became easily fatigued, so he stopped weightlifting.

All of this changed in 1994 when Renzo Gracie, a BJJ legend, first came to New York, opened shop, and John became a full-time student. Those life connections that bring people to their destinations in life sometimes unfold organically; I call it fate.

When world-class UFC/BJJ fighters Matt Serra and Ricardo Almeida left their head instructor positions at Renzo's gym in order to open up their own schools, John stepped up as a coach. He practically lived at the school, training upwards of twelve to fourteen hours per day! The work ethic and sheer drive to better himself helped set John apart from the pack. He became the only non-Brazilian instructor at the club.

The physical, mental, and emotional demands John endured should be applauded. The sacrifices he had to make in order to be at a high level, and then exceeding that level, were a testament to his propensity and penchant for detail and commitment to never stray from his ultimate goal—at nearly any cost.

John confessed that he had several motivations for this. The first was financial; he had to earn money to pay for an expensive lifestyle in Manhattan, so he worked a lot. The second factor was that Matt Serra and Ricardo Almeida were world champions who had always greatly impressed John when they were teaching. He felt that he was stepping into big shoes and had to exert a large amount of effort in his new role to meet the team's expectations. "I felt like, okay, these guys were coached by very, very good people in the past; I need to get up to that level. So I began a fairly serious study of jiu-jitsu at that point."

At Renzo's gym, John always received the highest praise. He thought this was fascinating and considered himself extremely fortunate as a student, learning from excellent teachers and grapplers that would always make John ask himself: "Is there anything more I could be doing to make myself and the people around me happier?" These questions were quickly answered by attending the Renzo Gracie Academy. Over the years, he learned a number of beneficial lessons from world-class athletes, who also impressed him on a personal level; he felt that he owed so much to many of these people.

One of the individuals that came through Renzo's doors to work with John was Canadian standout and now one of the best pound-for-pound fighters in the world: Georges St-Pierre. John met him when he was a young fighter in the now defunct "TKO" organization in Canada. Back in the day, it was a breeding ground for Canadian MMA. Georges was a blue belt when he arrived at Renzo Gracie Academy, which at the time was located on 37th Street and 8th Avenue. "Georges, at that time, spoke no English whatsoever. He would come in, put on his gi, and train with his blue belt on and he was like a big tough kid. He didn't have too much technique, but he had a lot of enthusiasm," John recalled with a menacing smile.

The funny part was that Georges' grasp of English was as weak as John's French, so the two of them had to get creative in their communication with each other. Georges was a young, hungry fighter who traveled six hours by bus on Friday evenings to reach his destination. He trained until Sunday and went back home to Montreal to train at his home gyms. During this time, he was working as a garbage man, and John proudly professed that he remembered even then being incredibly impressed by the dedication of this young man who came to train and live in the Big Apple a few nights a week with no money at all.

John would teach him for free because he admired the dedication of this young man who was making such an effort. When Georges began training with Canadian Top Team, he stopped coming down to the city for some time, which was around the time he first entered the UFC. Georges left Canadian Top Team close to the time when he fought B.J. Penn for the first time, after which he became a full-time student of John's. "He came down and asked me. By now his English was much better, and he was an established athlete. He'd fought for the world title… I cornered him in his first fight against B.J. Penn. That was a thrilling fight. That was an important test for me, also, because that was the first time I actually cornered Georges and the first time that I created a game plan for him."

John stated that there were actually two game plans for that fight. The first was engineered by Georges' kickboxing coach, who was his main coach at the time. He would fight B.J. in a conventional striking bout and look to win by knockout. John warned Georges that B.J.'s boxing was much better than most people believed and that a better strategy might be a wrestling strategy against defense followed by ground and pound from the top. However, because John was the new man in the corner, he didn't try to push his strategy hard, "But I said, 'let's go with the kickboxing strategy in round one, and if it works, continue with it; if it doesn't work, we will switch to the other strategy.'"

B.J. won the first round very convincingly, during which Georges had some bad luck. He took a terrible poke in the eye very early on and got clipped on the nose, resulting in a lot of bleeding. Georges showed tremendous fortitude and power to come back, switching strategies in the middle of a fight against a world-class player like B.J. Penn.

That's not easy. He achieved it at a relatively young age, came back and won two very tough physical rounds, and ended up taking a very narrow decision of two rounds to one. John proved to be an important factor in that tough battle to bring GSP, as Georges was often referred to, closer to his championship belt by astutely formulating a strategy that proved superior to B.J. Penn's.

John then cornered GSP in his very successful fight against Matt Hughes, in which he won the UFC world welterweight title. That was a very different fight because the idea was to make it more of a kickboxing match. Most of the training that John did with GSP was geared toward anti-grappling. Georges impressed John with his mental attitude and his relatively dominant performance in that fight. After the fight, major problems began to arise because of the simultaneous ascendancy of both Georges and Matt Serra, bringing the two fighters into a conflict that created a new round of problems. John was friends with both fighters, and he was thus put into an awkward position.

Switching gears to John Danaher as a globally sought-after coach, I wanted to know his thoughts on why the best fighters and grapplers in the world, such as GSP, would line up to train with him. He was very modest with his answer, like a true warrior exuding a humble spirit. He replied that he thought of himself as just a teacher, but not a special teacher. He stated that he thought there were many people out there who could teach just as well as he, if not better. He thought it would be a mistake to imply that he was better than others.

He shared his thoughts that Georges would still be world champion, even without his help. "Yes, I've helped him, but he is a remarkable character, and he would have done very well even if I never existed. My overall answer to your question is that there are many fine coaches in jiu-jitsu and it's my privilege to be named among those, but I don't consider myself entirely unique or superior."

However, within the business, John was praised. Professor Bruno Fernandes of Gracie Barra Montreal, who was a world-class black belt in BJJ, had only positive words: "I think John Danaher is beyond any category. He is in a category of his own!"

During our conversation, I had to ask if it was indeed true that John had attended Matt Serra's wedding wearing his rash guard. In my research, I noticed that John would wear his rash guard everywhere he went, but it really caught my curiosity as to whether he actually wore it to Matt's wedding, and the answer did not surprise me. "I'm ashamed to say, yes. In revenge, (he said) he would attend my funeral in his rash guard," John's eyes lit up with affection and laughter.

As for the future of Brazilian jiu-jitsu in MMA, John was a large proponent of the cyclical theory of MMA. He believed that there were and will be fashion trends in MMA. Those trends are influenced and dictated by whoever are the dominant athletes at the given time. Sometimes they would be predominantly strikers, other times they would be predominantly wrestlers, or sometimes jiu-jitsu fighters.

John explained that "what happens is you have certain players who through their athletic gifts dominate the sports in different ways at different times, and people tend to follow the leaders."

John also pointed out that strong athletes would be needed that exhibit world-class jiu-jitsu skills in the heat of competition, in order to bring the popularity of jiu-jitsu in MMA back. He believed it to be an incontestable, well-established fact that in order to succeed in modern-day MMA, an athlete must be strong in ground grappling, grappling in the clinch, striking in the clinch, and striking in the open position. Not being competent in all of these areas, an athlete would quickly be exposed.

Danaher opened up further on the topic: "How important it is relative to the others? I believe it changes over time, depending on what kinds of things are going on. And always remember that as one part of the mixed martial arts curriculum falls out of favor, it's only a matter of time until people tend to disregard it or downplay it, and then a new player can come in and exploit that lack of training in that one area and then rise to the top through that exploitation.

And then once again, the fashion cycle begins anew and suddenly that disregarded area of mixed martial arts comes back into favor. So, even though everyone would agree that we know that mixed martial arts must be studied as ground grappling, clinch grappling, clinch striking, the only question is which is the most important, and I believe, as the answer to that, well, it depends on the time and era in which you are fighting."

I had John where I wanted him, immersed in the discussion of his craft as he was opening up more and more, delving into his complex mind. I asked the million-dollar question: what did it take to be the best in the world in any given craft, whether it be MMA or jiu-jitsu?

He stated that one must look at themselves as a world champion, and, more importantly, be prepared to do the things necessary to be the world champion. "If you want to be better than other people, just train more than them; train more and train smarter and over time, barring some crazy mishap or accident, you would be better than them. The other guy is training six hours a day, and if you're training eight and you do that for five years, you'll probably beat him."

I also recounted his speech to the practitioners at the Paradise Warrior Retreat. He spoke about not dipping one's toes in the art, but to immerse oneself fully to reach one's true potential. He reiterated that it was very important to do things right and not put half-energies into preparation, but doing it completely immersed in the craft.

John saw a simple but forgotten element to becoming better than an opponent, which was to maintain a state of relaxation as you breathe. John pointed out that it would be hard to achieve that while operating at 100% of your physical capacity. "If you're completely exhausted, you're puffing like a steam engine pulling a long train, but if you're operating at say sixty-five to eighty percent of your physical capacity, then you still have the capacity to think. And if you can think and reason, then you can start the plan. When you can plan, you can plan a hit. When you can plan a hit, you have a good chance of a hit."

John also had an interesting approach to mental toughness in that he did not believe in it. He explained that anyone could be broken mentally, as this had been proven through history, such as in interrogation studies. By simply depriving people of sleep for seventy-two hours, they would break regardless of who they were.

As he must have seen my puzzled face, John was kind enough to break it down in terms I could understand. He stated that by putting the toughest human being in a completely unfamiliar situation, they would be lost, confused, or would break. "You can give me the toughest guy in the world, the toughest, roughest, meanest man, if he can't swim when thrown in the ocean, he'll break in three seconds. But you take a fourteen-year old kid who had six swimming lessons, thrown in the ocean, he would be fine. What people call mental toughness is much more the case that they have been dropped in these situations that most people will break in, but they're so familiar with them through repetition, through immersion, through being put in those tough situations so many times that they feel comfortable enough. Because they're comfortable, they can formulate a plan of escape. They can hatch a plan for victory, so they can endure tremendous hardship and prevail."

Fighters and egos were a conundrum that I had thought about at length. I have seen martial artists act humbly while suppressing their egos on a daily basis, but just as I had learned through my API stay, fighting is in our DNA, taking us back to our most basic roots, and we partially become interested in the sport because of our egos. I figured John was the right man to consult on the matter.

John briefly collected his thoughts and, just like his previous answers, astutely pulled wisdom from his vast library of experience and comprehension. "Cohesively, I mean ultimately, we fight in order to promote the physical needs of the social selves, and the bigger ego is the more liable way to do this."

John also explained that if we had no egos, we would have no conflict. So, it's unsurprising that people who are attracted to fighting are generally people with a strong sense of who they are. John concluded, "Sometimes they are overwhelmingly strong. But that's not really surprising."

I asked John who his dream match would be, and after stating Gandhi, he revised his answer to the master strategist Sun Tzu, author of the famous *Art of War*. He stated that combining a few months of jiu-jitsu practice with his competency, Sun Tzu may have well been unbeatable.

I wanted to know what a man with so much complexity had as a plan and ultimate goal for his jiu-jitsu career and life. Truly, he could not have put it any simpler (or more complex): "Same goal as everybody; to be happy."

John was a unique individual; his mind worked on different levels at all times. In my research I read about reporters being deathly scared of interviewing John because he would rip them to shreds intellectually when asked mediocre questions. My friend and fellow reporter Gary Whitaker made this statement right before my interview with John, but in all honesty, it made me want to interview him all the more.

I breathed a sigh of relief on the few occasions when John smiled and stated "good question" before pondering his answers. He was very welcoming and generous to me as well as to all of the students he was teaching at Tristar gym, where I was fortunate enough to watch a practice. His way of looking at the most basic ideas and dissecting them into minuscule increments to perfect the overall product was a thing of beauty. He had some of the best fighters in the world coming to him for help on a regular basis, but he also had a large following of bankers and business moguls, all because one day he decided he had to put all of his energy into teaching. John was the epitome of success and a person who forged his own paths in life. He willingly strayed from the crowd to satisfy his inner ambitions and venture to new heights of success, which is an admirable quality.

Quick Round
If you could grapple anyone in the world who would it be?
Sun Tzu, author of *The Art of War*.

What is your biggest strength?
My stupidity.

What would you say is your biggest weakness?
My stupidity.

Who are the best fighters in the world in your eyes?
B.J. Penn, Georges St-Pierre, Anderson Silva, Lyoto Machida, Shogun Rua, Frankie Edgar, Jose Aldo, Miguel Torres.

What's your favorite thing to do with friends and family?
To enjoy simple physical activity and complex mental pressures.

Anything that you would like to add or have portrayed to your fans around the world?
Always ask yourself: is there anything more I could be doing to make myself and the people around me happier?

Chapter Ten

MORE "SUGAR" PLEASE

"We are what we repeatedly do. Excellence then, is not an act, but a habit."
—Aristotle

Rashad Evans grew up in a large family of seven brothers and sisters in Niagara Falls, New York in a single-parent household. Unfortunately, Rashad's father passed away when he was only a teenager. It was really tough, and the large family had a lot of hardships growing up, but Rashad did confess that family support made things a lot easier.

Rashad recalled that his mom was always working. While she spent long hours at the hospital, Rashad helped his siblings in any way he could. When he was younger, Rashad gravitated toward football in the athletic realm, but his first martial art was Tang Soo Do, a form of karate. His coach, Carol Massimo, would let Rashad train in exchange for cleaning the dojo, as Rashad didn't have the money to pay for a membership. After four years, Rashad's knowledge base was growing, as was his love for fighting.

As fate would have it, Rashad got into amateur wrestling purely by chance. His football coach was also the school wrestling coach (Rashad imitated him with a Godfather-like imitation): "Guys, in order to be very good football players, you need to be good wrestlers!" Rashad took that message to heart and began to wrestle, but at first didn't really like it. He tried to quit on a few occasions, but his coach had other plans; every time he would concoct a different reason to make him stay on the team.

Rashad beamed as he recalled the past, "If we had a practice on Saturday and I missed it, he would find where I was at and bring me to the practice."

Rashad fondly remembered watching and idolizing an icon in the fight world while growing up: Bruce Lee. Rashad's mom would watch the movies with him. He also looked up to Chuck Norris, as his discipline was the same as Rashad's, Tang Soo Do.

Once UFC hit the scene, Rashad was a big fan of Royce Gracie. "Royce Gracie was the man. I couldn't believe someone that little, not physically imposing at all, was just doing his thing. At that point you saw other people go in there in their gi and say 'that karate dude is about to get mopped up.' Then you'd see Royce go in there and submit people left and right!"

Rashad did confess that his dad was very athletically gifted, particularly at basketball. His mom and dad had Rashad's brother when they were young, so the right thing to do was to take care of the family. His dad bypassed a college career as a basketball player to work at a factory and put food on the table. His dad was 6' 3", gifted at any sport he tried. "He died when I was seventeen. I think a big part of it was just that he never achieved his dreams. He died of a broken heart, you know? He worked in a factory, and then he ended up losing his job because they got bought out. The regret that he had in his life was too much to bear. "

Rashad spoke about life's inconsistencies and tribulations, reminding me of my father's tough life in the factory and how I lost my mom at an early age. That does something to the psyche of a youth; it either switches on a deep, burning fireball of ambition or implodes your dreams. Rashad revealed considerable layers of his mental strength living through the situation, "I definitely got a lot of my mental toughness from the entire situation. My upbringing was just like … have you ever asked God why? Why you? Why was I the one born not having anything and this person was born with this and I'm stuck with that? What did I ever do wrong? You start getting this whole pity party, upset mentality but it's something really hard to break sometimes. I used my sports to get over that. Before a football game or when I wrestled, I would just think about all the shit that was going wrong in my life, and I would just go out there and give it all I had."

Anyone who has been alive long enough could directly identify with what Rashad was saying. Life is not fair; circumstances can weigh heavily on the mind and soul, making it tough to soar in life, but by putting all of that energy into something positive and using that life experience to benefit us and others, good things happen.

After college, Rashad worked as a security officer on the metro in a tough neighborhood, making sure the kids were behaving. He called this part of his life "a hustle." Having graduated college, he had this idea that he would be able to land a $60,000–$70,000 job and really start living his life after putting so much into school.

Unfortunately, real life was not what he expected and he could only land jobs worth about $25,000 a year. Rashad was disheartened as he struggled to find his place in a seemingly indifferent world. He longed to find his niche and comfort zone that he could call his own, and do what he wanted to be doing.

Rashad wanted to become a police officer in Michigan, but the state declared a hiring freeze during the big economic scare. Michigan didn't want to cut back, so they implemented a hiring freeze for police officers among other professions. He began working at a hospital in hopes of gaining additional security experience before applying for the police force when openings became available.

During that time, he was also a JV wrestling coach and was doing a good job, but he had a revelation that he was still very competitive. He found himself getting too competitive with the students; for instance, he knew he had to let them get the takedowns so that they would see that it worked and do it in their matches, but it was difficult for him to resist the urge to get the upper hand. That competitive drive would lead him to bigger and better things.

As a bouncer at a bar, Rashad put someone in a rear naked choke when a fight broke out one night. Another guy ran up to him and exclaimed, "Hey! You just got this guy in a rear naked choke!"

Rashad was quite familiar with the terminology because he had watched the Ultimate Fighting Championship since its inception. They started chatting, and he told Rashad about a club he trained at that was NHB (No Holds Barred) in Lansing, Michigan. He invited Rashad to come and that he would even pick him up.

The man stuck to his word and drove Rashad to this gym, "I'm thinking it's like a bad fucking set-up. It's in the bad part of Lansing, Michigan. It's this broken-down abandoned factory. It had this smell and reek of dead cats and skunks throughout … this has got to be a set-up. I was just waiting to walk up to the room and have someone try to rob me!"

As Rashad vividly described the situation, I had a hard time pulling my mind away from the *Hostel* movies; he was accurately describing a horror movie scene. Before Rashad opened the door to enter the gym, he heard screams coming from the other side of the large door. I had to give it to the man, Rashad walked through the doors confidently, while most others probably would have turned and ran away.

Rashad walked into the small ten-by-twenty-foot room to be greeted by more sounds of screaming and shrieking. There must have been about six guys training their guts out in the small, confined space. Rashad felt the heat wash over him and the strong odor of sweat penetrated his nostrils in the humidity. The practitioners were beating the snot out of each other. Rashad even recalled blood stains covering the walls.

During his first session, he managed to do well because of his wrestling background. Rashad was hooked on the raw experience of fight training. He was thrown into the lion's den and had held his own; the feeling must have been very rewarding. He was completely enamored with MMA, and three months later he had his first bout.

The fight was in Angola, Indiana, at a Dan Severn tournament known as "Danger Zone." Rashad was frank and disclosed that he really only wanted to take one fight just for himself; the $500 was just a bonus. At the time, there weren't many places to fight legally aside from Connecticut, New Jersey, Las Vegas, and Native American reservations. Rashad fought in some underground, unsanctioned fights, and thus his record does not accurately reflect his wins/losses. Sherdog can't report fights they don't know about. As for his first outing in the tournament, he won not just one fight but all of his fights to become king of the hill.

As he walked into a match one night at a bingo hall, and some rednecks were yelling "whooooo hooooo—whoop him, boyyyy!" He wasn't sure if he was going to find trouble being an outsider. It turned out quite the opposite; they were great fans and cheered Rashad on to his win. There was one thing he would change, though: he would have made it a non-smoking room. Everyone in the room was smoking heavily, and a thick, foggy cloud hovered above the fighters in the ring, although it did add to the atmosphere!

Back when Rashad was training in Lansing, he was one of six practitioners, and they all agreed they had to open up their circles to train with others. Will, one of the other fighters, threw out the idea to train with UFC legend Dan Severn's gym in Coldwater.

Unexpectedly, the Lansing gang demolished the guys at Dan's gym. Rashad's teacher and close friend, Matt Torres, continually taught Dan Severn's students afterward. The entire Lansing club helped teach the guys in Coldwater, and they developed a better relationship with Dan Severn as they became family. Dan even got them into fights and shows.

Dan was inducted into the UFC Hall of Fame and was asked to refer one of his fighters to apply for Ultimate Fighter, which was a reality-based show that followed fighters who wanted a shot at a six-figure UFC contract. The guys competing for the chance stayed in one gigantic house with no television, no phone calls permitted, and with a lot of testosterone and high-quality training with famous coaches. They went through tournament-style elimination until one person would get all the spoils—the six-figure contract.

Dan approached Rashad with this opportunity; he still had to go through the selection process but he may have been favored, as he was one of Severn's boys. Rashad compiled a tape to send to the UFC for the first phase of the audition in which he was sparring with Matt Torres. The video was set to some R&B slow jams, not on purpose, but that is how they used to get down. To this day, Rashad is surprised he made it onto the show with the unorthodox music in the background.

Rashad showed up to the Ultimate Fighter interviews at 225 pounds, but he had to get up to that weight from being a strong 205–210-pound fighter. He arrived at the interview room, where Dana White, the UFC president, and Craig Piligian, the show's producer, were waiting. Rashad re-enacted the interview, accents and all.

"Dana says, 'Phewww. What you want to be on the fucking Ultimate Fighter? This is fucking heavyweights!'

I said 'Yeah, I know....'

(Dana remarked) 'I'm fucking bigger than you, are you fuckin' kidding me?'

I said 'What, what, what's wrong?'

(Dana must have been waiting for this question, as he had his punchline prepared.)

He says, 'I had guys so fucking big that they had to fucking duck to get through the doors! How the fuck do you think you can compete with guys that had to fucking duck through the door to get in here? You're fucking what, like five-foot-fucking-ten?'

The other guy, Craig, was like 'Yeah, you, Cuba-fucking-Gooding-Junior-looking motherfucker! You think you can beat these guys?'

(Rashad found himself in front of the firing squad, but rebutted quickly.) 'Dana, listen. You know when heavyweights were heavyweights, those guys weren't big and they weren't cumbersome. You take Muhammad Ali, Joe Frazier, you take Mike Tyson; those guys would weigh in 211, 212, 217 (pounds). That's when the heavyweight division was exciting to watch. If you just want to watch a bunch of big guys lie on each other, then go ahead, be my guest. You may have all of these big guys, but if you want excitement, you have me, Rashad.'"

Rashad's face beamed, recalling the day long ago that cemented his legacy as one of the best mixed martial artists to step into the octagon. He wasn't sure if that was the line that sealed it, but they let him on the show.

Rashad went on to win the entire tournament, just as he had his entire undefeated career up to that point. He was pitted against one of the monsters Dana White was talking about, such as Brad Imes, who stood 6' 7" and weighed 265 pounds. Rashad wore his heart on his sleeve in the fight and not only won by unanimous decision, but was crowned only the second UFC Ultimate Fighter in history, claiming his place in the most prestigious fighting organization in the world: the UFC.

Another significant milestone in Rashad's career occurred on January 2, 2010, when Rolles Gracie, a third-degree black belt, presented Rashad his BJJ black belt in the locker room, completely surprising Rashad before he was to face Thiago Silva. Rashad had trained extensively with Rolles; given the accomplishments that Rolles had achieved in the BJJ world and the fact that he had the esteemed Gracie name, receiving the belt felt so much more honorable.

However, some fans and keyboard warriors contested the move because Rashad was not a gi-trained jiu-jitsu player, as tradition dictated. But Rolles Gracie was recognizing Rashad's high-caliber skills, and even if they were no-gi skills, Rashad held his own with elite fighters, which could not be disputed. I asked Rashad which event felt better: the win against Thiago Silva, who was a tough main-event opponent at UFC 108, or obtaining the black belt from Rolles Gracie. He hands-down stated that the belt was more significant.

With my first interview in the books, I gained a lot more respect for Rashad. I saw his personal side and learned more about his raw talent and skills. It took a couple of years before we would meet up again, mainly due to my stubborn attempt to conduct our interviews in person. I really wanted to be able to feed off his energy and read his thought processes, which would be diminished over the phone. He has always been a class act, and gave me and other fans time and attention. At the UFC expo, he was being rushed to an autograph signing, but still managed to sign autographs along the way and catch up with me as organizers rolled their eyes.

Rashad was back in Ontario for a meet-and-greet circuit, and he texted me with an affirmative to finish our interview. Unfortunately, I was nursing a cold that had been going around the Member of Provincial Parliament's office. I ingested a bunch of cold and sinus pills, took my Kleenex with me, and my wife and I set out toward Rashad's hotel, which was 1½ hours from my home in London. He pulled up with his assistant, Peanut, who helped set up our meeting at 10:30 p.m. after a busy day of meeting fans. Rashad not only opened up about his life and strategies again, but also stayed up until past midnight to chat about the finer details of the fight game.

Since the last interview, I learned about a personally gratifying encounter that Rashad had with someone he had looked up to for many years: boxing legend Roy Jones, Jr. There was a backstory though; while in college, Rashad had ordered some Roy Jones, Jr. bootlegged fight DVDs off the Internet. He was obsessed, watching them over and over again. He began emulating the boxing great, shadow-boxing every chance he got. One day, he went to cut his hair in the bathroom, and when he came out, his ex-wife (who he was dating in college) asked, "Did you just cut your hair like Roy Jones, Jr.?" He was very embarrassed.

Rashad had a lot of respect for the boxing legend, who trained with Rashad and gave him pointers in the "sweet science" of boxing. It was one of Rashad's fondest memories. He humbly told me that he could not believe this was his life, that moments like that were when he got a glimpse of how far he had come, to have one of his idols tell him that he was a big fan. Rashad felt honored.

I asked him about the best advice he had received during his career. Not even a moment of contemplation was necessary. The advice came from another legend in the sport, Randy Couture.

It was right before Rashad's fight with a man that dominated the light heavyweight division and had knockout power both in his hands and kicks: "The Iceman" Chuck Liddell. Another legend, Randy Couture, was staying in the same hotel a floor lower than Evans, so Rashad approached him for advice. Rashad was still working his way up the ranks, and Chuck Liddell was a big hurdle to overcome. Few people felt Rashad had a chance in that fight. The words of others who told him he would be destroyed weighed heavily on his mind.

Rashad told Randy that he was scared and nervous going into this fight. Randy acknowledged that he knew exactly what Rashad was going through and that he needed to make friends with the worst possible outcome of the match. He told him to truly make friends with the feelings, and imagine the most embarrassing things happening to him. Only then would he be able to compete to the best of his abilities, being content in the fact that no matter what, the sun was still going to rise the next day and the people who loved him would still love him the next day,—life would go on.

Rashad accepted the wisdom, but the full meaning did not dawn on him until his head hit the pillow that night and his mind started to wander. He thought of everything that could go wrong and started to take Randy's advice. An epiphany started to occur as Rashad began letting go of the psychological "what ifs." It empowered and freed him, allowing Rashad to focus on what he did best.

"I remember every single time. I was like, I don't give a fuck, I don't give a fuck, and I'll just say that to myself, I don't give a fuck, I don't give a fuck, I don't give a fuck, I don't care, I don't care, I don't care, and I'll say I don't care not because I didn't actually care, it was that I just, I was not caring about all those feelings, all those negative thoughts, all those, the baggage that I was carrying with me. I just let it go, and so I don't give a fuck no matter what, you know, I'm going to go out there and compete, and whatever happens, happens, I don't give a fuck."

Rashad even remembered how free he felt when he walked out to the cage the following night. When he hit mitts with Chuck Liddell in the center of the cage, he was ready and free to show off his talent, not weighted by psychological baggage. Rashad put together a riveting performance, finishing with a devastating hook that left the legendary Chuck Liddell sprawled unconscious on the mat.

The limelight has been shining on Rashad ever since, and coping mechanisms for dealing with the glitz, reporters, and constant tours that detach fighters from their training schedules was a variable in the fight game that I wanted Rashad to disclose.

Rashad admitted that dealing with the media was hard. The style and magnitude of media attention was different for every fight. "So that's actually another fight in itself." He disclosed that once a fighter reached a certain level, they had to talk to the media. It was something that he and many others had to prepare themselves for.

Rashad laid it out for me: in getting ready for a fight, physical preparedness is the easy part of the equation. The mind is usually the last to be fortified and ready. The media plays a part in the equation, completely draining the fighters as they give assembly line interviews; the fighter knows every single question by heart, but isn't allowed to be upset about it. Rashad explained that it is all part of the game, even though sometimes he realized that interview questions were often identical to those from another interview.

Patience and a bit of a detached persona were key factors to success when dealing with the media, as Rashad further explained, "You got to be mentally able to just be a character at a point, not so much yourself, but just be a character so that you can play the game and you can answer the questions and you can sell the fight and you can smile and you can joke around and make it look like you're not even mentally fazed by any of it. So that's the hardest part about the media. I say the media is probably one of the hardest things to deal with."

I asked Rashad about the difference between his alter ego, "Sugar," and Rashad. The man, as I could attest, was soft-spoken, very humble, and at times withdrawn. The character was the flip side: loud and a jokester, with a flare for personality. Rashad explained that fighting is an art form, and with all art forms there comes a form of expression. When a person expresses his or her art, the character is released. But you can also practice an art form to express another side of yourself, and that was exactly what Rashad did by unleashing "Sugar" into the world during fights. He was expressing another side of himself that would normally stay locked away. He is not a cocky person, even though "Sugar" could be such during a fight competition.

Rashad revealed that he was motivated by "Sugar," who fueled his fighting abilities. "Sugar" was the cocky one. Winning wasn't enough; he wanted to embarrass his opponent for even thinking he could beat Rashad. Muhammad Ali brought a similar attitude to his fights. Rashad, the man, added that it was a privilege to step into the cage with such great opponents and he was thankful to be there, but he also had to flip that switch. I couldn't argue his philosophy, especially because his opponents were there to knock him out as well. Being a nice guy in the ring doesn't correlate well with winning.

A spinoff effect from reaching Rashad's level were the spoils. Did the younger Rashad ever believe in a million years the he would be in movies, have action figures made of him, be a character a in video game, or have fans wait for hours to get his autograph? He said that it felt like another life; the world he grew up in was full of struggle and harsh reality. He never imagined that this would be his life. He was genuinely appreciative when shaking the hands of fans while signing autographs. When he was younger, he played with action figures of his television idols, and now *he* was in that category. It was surreal that so many positive things resulted from simply doing something that made him happy.

It struck me how grounded he was. Rashad mentioned that he always says "thank you" prayers because it was easy to get complacent about the good things in life. It would be easy to take it all for granted. People would ask him if he was tired of things, and he had to admit that sometimes he was, but he would just remember that it was one moment in time. When he found himself in situations that seemed like they would never end, they eventually did pass. He consciously enjoyed as much as he could, knowing that it wouldn't last forever.

Hard work was what got Rashad into this position, along with his formula for success and what he centered his existence around. Rashad recalled a teammate on his college wrestling team who didn't have the best technique, but won matches because after practice he would stay and drill on the wrestling dummy when everyone else went home. He would drill shots over and over again for at least thirty minutes to an hour.

Rashad modeled his work ethic after Georges St-Pierre, who would drill things he learned in practice over and over again until his movements were perfect. Rashad also mentioned that Jon Jones was always drilling, sparring, play sparring; he put the time in. These guys built up their rhythm, muscle memory, and confidence.

Rashad once read in the book *Outliers* that an investment of 10,000 hours into something is required to become a master. Rashad observed that great fighters put in those added gym hours. Discipline was the path to the next level.

The double-edged sword to training long hours was overtraining, and Rashad agreed that it was no myth. He had seen guys who were in great shape, but they would push too far with everyone cheering them on. It can turn into an addiction, something you want to do over and over again. Their bodies would approach a peak, but after some time it would drop off. Some fighters don't know how to taper and listen to their body, pushing through to hit the wall just before a fight, negatively affecting performance.

Rashad was one of the most confident fighters on the UFC roster with one of the best fight records; I asked him how he brought "Sugar" to life to make this happen. Distracting thoughts and feelings would get dumped out on paper; he wrote everything down. He said that he often felt "emotionally constipated," meaning that he felt a lot of emotions but couldn't get them out. Writing down his feelings, fears, faults, and positive affirmations helps him cope. "I write down all the things because what it basically comes down to is when you have a fight, you're fighting yourself more than anything."

Rashad went on to talk about the ability to impose his will on his opponent in order to win. It didn't matter what his opponent was going to do, but what he was going to do to his opponent by believing in himself and fighting to the best of his ability. But believing you're the best is always difficult.

Rashad referenced the fact that some of the best fighters in the world were "fucking crazy because they're out of touch with reality." But he added that this was also the thing that made them great. "You got to be a little bit crazy, because that's what it takes, because if you're logically thinking … sometimes if you logically think (about things) you can talk yourself out of a fight for sure. Just by looking on paper, you can talk yourself out of (a fight), but if you are a little crazy, if you know how to hype yourself up a little bit, lie to yourself, then you can go really far."

Being crazy or delusional helped. Inside the cage and exchanging, Rashad is a self-described blank slate. There was not one single thought or feeling he could put his finger on because in the fight game, it was all split-seconds. Had Rashad taken the time to mentally process anything, his opponent would be two or three steps ahead of him.

But there was also an intense thought going on; all focus was on the match. Before a fight, his mind would blank, and the last thing he would remember was "Oh shit, it's going down!" as he smiled, reminiscing. He would have little gaps of consciousness used for thinking or listening to someone yelling from the crowd, but once the fight was over none of it was retained. Rashad would watch videos to find out what had actually happened.

A five-minute round felt like an hour, as his presence in the moment seemed to make time slow down. He would ponder about how slow his punches were in a fight while being alert/focused, determining that he needed to add some thunder. Watching it later on video, it actually looked like thunder.

He did admit that in the moment he almost blanked out; there was no planning or thought processing, but just working off his own reactions. Reacting put Rashad ahead of his opponent, who was trying to plan, but that also made Rashad faster at achieving his desired results. His reflexes and muscle memory reacted in positive ways because while in training, Rashad was not only training his body to get into shape, but also training his body to react with proper technique without thinking. That way, even if knocked silly in a fight, his body would react much faster than his mind by the time he could regain his bearings. It was that higher spiritual area that allowed a fighter who'd prepared his mind just right to unlock greatness in his performances by being "in the zone."

As MMA is a battle of the minds as much as it is a battle of physical attributes, we discussed the logistics of how to break down an opponent and achieve victory. By imposing his will, Rashad had managed to break some of the best fighters in the world. Rashad thought about it and added, "It's like this is the weirdest thing. I've been in a fight and I remember just seeing a look in their eye and I knew they can see that, in effect, that they were going to lose, and it's like a weird thing, like there are certain agreements in a fight that we unconsciously make."

That was when Rashad would pounce and go in for the kill, the minute he would feel it, even if the indicator was something simple, maybe a look in his opponent's eyes or his opponent looking at the clock. As soon as Rashad would get the feeling, he was more than happy to bring his opponent to that breaking point.

I changed focus a bit, asking Rashad about the "bread & butter" that got him where he was today: wrestling. He said that in MMA, wrestling was the glue that brought the disciplines together. It didn't matter what discipline someone excelled at, there would be a point at which fighters would get locked up in wrestling positions and a striking match can only last for so long. It was very important for a fighter to excel at wrestling.

His wrestling abilities helped him to reach a title fight against Forrest Griffin at UFC 92. Both fighters wanted to claim the number one spot in the world, but Rashad was destined to have the gold UFC belt strapped around his waist. Winning the belt was a great experience for him, as it all came so fast. At first, he honestly did not know how to feel; everything seemed surreal and new to him. He had finally gotten a major break. He was in a slight state of shock and could not believe that this was happening for him. After the fight he went out, but did not party, he did not drink or eat anything and barely said a word. He sat there in a state of euphoria, hypnotized by watching everyone around him as he absorbed the power of the moment. "This shit has really happened. I'm the UFC champion."

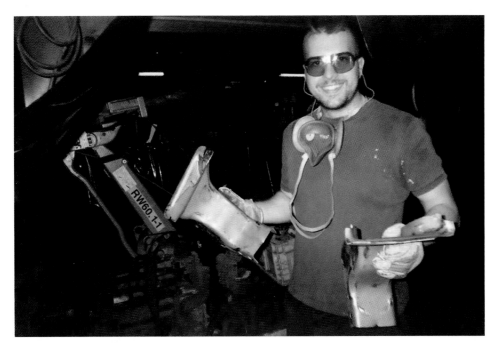

Top: Holding welded parts at my factory job, working in high heat.

Above Left: Receiving my Caveman certificate from Matthew Olson at Athletic Performance Inc.

Above Right: After a hard training session Sean Sherk and Nick Thompson take a break to snap a picture with me at the famed Minnesota Martial Arts.

Top: I found out that pulling a pickup truck was much harder than pushing one during a workout session at Athletic Performance Inc. (now Fitness Solutions) in Minnesota after my certification.

Above: Sean Sherk taking a break in between signing autographs at the Toronto UFC expo. (*Photo by Christopher Olech*)

Top: Sean Sherk showing some boxing techniques at a seminar in Burlington, Ontario at Academix Academy Martial Arts. (*Photo by Christopher Olech*)

Above: Sean Sherk showing his famous wrestling techniques at a seminar in Burlington, Ontario at Academix Academy Martial Arts. (*Photo by Greg Bartnik*)

Top: Sean Sherk performing a fast paced caveman routine pushing a heavy tire. (*Photo by Christopher Olech*)

Above: Goofing around with Sean Sherk, I did not stand a chance. (*Photo by Greg Bartnik*)

Opposite: Sean Sherk using a 45 lb weight for a shoulder workout. (*Photo by Christopher Olech*)

Top: The trainers at the Paradise Warrior Retreat in Mississauga, Ontario (from left to right) Renato Sobral, Chris Horodecki, Matt Serra, Demian Maia and Rob Kaman. (*Photo by Christopher Olech*)

Above Left: Signature fight pose with legendary striker and actor Rob Kaman at Canada's first Paradise Warrior Retreat. (*Photo by Jeff Phillips*)

Above Right: Practicing my leg kick against Jeff Phillips at the Paradise Warrior Retreat at Kombat Arts in Mississauga. (*Photo by Beata Olech*)

Top: Getting into the limousine next to the legend Bas Rutten before hitting the night-life in Toronto after the Paradise Warrior Retreat seminar. (*Photo by Jeff Phillips*)

Above: Inside Boston Pizza. Left to right: Matt Serra, Bas Rutten, Chris Horodecki, Demian Maia (kneeling), Rob Kaman, Boston Pizza manager Todd Taylor, David Loiseau and Renato Sobral. (*Photo by Jeff Phillips*)

Top Left: Zofia and Edward Ring shortly after World War II.

Top Right: Filling the storage full of coal for the winter proved to be a great workout with doggy Aza in Poland. (*Photo by Beata Olech*)

Above: Preparing for war mentally while imitating a Viking warrior in Bedzin, Poland. (*Photo by Beata Olech*)

Top: Training with Polish kickboxing and Savate champion Rafał Chwałek in Bedzin, Poland. (*Photo by Beata Olech*)

Above: At Tristar gym in Montreal with (from left to right) Kru Phil Nurse, Firas Zahabi, Joe Ferraro, the author, and John Danaher. (*Photo by Beata Olech*)

Top: Jon Jones watches on as John Danaher demonstrates a leg lock on Firas Zahabi at the Paradise Warrior Retreat in Montreal at Tristar gym. (*Photo by Christopher Olech*)

Above: Author with Joe Ferraro and Rashad Evans in the empty Tristar gym after taping a segment for UFC Central. (*Photo by Beata Olech*)

Top Left: At Gracie Barra Montreal with Mark Colangelo after his Brazilian jiu-jitsu class wearing Professor Bruno Fernandes' gi. (*Photo by Glen MacKenzie*)

Top Right: John Danaher at The WAT in New York City. (*Photo by Christopher Olech*)

Above: John Danaher showing the class a jiu-jitsu move at the Paradise Warrior Retreat in New York at The WAT. (*Photo by Greg Bartnik*)

Top Left: After our interview with John Danaher at Tristar gym in Montreal. (*Photo by Beata Olech*)

Top Right: A good old fashioned stare down with Rashad Evans at Tristar gym. (*Photo by Beata Olech*)

Above: Rashad hitting pads with champion kickboxer Tyrone Spong. (*Photo by Ryan Loco*)

Opposite: John Danaher at The WAT in New York City. (*Photo by Christopher Olech*)

Top: Rashad hitting pads with the famous Henri Hooft at the Blackzillian camp. (*Photo by Ryan Loco*)

Above: Rashad Evans resting at Jaco Training Center at the Blackzillian camp. (*Photo by Ryan Loco*)

Opposite: Rashad Evans resting between rounds. (*Photo by Ryan Loco*)

Top: Taking down my opponent at the Grapplers Quest BJJ tournament in London Ontario during my championship match. (*Photo by Greg Bartnik*)

Above: With my brother-in-law, Greg Bartnik, and sporting my gold medal in BJJ at the Grapplers Quest tournament. (*Photo by Beata Olech*)

Opposite: Professor Bruno Fernandes at Gracie Barra Montreal.
(*Photo by Christopher Olech*)

Top Left: Boxing champion Tomasz Adamek hitting the speed bag during his training camp for Kevin McBride in the Pocono Mountains. (*Photo by Greg Bartnik*)

Top Right: Perfecting my boxing skills with legendary boxing coach Roger Bloodworth in the Pocono Mountains. (*Photo by Greg Bartnik*)

Above: Sitting on the edge of the ring interviewing the boxing champion Tomasz Adamek after we both had exerted ourselves training. (*Photo by Greg Bartnik*)

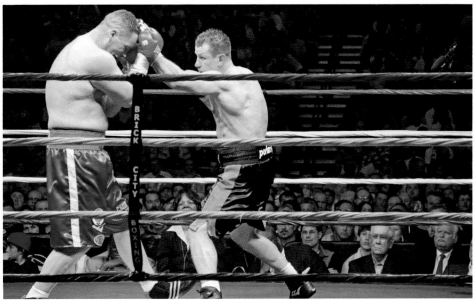

Top Left: Tomasz Adamek landing a stiff jab to Kevin McBride at the Prudential Center in New Jersey. (*Photo by Greg Bartnik*).

Above: Tomasz Adamek jabbing Kevin McBride at the Prudential Center in New Jersey. (*Photo by Greg Bartnik*)

Top: Tomasz Adamek warming up in the locker room prior to his fight with Kevin McBride. (*Photo by Michal Gladysz*)

Above: Kru Phil Nurse posing at The WAT gym in New York. (*Photo by Christopher Olech*)

Top: Kru Phil Nurse shadow boxing, throwing his special "left superman" at The WAT gym in New York. (*Photo by Christopher Olech*)

Above: Using my Muay Thai skills to keep up with Kru Phil Nurse at The WAT in New York. (*Photo by Greg Bartnik*)

Top: Presenting the *wai* (bowing with clasped hands in Thai tradition) to show my gratitude and respect for Kru Phil Nurse after our intense training session. (*Photo by Greg Bartnik*)

Above: Kru Phil Nurse chatting with UFC light heavyweight champion Jon Jones at a Paradise Warrior Retreat in New York at The WAT gym. (*Photo by Christopher Olech*)

Above: A stare down with Rich Franklin at a restaurant in Woodstock, Ontario. (*Photo by Beata Olech*)

Top: Fight pose of Rich Franklin in the cage at MMA World Academy in Toronto, Ontario. (*Photo by Christopher Olech*)

Above: Close up of the coveted UFC championship belt as the author interviews Rich Franklin at MMA World Academy in Toronto, Ontario. (*Photo by Beata Olech*)

Top: Rich Franklin in deep thought during an interview at MMA World Academy in Toronto, Ontario. (*Photo by Beata Olech*)

Above: Rich Franklin hanging loose after our interview at MMA World Academy in Toronto. (*Photo by Christopher Olech*)

Top: Fedor Emelianenko at a press conference in Edmonton, Alberta. (*Photo by Christopher Olech*)

Above: The author interviewing Fedor Emelianenko with Ioulia Reynolds of *The House-wives of Vancouver* fame as the translator. (*Photo by Greg Bartnik*)

Top: Fedor Emelianenko looking as mean as ever as he teaches striking techniques at a seminar in Calgary at Canuckles gym. (*Photo by Christopher Olech*)

Above: Fedor Emelianenko showing how far a shoulder can rotate while teaching a kimura at a seminar in Calgary at Canuckles gym. (*Photo by Christopher Olech*)

Top: The author in business attire and Fedor Emelianenko in MMA garb showcasing that MMA philosophy and applications can be transferred to the business world. (*Photo by Hector Quintero*)

Above: Fedor Emelianenko teaching a move he used to defeat many of his opponents, the arm bar, at a seminar in Calgary at Canuckles gym. (*Photo by Christopher Olech*)

Top: Rory MacDonald teaching striking techniques at a seminar at Lanna MMA in Toronto, Ontario. (*Photo by Christopher Olech*)

Above Left: A close-up of one of the sport's pound-for-pound best champions, Fedor Emelianenko. (*Photo by Christopher Olech*)

Above Right: The author interviewing Rory MacDonald in the cage at Grant Brothers Boxing & MMA Gym in Toronto, Ontario. (*Photo by Beata Olech*)

Above: Rory MacDonald being interviewed in the cage at Grant Brothers Boxing & MMA Gym in Toronto, Ontario for mmacanada.net. (*Photo by Beata Olech*)

Top: Firas Zahabi and Rory Macdonald after an exhausting training session at Tristar gym in Montreal, Quebec. (*Photo by Christopher Olech*)

Above: Firas Zahabi teaching a technique with Kru Phil Nurse at the Paradise Warrior Retreat in New York. (*Photo by Greg Bartnik*)

Top: Hanging out with Firas Zahabi and Kru Phil Nurse after our spontaneous grappling and sparring session at The WAT in New York. (*Photo by Greg Bartnik*)

Above: Firas Zahabi looking to take down Rashad Evans at the Paradise Warrior Retreat in Montreal. (*Photo by Christopher Olech*)

After beating Forrest Griffin, he carried an undefeated professional record of thirteen wins to one draw and no losses. It was a gift and a curse for the Niagara native. The good part was that, at first, when he went into a fight, he was pursuing his passion. However, becoming more successful made it more difficult to have fun, due to the expectations. He was no longer the guy that would go in and whoop people's asses and then go back to his job, living his life. When fighting is your profession, it counts a lot more. He was now fighting to make money; his livelihood was at stake, so success was the only option.

The added element of pressure took fighting to a different level for Rashad. After his title claim, he lost to Lyoto Machida, causing Rashad to revisit his initial perspectives on the fight game. He asked himself why he had started fighting, what all of this was really about, whether he loved it, and whether he could handle losing; he rediscovered that he could take a loss and that he did love fighting, and went into his next fight as if he had never lost a match.

He also had an opportunity to return to The Ultimate Fighter (TUF) show, which had originally helped him make a grand entrance into the UFC. But this time, he could give back by coaching the new wave of fighters with the same UFC dreams that he once had. Fans saw Rashad's warm side, as he put his students first, mentoring and teaching them to the extent possible in the limited time frame. Rashad had an amazing experience. He cemented his love for coaching, giving praise to all of the amazing coaches he had throughout his career.

He took lessons from of each of his coaches and pieced together the concept of what he thought an ideal coach should be, working hard to be that person. A humble man, Rashad went on to discuss his appreciation for living a blessed life. He often reflected on how far he had come; he was once in the same position as his students, understanding the trials and tribulations they still had to go through. He was honored to be a coach on TUF.

Rashad was making a name for himself as a top-tier coach. Vitor Belfort had come to Boca Raton, Florida, to enlist Rashad as his head coach in preparation for his fight with Jon Jones. Rashad enjoyed the experience, particularly because he had been watching Vitor fight since Vitor was nineteen and lighting the MMA world on fire, providing a glimpse of what MMA would be like ten years later. He spoke volumes of the "phenom" Vitor Belfort, who came close to taking the belt from Jon Jones at UFC 152 with a near arm bar submission.

Going with a quote I had read, "Great achievement is usually born of great sacrifice and is never the result of selfishness" by Napoleon Hill, I asked Rashad what sacrifices he had made to achieve success. There were many, but time was something that stood out for him. Time was the only thing we as humans really have as complete value, in existence it was time itself. He sacrificed time with his kids to pursue his dreams in an attempt to give them a better life. Sacrifice was not on his mind while training, but the stark realization was that moments such as his children's first steps were gone forever.

MMA was a spiritual journey for every practitioner, and Rashad agreed that MMA had made him a better person. Every time he fought, he would learn more about himself. Training camps were a journey themselves; embracing the rigorous preparations and being open to learning new things would strip away weaknesses. Those journeys also sharpened his spiritual and mental resources, which would be necessary in a fight.

I asked Rashad which of his fights was most difficult, and he responded that they were all hard because of what it took to get there. Rashad, an avid student of the game, always spoke with many fighters, some with nearly 100 matches under their belts. All of them agreed that every single fight felt like the first one.

As soon as it was over, the win would be in the rear-view mirror, and the desire to go through the experience again would immediately surface. Rashad also mentioned that within a week, that feeling of being on a mountaintop would be forgotten, "That feeling is like when you're in the room and everybody has gone and you said your goodbyes. Then it's just you and it's really like the moment of truth. It's like, not even a moment, it's just like a long period of time when you're just alone with your thoughts, and sometimes that can be a scary place to be."

The night before a fight, however, was different for everyone. Rashad never slept well the night before; he would go over the fight in his mind a million times in one night, waking up five or six times throughout the night. On fight day, 6:00 a.m. approaches quickly, his mind red-lining with thoughts, worries, and anxieties. Rashad loved the fast pace of the fight, but the lull before the fight was not enjoyable.

"So every time I do fight, it always takes me on a different journey and it takes me to a place where I learn a lot about myself, because when it comes down to it, everybody helped me prepare and stuff like that, but it's me—the one who steps inside the cage. It's me who has to face the weakest parts of me, you know? When you're held accountable and your back is against the wall, you're going to find out what kind of person you are inside. Some people like what they find and some people don't…"

Joe Ferraro, MMA analyst and the host of Sportsnet's *UFC Central* (TV and Radio), had definitively stated his view on Rashad Evans, summarizing my exact thoughts. "I think Rashad Evans as a person is one of the nicest human beings you could ever meet. He is by far one of the most misunderstood guys in the sport of mixed martial arts. If you look at the whole situation with Rampage and Jon "Bones" Jones, he calls it like it is and says it like it is and never backs down to trash talk. He is a natural athlete … he was one of those guys that was able to pick up the striking aspect, the boxing and kickboxing and really use it efficiently for his game. Rashad Evans has done a great job to put it all together."

I skipped through questions as we neared the end of our conversation. My watch indicated that it was past midnight. My final question was to ask what he imagined was in store for him in the fight game. Rashad's eyes lit up.

"I'm going to be UFC champion again, and that's the only thing that I feel like I need to really accomplish in my life and in my career, just because I know there is another level that I can hit and I feel like I've had sprinkles of that, you know? I always say to myself that I'm going to quit once I have the perfect fight, and I've not had the perfect fight yet. What would epitomize me having a perfect fight? It is me once again finding a way to master my emotions, master my thoughts, and to go out there and have a form in which I'm totally free."

He continued, "I'm not in a box, I'm not thinking about a game plan, I'm not thinking about what he is going to do. Where I'm just, like, totally free to just fully express myself, just do it, you know, and no hesitations, no fear … if I do this he may do that; none of it. I just throw caution to the wind as if after this fight no matter what happened my life will be over and this is all I have to give, like a true test and I just do it like that and I feel like if I go out there and compete from that position, then I feel like I will be the champion again and my career will thus be complete."

QUICK ROUND
What's your favorite thing to do with family and friends?
Watch TV.

Favorite city to fight in?
Vegas.

What city would you like to fight in that you haven't yet?
New York.

If you could fight anyone in the world, who it would be?
I want to fight Jon Jones.

If you could fight anyone in the world from any time, who would it be?
I guess that's tough. I want to fight Tyson, I'd love it.

What is your favorite junk food?
I must say Toll House cookies, when you just put some ice cream on them or something.

If we listened to your music playlist, what would we find?
Anything from the hardest hip-hop to Elton John.

What's your favorite movie?
I'll have to say *The Usual Suspects*, yes.

What's one of your favorite video games?
Mortal Kombat.

Favorite standup technique?
Overhand right.

Your favorite wrestling/grappling technique?
Outside single.

Favorite supplements?
L-Glutathione (antioxidant).

Please tell us one thing that most people don't know about you.
I'm afraid of the dark.

Chapter Eleven

THE PROFESSOR

"Whoever I am, or whatever I am doing, some kind of excellence is within my reach."
—John W. Gardner

Gracie Barra was a brotherhood and sisterhood where relationships ran far deeper than at a typical training gym. There was code among fighters who attended Gracie Barra, which housed some of the best fighters in the world from all realms of the game. Jon Jones had recently begun gi training as a white belt under the Gracie Barra banner… but I would not want to enter the white belt division in a tournament to face him! The training was meticulous and systematic, as each school followed a university-type curriculum. My own roots were in Gracie Barra London, even before it was classified as a GB school under Professor Fateh Belkalem in London, Ontario. I traveled to Montreal for a one-on-one sit-down with a very popular Gracie Barra professor, a man who was truly the yardstick of excellence.

Bruno Fernandes was born in Rio de Janeiro, where he lived for most of his life. He was always an avid sports player growing up, just like most of the children around him, which he loved. His parents entered him into competitive swimming tournaments as early as three years of age. His regular routine consisted of going to school, followed by swimming practice each day. From a very early age, he was used to the sports lifestyle.

At the age of eleven, he began training in one of Brazil's national sports: jiu-jitsu. It took only a few years for Bruno to choose jiu-jitsu over swimming. He trained under the Carlson Gracie kids' team, but at the age of sixteen moved to the city of Barra da Tijuca, where the famous "Team Gracie Barra" was born. He joined the team and has been one of their leading representatives ever since.

Surfing the turquoise ocean waves of Brazil was another one of Bruno's passions. It definitely helped that he grew up close to the beach. From the beginning of his surfing days at six years of age, it had become more and more a part of his warm Brazilian blood over time. Years later, living in Quebec, Canada, skiing was more the norm than surfing could ever be; however, Bruno made traveling to warmer locations around the world a priority five or six times per year to fulfill his insatiable thirst for the thrills and serenity of surfing.

As Greg Bartnik (my brother-in-law) and I sat with Bruno on the jiu-jitsu mats cross-legged on the second floor of his famous Gracie Barra gym, his laid-back surfer aura was evident, like nothing could faze him. His frequent bright smiles radiated a calming atmosphere and brought joy to the room.

Why had Bruno immigrated to the great white north of Canada when he had pristine beaches at his fingertips in Brazil? Education was always important to Bruno, and once he had finished his residency in ophthalmology, which is a branch of medicine that deals with the anatomy, physiology and diseases of the eye, he moved to Quebec to finish his PhD. After that, he was offered a postdoctoral study/research position and then was invited to stay at the university as a professor. He completed another year of training in Toronto, Ontario, and then moved back to Montreal for a position at McGill University.

Bruno was a professor at one of the most prestigious medical schools in the country; in addition, he spoke four languages. If that wasn't enough for his CV, he was also a world-class jiu-jitsu third-degree black belt who had won countless competitions, he held the title of Gracie Barra regional director for eastern Canada, and was the owner and professor of Gracie Barra Montreal, a gym catering to the best jiu-jitsu players in the world, including Georges St-Pierre and Mark Colangelo, among many others.

Growing up and gravitating to the sport of Brazilian jiu-jitsu, Bruno admired many others; in fact, he stated that it would be unfair to single one out. He particularly appreciated all of the people he had gotten to train with. He felt blessed to train with a long list of who's who of the sport, people who took the time to coach him—he knew he hadn't become great on his own.

Bruno had been in many ground game wars on many of the biggest stages in the Brazilian jiu-jitsu world, but there was one that was more memorable than the others. He was a brown belt, splitting his time studying for school and practicing jiu-jitsu, when he entered a prestigious tournament. During one of the rounds, he was pitted against an old Carlson Gracie teammate who had beaten Bruno at the Pan American championships in 1998. It was rare for Bruno to step onto the mats being the underdog, but in that instance, it was exactly where he found himself. Bruno not only won, but he won by a landslide of eight points to zero. He liked being the underdog who went on to surprise everyone with a landslide win—it was an exuberant feeling.

Bruno would always begin his training camp a month in advance of a tournament. Although a month seems short for a training camp, he also trained hard year-round. The biggest variable that he would really change when in training camp was his nightlife. As he was around eighteen years old and winning world championships, not going out was actually a big deal for him. He would enter a monk-like state by limiting his beach time and focusing only on his training. Bruno maintained his mental focus on the mats, giving him time to come up with a proper game plan and add smoothness to his game.

Given his other obligations, Bruno could only squeeze in one training session per day. He believed that one session of jiu-jitsu per day for up to two hours (one hour studying technique and one hour of hard rolling) was enough, and that other training sessions such as weights, stretching, or swimming should be implemented as a second session. Too many jiu-jitsu sessions could lead to joint pain, mat burns, fatigue, and injuries.

During the time when Bruno was tearing through the BJJ world, the grading system and ascension of belts was so tough that receiving the coveted black belt seemed nearly impossible. Bruno felt that most practitioners weren't focused on reaching the black belt, as the ones who did receive it should have been awarded them long ago. Bruno had won two world titles before being awarded a black belt himself. Looking back, he grew to like the striving to achieve the black belt, but did not think it should have been as cumbersome for the blue, purple, and brown belt promotions. For Bruno, receiving the black belt was recognition of everything he had done for the team and was an opportunity to represent the team at the highest level of the game.

When Bruno was younger, being strict with diet was not a priority given the efficiency of his metabolism. However, Bruno has always been known to be in optimal shape, so I asked him for the key to a healthy life. He had recently changed his diet by cutting out a lot of red meat, as well as animal-derived products such as milk, cheese, and eggs. He added superfruits such as acai, Brazil nuts, cashews, maqui berry, cacao, maca root, ginseng, ginkgo biloba, hemp seeds, chia seeds, flax seeds, and goji berries into his diet, which were lower in calories and higher in fiber than animal products. Within no time, he had lost ten pounds without changing his overall routine. He also reported having a lot more energy after tweaking his diet. Approximately eighty to ninety percent of his diet was derived from some form of fruit, nuts, or vegetables.

We transitioned to the subject of the mental game. The professor believed that this was something that could be trained. Not only could it be trained, but it should be passed on, with its importance stressed to students. He went on to explain that no one was born tough, but strength was built; it was his job to show his students how to increase their capacity for toughness. In pushing their limits just the right amount, they could do a little more while enjoying small victories. Bruno stated that this attitude should not be limited to the fighting realm, but is a skill adaptable to everyday life. "Whenever you face adversity, you have the guts to push yourself through. Take a good look at it, assess it, and come up with a good solution and fix it. If you adopt that mindset often, it just becomes natural to you, and that is when mental toughness kicks in."

As for his thoughts on gi versus no-gi, he thought it was two sides of the same coin. He never looked at no-gi as not being part of the same martial art. Without disrespecting any other arts, he mentioned that, in Brazil, a few guys trained without a gi, and ADCC, a large tournament that had no-gi fights, believed that the prominent gi-trained schools wouldn't stand a chance. However, ADCC proved that gi training was necessary in order to excel at the ground game, as the gi trained fighters had fared better in the tournament. In switching roles, no-gi didn't seem to show a benefit over the gi game, so Bruno felt that it was more efficient to train gi over no-gi. Optimally, one would train both.

On fighters and egos, Bruno thought that the ego could be a fighter's worst enemy. The ego could stop a fighter from excelling to his potential, and Bruno gave an example from daily training. The ego-driven fighter would not expose himself too much, being afraid of tapping or being scared of what others might say, hindering positive progress. Tapping a partner in training or in a competition could make some guys think that they were the absolute best, but on the other side of the coin, those egos were easily bruised. "If you don't live in a bubble, it is hard to maintain an ego without being delusional. Some advice for people that are starting a martial arts career: man, you will be beaten several times and that is the beauty of it because one day you will become the guy that kept beating you."

Once on Canadian soil, Bruno met UFC Welterweight Champion Georges St-Pierre in the infancy of the champ's career. GSP had just beaten B.J. Penn for the first time, and Bruno was a purple belt teaching Brazilian jiu-jitsu at the Tristar gym where GSP trained. GSP was one of the first faces at Tristar to train with the gi, which was unusual at the time, but not at the pioneering MMA Mecca gym. Their friendship grew from there, and GSP has been honing his skills with Bruno ever since.

When I asked why the professor thought that the biggest names in MMA came to train with him, he knew exactly why. Bruno was always honest about the way that he did not have a lot of MMA knowledge, but Brazilian jiu-jitsu was a different story, so he did his best to accommodate and stimulate a fighter's BJJ game. He didn't try to change their approach, though, he just tried to solve problems efficiently, without being arrogant or telling someone what to do in the grand scheme of the MMA game. His tactical and deep knowledge of the ground game was what he passed along to all of his students, and he was very gifted in identifying what a fighter needed to fill a void.

Having reached such success both as a coach and as a student of the game, he was kind enough to share his thoughts on how to become the best. An innate drive to achieve the goal was necessary, as he believed that everyone could achieve their goals with the right approach. It may take more or less time for certain individuals, but the drive had to be there. A person had to find what it was that motivated him or her and to have the right amount of discipline to follow through. The last part of the equation was to have patience and give it time. "No one is going to become a champion overnight."

Thousands of hours had to be invested into a craft in order to perfect it. Whether we are speaking about athletes, musicians, or office workers, goals are attainable by all, but the work and time are necessary components.

As for his coaching philosophies, he wanted to help his students but not push them into things; he always tried to meet them halfway. Each student had a different motive for attending classes, whether it was for self-defense, socialization, or weight loss. He didn't have the right to question their motives, so he provided them with the basic tools of jiu-jitsu. He would continue to share his knowledge and monitor their progress, encouraging them to keep working on their game and attaining their goals.

A mixture of world champions and individuals simply there to have fun made for a great environment, but everyone had the same goal of inching closer to perfection. Bruno admitted that a few of his best students were those who will never compete; they are content training on a daily basis, and he respected each student's decisions.

My Gracie Barra training in London, Ontario, had lineage to Professor Fernandes as he had presented my Professor Fateh Belkalem with his black belt. Bruno greatly admired Fateh, as he had been a practitioner of Judo for his entire life, giving him the discipline that a lot of BJJ schools lacked and didn't pass on to their students. Bruno thought that practicing martial arts without discipline was a mistake. Second, Fateh was humble enough to start a new sport when he wasn't in his prime, and he had started as a white belt and worked his way up. Bruno had never attempted to pick up a different sport like that, to take the leap, but that he admired Fateh to not only do that but also to achieve the highest rank possible in the new martial art.

I switched the focus back onto the professor, asking him what drove him to be so successful in such a wide range of areas in life. He seemed to have the golden touch. "It's not so magical, unfortunately. First, I don't try as many things as people think. The things I succeed at are pretty much the only things that I did. I never tried other martial arts, I never had a full career outside the mats. I suck at soccer, for instance, and I come from Brazil; it's almost shameful to admit. But I like jiu-jitsu, so I did not see a point in investing my time in doing something that I could get hurt in. I think the secret to success is knowing what you really like doing and then being able to put time into it. Always having that pursuit to improve yourself, never being comfortable, knowing you can get better."

Bruno went on to explain that he was happy with his achievements, but he was never too proud to stop improving. He was happy knowing what he had achieved, but knew he could achieve even more. This winning mindset was necessary for any successful fighter or member of society.

As we approached the end of the interview, I asked Bruno for his thoughts on the role of BJJ in MMA in the future. He thought that being well-rounded was very important; long gone are the days of a one-trick pony dominating in MMA. He noticed a shift, that it was becoming increasingly difficult to submit an opponent, as everyone was working on the ground game, or at the very least at their defense on the ground. As the sport has expanded and grown, it has become well-established regarding what a fighter needed to step into the cage.

Bruno also noted that a jiu-jitsu guy could take his opponent down and win the round, but not dish out much damage. He thought it was important for jiu-jitsu players to expect this and to not get frustrated in the same way that a striker wouldn't get frustrated if he didn't knock out his opponent out in the first round. Jiu-jitsu fighters were under added pressure to submit their opponents quickly, but successful fighters in the future would work past the pressure and dominate their opponents on the ground. They would then get the submission by a consequence of that fact.

Bruno was a legend in the Brazilian jiu-jitsu world; he had won the Pan American Championship master black belt division in 2014, and was always perfecting his technique. It was very evident why this was so. He had a constant drive to improve, even when it seemed impossible. The truth was that skills could be built to unfathomable degrees. He was an expert at living a balanced life of work and play, as he made sure to detach himself from his immense responsibilities to venture around the world, finding tranquility in nature's ocean waves. I knew I would be come back to train with the professor on the same mats were world champions had unrelentingly perfected their games.

QUICK ROUND
What's your favorite junk food?
Pizza.

What are your favorite two cities in the world?
Rio de Janeiro and Montreal.

If you had a dream match, who would your opponent be?
I would like to fight my idol, Rolls Gracie.

Favorite ground techniques?
I like sweeps; butterfly sweeps to be more exact.

Favorite submission?
Arm triangle choke.

What is your biggest strength?
I would say patience.

What is your biggest weakness?
Stubbornness.

What is one of your favorite movies?
Recently, I watched *Driver*.

If we looked in your fridge, what would we find?
Fruit and veggies. I eat junk food, but do not have any in the house.

Chapter Twelve

JOURNEY FOR GOLD

"Destiny is not a matter of chance, but of choice. Not something to wish for, but to attain."
—William Jennings Bryan

For the first time, having the time to train like a professional athlete allowed the realizations that I was ready, able, and, in fact, going to take first place at the prestigious Grapplers Quest national tournament. This was the first time that Grapplers Quest, one of the biggest Brazilian jiu-jitsu tournaments, was coming to Ontario. As luck would have it, they were coming to my backyard in London, Ontario.

I learned that Grapplers Quest would be held in October on the mixedmartialarts.com forum and informed my wife that I would definitely be participating.

As I was on another lay-off from work, the timing and location gave me a significant home-field advantage. This was my third tournament, following Alex "Pecker" Gasson's thirty-two-man tournament from Adrenaline. At the Toronto Classic, I passed through the first round to take a bronze medal.

For the first time, I used a lot of the advice collected for this book, testing the wise words of great fighters. I approached the tournament methodically; I was not going to be brazen with my approach, as I was in my two prior tournaments.

I carefully considered what I needed to do to enter as the best Chris Olech Brazilian jiu-jitsu artist possible, given the few months I had to prepare. I wrote it down.

1) Lose ten to fifteen pounds, placing myself in an easy position to cut to the 209-pound division. (I was 228 pounds at the time.)
2) Train twice a day on Monday, Wednesday, and Friday, with morning classes in either no-gi jiu-jitsu or Muay Thai at the Adrenaline Training Centre, and in the evenings, strictly focusing on gi jiu-jitsu at Gracie Barra London.

Tuesday mornings involved strength and conditioning simulating API caveman training routines for a good hour in the morning and Gracie Barra jiu-jitsu in the evenings.

Thursday mornings were rest days or cardio; I would listen to my body to determine what I was going to do.

Saturday mornings, I did some form of strength and conditioning, coupled with cardio.

3) I maintained a strict diet regimen that was high in protein, greens, and fruit. James Haourt from Adrenaline really helped me, showing me how important it was to cut all food out after 6:00 p.m. every night. Protein drinks after workouts were a godsend for flavor and energy. My typical shake consisted of a banana, protein powder, greens, flax seeds (whole flax seeds, not the ground ones, as they lost a lot of their benefits unless they were whole and then ground into my shake; humans do not possess the enzymes necessary to break down the flax seed coating) glutamine powder, berries (acai frozen berries, blueberries, or raspberries), and water.

4) Sundays were always rest days and cheat days for one portion of snacks, cakes, fast food, etc.

5) Give myself time to either meditate or pronounce self-affirmations regarding my skills, talent, and potential.

6) Train and prepare to my fullest potential. Be true to myself knowing that I was pushing myself hard, while at the same time listening to my body to get the proper rest while staying injury-free.

7) Give thanks to my immediate trainers and training partners donating their time, energy, and knowledge with me, as well as all the fighters and trainers in my book that shared their formulas. The way to give them thanks was by doing everything I could to prepare and compete at my fullest potential.

8) Have fun while doing it all!

This time around, not only did I make a list, but also I stuck to it. I was also fortunate enough to travel to Poland and Montreal to train with some great athletes during training camp. Having trained with Rafał in Poland gave me a mental edge. Although I trained in both kickboxing and Muay Thai, the difficult regimen coupled with the run-down conditions and never-say-die attitude of his students strengthened my mindset.

At Tristar and Gracie Barra Montreal, the educational experience in terms of the quality and volume of techniques that I learned from the elite fighters and trainers, including black belts Mark Colangelo, Rashad Evans, John Danaher, Firas Zahabi, as well as Glenn Mackenzie, Jon Jones, and many others in the realm of wrestling and jiu-jitsu, were second to none. My even larger advantage came from their stories of inspiration and toughness that filled a deep hole in my soul that have resonated there ever since. When two fighters with equal amounts of skills and physical attributes compete, the fight would be won by the one with more heart. Thanks to all of my great teachers and warriors, I was confident that there was no one with more than me.

I was a regular at both of my gyms, as I pushed myself every day to become better. I noticed that I was getting faster, stronger, and more fluid in my movements. However, my weight would hover between 216 and 218 pounds. No matter what I did, it seemed that the scale would always bounce back between those numbers.

One morning after running on the treadmill at Adrenaline, I jumped on the scale and was shocked that it read 220 pounds. With only a couple weeks until the competition, it lit a fire under my ass. I got reasonably pissed, even with my training and diet regimen my body was doing whatever it wanted. I saw LIUNA-sponsored fighter Chris Clements, who made it to the UFC a few years later. He put on a Bas Rutten CD; on the disc, the legend himself yelled out combinations that we followed by mimicking.

I joined the veteran on the empty wrestling mats, as we had half the gym to ourselves, and we listened as one of the all-time greats relayed combinations and exercises while we acted out the words. I wanted to maintain a steady pace with Chris as we punched, elbowed, and kicked the air, shadow-boxing. Bas threw sprawls and push-ups at the moments when my lungs needed to rest the most, and I loved it! Time passed as we became drenched in sweat, perfecting our form. That day, I learned the hard way that Bas's particular workout is near thirty minutes long without a single rest. Toward the end, Chris encouraged to finish strong, providing the much-needed motivation to throw crisp combinations even faster than when we started thirty minutes prior. Once the session was over, I collapsed to the mat to regain my composure and try to breathe. After a bit of stretching, another local kickboxing legend, Leo Louckes, who was present helping the pros train, came over to congratulate me on a great job during the session; it meant a lot to me.

The day before the competition was a cold, cloudy, and windy October afternoon that I will never forget. I was shadow-boxing in my basement, sporting a sauna suit to lose the extra weight. I weighed 219 pounds and had to lose ten more before the weigh-ins, scheduled for early evening. I lost a pound for every ten minutes of bouncing around in the suit. After an hour and ten minutes, I lost seven pounds, but I was getting a bit dizzy and feeling really off. I decided to listen to my body and take the suit off. I had not eaten or drank anything since 5:30 p.m. the previous day.

My wife drove me to the local gym, which had a sauna I could use to shed the remaining three pounds. In the sauna, I was again drenched in my own sweat, and I started shadow-boxing, as I believed that the water was not coming out fast enough. I received some confused looks through the entrance window as I was uppercutting the air in high heat. The weight scales were all irregular at the club, as all of them had put me significantly over the limit. I thought that either my body was out of whack or their cheap scales had to be the cause. But to be sure, I kept entering the sauna and shadow-boxing for as long as I could stand, taking a break only to do it all over again four times over. The scales read 209 pounds, and I was ready to make my way to the weigh-ins as my body was begging for vitamins and water. The faster I got this over with, the sooner I could eat.

As I ran to the car, cutting through the forceful winds, I had the prize on my mind; nothing was going to stop me. Once at the weigh-ins at the Western Fair, the lineup of competitors was massive. After nearly an hour, my time had come to stand on the scales; I felt like I was a matchstick that was going to topple over. I weighed in at 207.3 pounds, nearly two pounds under weight for my division, thanks to those wonderful scales at the gym!

I ate some chicken and drank electrolytes right away and proceeded to the group meeting at Gracie Barra London to review the point system and rules for the tournament. Once there, all of my friends from Gracie Barra Montreal were present, including Professor Bruno Fernandes, Mark Colangelo, Glenn Mackenzie, and others. After a group photo, I went home to sleep.

The next morning, I felt surprisingly refreshed and powerful. I looked in the mirror and noticed that the lines of a six-pack had formed; I was physically and mentally jacked, ready to put my skills to use. Many fighters have mentioned, "I do not get worried before a fight if I know I did everything I could during my training camp." I could easily second that statement that morning.

The competition drew thousands of spectators and competitors from throughout Canada and the U.S. The super match pitted legends Saulo Ribeiro and Joao Assis against each other. The two true world-class athletes of Brazilian jiu-jitsu went at it. Joao Assis picked up the win, besting the legend and giving me more motivation to bring my best game forward.

Greg, my brother-in-law, and some friends arrived halfway through the day to show their support, but it seemed as if my turn would never come. The waiting was excruciating. I was going through moves and variations as well as how I would get out of tough spots in my mind. The Gracie Barra Montreal and London guys were also there to cheer on. Glen Mackenzie was a true warrior in his matches. Incredibly, Mark Colangelo won gold in the black belt division; he was a brown belt at the time.

The end of the tournament inched closer; the spectators were quietly leaving for home. My turn was finally approaching, scheduled for after 6:00 p.m. I noticed some of the guys crowding in the waiting area, and I thought to myself that I seemed a little bigger than they were. My cut must have worked, and my adrenaline started pumping right at that instant.

There were a couple matches before mine, and I chose not to watch them. I went behind the stands to do my warm-ups and stretches. I did a few short sprints and ballistic stretches. Not only was I warming up my muscles, but also I was preparing my mind for battle. I kept repeating simple phrases to give myself a mental edge: "I am unstoppable. I deserve to be here. I will win the gold!"

When my name was called, I was stone-faced, not noticing anyone in the stands. The spectators included Glen, Beata, Greg, and my head coach, Fateh, as I made my way onto the mats. All I could focus on was my opponent; I was fully immersed and in the zone. My tunnel vision kept me calm, collected, and, most of all, determined, and this guy was not going to stop me.

We both came out at a fast pace and never let off the gas pedal. As we grabbed each other's gis, it was immediately evident that I was stronger. After a short tugging match, he opted to jump into his guard to prevent being forcefully taken down. He must have been pretty comfortable with his guard game. As quickly as I had this thought, he was switching his hips and throwing his legs over my face for an arm bar. I kept circling along with his hips, not willing to give him the angle he was looking for.

My opponent was from Toronto BJJ; Jorge Britto was his instructor under the Ribeiro banner. He was good and worked efficiently to keep me off of him, even when I worked my way to the half-guard, he almost reversed me. Toward the end of the round, he shot in for a single leg and I hopped backward, using my balance until I found myself on top of him as he went into the turtle position. The round ended with me trying to get my hooks in as I was taking his back.

The win felt good for a second, but I was already thinking about my next match as I stepped off the mats. My competitor came up to me to congratulate me and told me to win the tournament, that since I beat him he was rooting for me. It was a solid gesture of camaraderie.

My second opponent was as tall as I was and jacked. He did not have an ounce of fat on him; he wore a Chuck Liddell-style short Mohawk and hailed from Montreal, where he trained out of the TapouT gym. I had to wait for him to finish a match he had on the other side of the mats, as he signed up for two separate divisions. The referee just came over to me to let me know it could take a while, as he was allowed to refresh before our match. I responded kindly, "Let him rest up as much as he needs; I will be behind the stands."

A good fifteen minutes later, I continued my small workout regimen behind the stands; the worst thing I could do was to let my muscles get cold. Emotions surged through me, and I began praying to God. I prayed to my family members who had passed into the next life for strength, guidance, and to let them know I was doing this in their honor. Everything I had endured in life rushed into my mind, adding fuel to my ambitions.

My name was called, and my opponent and I were all business; I think we both watched one too many "The Axe Murderer" Wanderlei Silva matches, as we maintained straight faces at each other. But neither of us was intimidated by the other.

We clinched forcefully, grabbing onto each other's gi lapels, trying to force each other to the mats. Our goals were the same: top control on the ground. I was told that he had a good top game, as did I, so I tried everything to get the dominant top position on him. I used Judo variations to sweep his ankles in an attempt to take him down by forcefully projecting his upper body in the opposite direction. It was a no-go. He was super strong, and our strengths canceled out our advantages in the takedown.

We were like two bulls with locked horns, fighting for leader of the herd. We were equal in many ways. I would try to throw him one way; he would try to throw me the other. He pushed; I pushed back. Our primitive natures came out as we tried to best each other, yet I had the better game plan that day.

My fingers lost all feeling from grasping his gi top so hard and violently for the entire five-minute match, so much so that I had to pry them off. But before I did, I had to be the one to finish in aggressive fashion. Playing it safe, I went for one single-leg attempt but didn't attempt any throws as he could have countered, and the win meant more to me than showing off any fancy skills. With thirty seconds left, our fingers bit into the other's gi like rabid pitbulls clenching with jaws of death. I began pushing him backward, attempting more leg sweeps. One threw his base off, and he took a wide stance mid-air in an attempt to save himself from falling to the mats. The buzzer sounded to end the match, and even though we were leveled in skill and strength, I knew I had done everything I could, and that was enough.

My hand was raised at the end of the round. My opponent was not happy, but the referee let him know that it was a very hard match to judge and that I had aggressively done more, pushing the decision in my favor, and that was good enough for me. I was ready for my championship match.

I was given rest time before taking on someone just as hungry for the gold, another practitioner from Toronto BJJ who trained under my friend and black belt Jorge Britto. In my safety zone behind the stands, I once again said a quick prayer, affirmed my place, loosened my shoulders, and took my last deep breath before stepping onto the mats to take what was mine.

My last opponent was much shorter than me but had a strong base and wide shoulders. He started slowly with a low stance, making it harder for me to shoot in for a successful takedown. As he went to grab my gi collar, I faked throwing my hands up to his collar and shot in for a tactical double-leg takedown. But as quickly as we hit the mat, he was already looking for submissions. I had left my arms on the mat, a big mistake in jiu-jitsu, especially with my long limbs. He tried to manipulate my elbow joint but I pulled my arm out to safety. He transitioned to crossing his wrists while pulling on my collar to choke me. I immediately looked up, took a deep breath and put myself in a calm state; I was in no real trouble.

He then tried to sweep me from the bottom, and we scrambled as he tried to take my back. My extended arm reaching over his back was all I had to stop him as I thrust it into the air. He was inching closer to take my back, and I capitalized by twisting into him; I grabbed his heel, throwing him off balance and onto his back again, adding more points in my favor. He had good hips, as every time I tried to pass his guard he switched his hips and put me back in. Keeping weight over him, I worked hard to maintain position. I was not going to give him an inch in our struggle.

With ten seconds left, I heard Fateh clearly yelling, "Breath Chris, ten seconds! Stay in position! You got this!" Fateh was like an angel on my shoulder. I tried doing everything he said throughout the match, and it was clearly working. The timer buzzed, signaling the end of the round, and immediately I raised my hands in the air, knowing I had climbed the mountain and earned my gold medal.

I could not have done this without every single person that helped me along my journey, Greg, my wife, James Haourt from Adrenaline, Scott and Matt from API, Bruno Fernandes, Mark Colangelo and Glen Mackenzie from Gracie Barra Montreal, all the guys teaching at the Paradise Warrior Retreat, and, of course, my head coach, Fateh Belkalem, and the boys at Gracie Barra London. The discipline and hard work had paid off, and it felt good to have an army of great people behind me to celebrate.

I had yet again learned how to approach my goals systematically to get the best results. I sacrificed time with my family, took away the things I craved (food), outworked others in preparation, and kept a strong mind and focus on the prize as I resisted situations trying to pry that focus away. This was the winning formula—one that I could also apply to my everyday life experiences and to help others as well.

Chapter Thirteen

A THROWBACK TO ROCKY!

"Not everyone could be a champion. You can practically count the amount of champions on your fingers. I would not be here without hard work. Everyone in life has a mission to fulfill and I hope I am on the right path in my life."

—Tomasz Adamek

Tomasz Adamek is a very talented boxing champion with the heart of a lion and a chin made of granite. Naturally, when I was looking at prospective boxers to interview on my journey, Tomasz was at the top of the list. Setting out, I promised myself that I would get the best fighters and people from all realms of the fight game, and having this opportunity was one that I ran with. I set up a trip to his training camp in the Pocono Mountains in Pennsylvania, where I would have the time to get to know the champ, see his training regimen, and find out more about his fascinating life story.

As the time neared for the eight-hour trek from Ontario to Pennsylvania, I was ecstatic to feel welcomed by his camp. In the boxing world, it is not very common to be able to crash a training camp, especially two and half weeks before a scheduled bout.

My brother-in-law, Greg Bartnik, would be accompanying me again to help with the photos, camera work, and to correct me with any twisted Polish that I might have muttered. I've always had a tendency to mash Polish and English words together to create my version of "Polglish." Tomasz spoke and understood English, but it was definitely easier for him to communicate in his native tongue.

To prepare for the trip, I did my usual paperwork, preparing the questions and doing research. I was also boxing a lot to prepare in case the camp would let me train. I devoted all of my training sessions to boxing. Honestly, it was a lot of fun to work on my standup. I would always end with three, three-minute rounds of shadow-boxing sessions, trying to improve my speed and footwork while maintaining proper technique. My last training session was great; I felt fast like a lightweight, and as strong as a heavyweight, and my confidence was soaring before the upcoming adventure.

Back home in London, I was working like a dog for a house builder, pulling long hours in the broiling heat for close to minimum wage. What didn't cover the bills was made up for by credit. Taking a trip south to Pennsylvania and nearly maxing out my line of credit for my book project and the chance to train with and interview the best in the world was always in the back of my mind—the ever-revolving "stress wheel," as I called it. Realistically, I had no other job leads, I was getting sick of the creditors calling, my body was deteriorating at an alarming rate, and it was stressing my marriage dynamics, as financial woes always do.

We piled our luggage and junk food into Greg's Mitsubishi as we got onto the highway for our seven-to-eight-hour drive, or so we thought. I had worked hard on the construction site that day lifting stairs, holding the side wall for the framers, and throwing lumber into the garbage trailer. I was spent, but the thought of the trip kept me up. We ventured out at 8:00 p.m., thinking we would make it by 3:00 a.m. It was a cold March evening as we crossed the border to the U.S., following our GPS directions through the side roads in an effort to avoid toll roads; what is it with all the toll roads!

The night air was dense with the cold, which probably kept many people from venturing out, but not us—we had a mission. The farther we drove, the more frigid the night became—we had not seen anything like this in a long time. We had to make pit stops every twenty minutes on the highway shoulder to scrub the ice from the freezing rain off the windshield. We were bombarded with a cold wind, freezing rain, and had poor visibility, as even through our windshield wipers were going full tilt, the window was literally freezing in front of us like a commercial promoting frosty mint gum.

Greg and I had a ritual of eating junk food and having way too many Xyience energy drinks when we went for our fight trips. And this time was not any different, we would stop at the local gas station convenience stores to stock up every few hours, having some lengthy conversations with the locals in the middle of the night.

Due to the weather conditions, we arrived well after 5:00 a.m., amped on energy drinks and junk food with only three hours of sleep in front of us before we had to be at the gym. I had a full head of thoughts of what the day would bring as my head hit the pillow, but my exhaustion took over as I passed out close to 6:00 a.m.

The alarm rang at 8:00 a.m., preparing us for a great day, regardless of feeling like zombies. I got a better view of the area as the sun made its appearance, revealing the beautiful mountains and small-town feel of Bushkill. I really felt great despite the lack of sleep, as the air was crisp, the sights were breathtaking, and I was about to meet the champ!

Bushkill is a small-town scenic wonderland, with trees covering the hills and mountains. A small lake was parallel to the hotel, which was more of a resort on a compound surrounded by paradise.

Bushkill, Pennsylvania had just under 7,000 inhabitants. The town is a great family retreat as well as a lover's paradise, and experiences a significant influx of tourists during the summer and winter months. Scanning the scene outside the hotel, my eyes took in the different shades of green, while my lungs enthusiastically took to the uncharacteristically fresh air. I could breathe easily through my nose, which was a new experience for me. At that point, I completely understood why Team Adamek had started their camps in Bushkill. They weren't hounded by media or fans, the air was fresh, the surroundings set the mind at ease during intense training, and the training at elevation was helpful for adapting to the lack of oxygen. The increase in red blood cell mass gave fighters a competitive edge; one that would last for approximately ten days while venturing to a lower altitude before a fight.

We grabbed our usual gear: cameras, tripod, recorder, question sheets and fight gear, and proceeded to the famous Bushkill boxing studio. Once inside, we noticed that there were a handful of other reporters present for the media day. I began scouting the gym walls, which were adorned with boxing posters and pictures of the famous boxers that had trained and even fought at the hotel. There was a signed picture of James Tony, a boxing legend and someone better known to MMA fans for his quick MMA stint with the UFC when he stalked UFC president Dana White across state lines until he could get an MMA fight. I was inspired by the many boxers who had walked through those gym doors.

Tomasz came walking in, wearing the Team Adamek sports track suit. He was followed by his legendary trainer of champions, Roger Bloodworth, who reminded me of the Mickey Goldmill character from the *Rocky* movies.

Rap music began blaring through the speakers along the gym walls, and Tomasz started dancing. He had a comedic side to go with his torpedo punches. Tomasz then started stretching as Roger prepared his gear. Once the open workout started, I could not believe his perfect form and lightning speed as he gracefully popped the pads. He did not just shuffle his footwork, but glided across the ring.

As Tomasz effectively moved his feet, he stayed in one place long enough to fire with hard precision and efficiency that resonated with loud pops across the gym. He cut his corners very well, barely breaking a sweat. Roger was much shorter than Tomasz, and his quick movements and absorption of every shot thrown his way defied his age, which was revealed only by his gray hair. I was witnessing a fluid and gentle art performed in an austere and dispassionate manner. We could have heard a pin drop as everyone stood in awe.

Tomasz did a few rounds with Roger as they danced in the center of the ring. They then proceeded to the heavy bags on the side of the ring. Tomasz went to town, mercilessly battering the poor bag as he displayed superb head movement and power. I felt sorry for whoever would have to step into a ring and take those shots!

Punching the speed bag, Tomasz's forearms bulged like Popeye's. The small bag was a blur as it swung back and forth from Tomasz's taps. The noise was hypnotic to the point that I practically fell into a trance after two minutes of listening to the rhythm.

After an hour, Tomasz did some cool-down exercises and managed to crack some jokes. It was like he was made of ice and granite when doing his rounds, but in-between he was smiling and telling jokes. This guy was amazing ... raw talent, with an amazing personality.

After my interviews, I managed to weasel my way into a one-on-one session with Roger Bloodworth, a true boxing legend. I was giddy with anticipation until I noticed that I'd forgotten one of my training gloves in the room. Not wanting to lose the opportunity to train with one of the world's best boxing coaches, I ran down the stairs like a cheetah. It was a good warm-up, as I got back within seconds, out of breath and a smile on my face.

I bowed and thanked Roger before our training period and took in a deep breath of confidence. We started slowly with some jabs and crosses. Once Roger assessed that I had at least some competency, we circled the ring and added thunderous hooks and uppercuts to the mix. I was doing my best to always bring my hands back to my face as I had just witnessed Tomasz do. I threw torpedoes at Roger's pads and he took every single one; I tried using speed, knowing that I had to perform at my highest level. For a couple of seconds, I felt like a pro boxer, flowing, swaying, and retaliating in that ring. It was fun; all of my worries seemed to melt away, and my confidence soared high above the Pocono Mountains. I threw a perfect jab; I stepped into it, tucked my chin, rotated my hips, and turned my wrist slightly as my jab echoed across the entire room with quick precision. I followed it up with a torpedo right. At that moment, I knew that all the effort had been worth it.

Those thoughts hit me as hard as Tomasz's punches: life was good, even if only for that moment, and it was something I could take with me as a potent life experience, something I could proudly retell to my grandkids one day. I was far from home, far from my family, and chasing my dream with zero certainty of what my future would bring. I was following my heart, and even though my mind was not at ease, my soul felt cleansed.

When I popped off the last combination, I thanked Roger from the bottom of my heart. I had added a few new tricks to my bag. Roger informed me that I was a little too upright and that my toes were pointing in too much. I had to use my rear leg to torque my hips more to project the power needed for every punch and jab. Roger congratulated me on my overall power and speed, but more importantly, the foundations were all there! All those training videos and years of practice with great coaches such as Jeff Joslin were paying off.

In my interview with Tomasz, he was funny and personable. He really wanted to know about my life and background. It was a reversal of roles, as he interviewed me, revealing his caring spirit.

Tomasz and I sat on the end of the rustic boxing ring as I began to uncover what makes the champ tick. Tomasz grew up in the town of Wielowice, Poland, without his father, who had unfortunately passed away when Tomasz was two years old. Life wasn't easy for his mother, but Tomasz did what he could to help on the farm and with daily chores. He was drawn to boxing when he was young, but never in a million years would he have expected to become a world champion.

At the age of twelve, his older friends talked him into training at a boxing club in the town of Zywiec. It was unheard of for parents of a twelve-year-old to allow their son to travel over 10 miles (17 km) to the gym after school on two different buses. Tomasz did just that, and had his mom not allowed him to follow his passion, Tomasz put it best, "I probably wouldn't have become who I am today. I wouldn't be in this spot here today doing this interview today, so I believe this is my destiny."

Tomasz has four sisters, who all reside in the town of Milowice near Gilowice. They taught him to be diligent, and he grew under the influence of the Roman Catholic Church. Religion was a large part of their family life, as they prayed together and strove to make wise choices.

Tomasz worked at local clubs as a bouncer, a path followed by many great fighters on the journey toward fulfillment. He did get into a few scuffles and occasionally had to use a bit of force. Looking back, Tomasz confessed that working the clubs may not have been the smartest profession because any bone breakage could have meant a premature end to his boxing career.

His mom was never opposed to him training, although he chuckled that she did once mention that if she hit him on the head a few times it might discourage him from boxing. That never happened, of course. She was a tough woman and had taught Tomasz and his sisters very well. She instilled strong discipline from an early age and would spank them when they got out of line. She did everything for them and wanted her children to succeed in life, especially because she had reared them alone.

Tomasz's mother has told him that she wouldn't mind if he decided to hang up his gloves, a decision that would likely lower her blood pressure. But Tomasz's response validated his place in the sport, one that most champions emulated: "Mom, what would I do if I didn't fight? That's my lifestyle, and I have a talent for it. It was given to me by God, and I don't think it's the end of it yet; I think I still have a lot to achieve."

I asked Tomasz about growing up as a highlander, living in the mountains. His first reaction was that he disliked winter. There was more winter than summer in the mountains, meaning that there was a lot of snow. He also thought that children who grew up in the mountains and that had tough, militant parents were by nature going to be mentally tough.

Tomasz had the typical fighter life: plenty of obstacles to work through when he was younger. The loss of his father at a young age, growing up in a harsh environment, having a heavy workload, and watching his mother maneuver through life without her soul mate by her side was more than any kid should have to deal with. These challenges drove him to surpass his goals as an athlete, giving him that edge and ambition. As he spoke, his love of boxing was clear.

Tomasz said that the experiences and lessons learned while growing up are what really shape people. He understood the importance of prayer and building character at an early age. He thought that it was paramount to provide positive examples as a parent. He actually built a house next to his mother's house while in Poland. He holds his mom and his homeland of Poland close to his heart, although at the time of this interview, he lived on a separate continent, chasing his dreams. He felt New Jersey was his place to be at the moment; it was his destiny.

Tomasz got married at the age of twenty-one and turned his life around. He learned to focus his stamina and energy in the boxing ring. At the time of our interview, Tomasz was thirty-four years old and was working harder than ever. He was in his self-proclaimed best form. He confessed that he felt better at thirty-four than he did a few years back when he had to cut weight and maintain it.

He circled back to his youth, recalling that it was a careless time for him but that he had grown wiser since then. He spoke about the importance of properly rearing his children. He discussed the circle of life and how he was now responsible for looking after his children. One thing was for certain: family was important.

Tomasz moved to the U.S. because there was an upper limit to his growth as a boxer in Poland. All of the tools and resources he needed to follow his dreams were in the U.S. Tomasz abandoned everything that he knew and moved his family to New Jersey. He was willing to move from the house he built next to his mother and trek to a different country to reach his goals, and the risk had definitely paid off. "For example, basketball is the same way. There is no possibility of achieving the same successes in Europe as in the U.S. I grew here as a boxer, a fighter...."

I asked the champ how he physically prepared for his bouts. Tomasz smiled and mentioned that boxing is a grueling sport and that stamina had a big role to play in training. He worked on technique every day, including approximately six rounds of pad work with Roger Bloodworth. Tyler, his strength and conditioning coach, would travel to the Pocono Mountains and they would conduct a wide variety of traditional exercises to push his cardio at various stations, focusing more on cardio and conditioning than on weight training. Tomasz spoke about the importance of being able to last twelve hard-fought rounds; if someone was not physically fit, they had no business stepping into a boxing ring to fight for thirty-six minutes, as doing so could lead to injury and pain.

Aside from physical training, diet was paramount, and Tomasz opened up about the importance of keeping to a strict, year-round healthy diet regimen. He felt that athletes who regularly strayed from healthy eating were only hurting themselves by shortening their athletic careers. Portion sizes and meal timing should be highly regulated, and late-night eating was out of the question. His trainer would cook at their cabin in the mountains. There were no excuses.

Being a food guy myself, I asked what types of foods he would eat. Among other things, he ate organic chicken, duck, veal, fish, and beef, which were all simply cooked and never fried. One advantage of fighting at the heavyweight division was that he could eat until he was full, but while he fought at the light heavyweight and cruiserweight divisions he really had to restrict his portions, which was not very enjoyable.

He mentioned that while at cruiserweight, he was not content or satisfied with the weight cuts or the toll it took on his body. He made the right decision in moving up two weight classes. At cruiserweight, he was sluggish and irritated from the lack of food and energy, but as a heavyweight he approached his training sessions with a positive attitude and vigor. Not having to go through weight cuts gave him more to look forward to.

He also said that if an athlete were to eat only Polish traditional fatty foods, he could kiss a good body and athletic career goodbye. Growing up, Tomasz loved eating pork on a daily basis, but unfortunately this was not included in his fighter's diet. It was clear how much he sacrificed to cut all the amazing pastries, perogies, and fatty foods, which I loved so much, out of a diet for good. I'm not sure I could do the same; my taste buds would start giving me nightmares, and I'd break down to reach for sweet goodness.

However, pressed a little harder, Tomasz did confess that he would steal a jelly-filled Polish donut (paczek) when his wife baked them. He only infrequently let his human weaknesses get the better of him. It was another indicator that these athletes were both physically and mentally strong, but that they were also human and gave in to their weaknesses on occasion.

The conversation reminded Tomasz that he was due for a protein shake, as he had gone through a rigorous workout and needed to replenish after his training session. He also took multi-vitamins and natural products to keep his body fueled. In the U.S., there were plenty of choices and natural sources for supplements, and he was lucky to have access to them; in Poland, he may not have had the same quality of supplements.

I asked Tomasz to take us through his typical day, starting with waking up in the morning. He begins his days with a hearty breakfast: oatmeal with a spoonful of honey, yogurt, a banana, and coffee. He doesn't eat a lot right before training because it makes him feel heavy and full. Approximately two or two and a half hours after breakfast, he would train and have a protein shake. After the training session, he would eat a full meal; Roger would be preparing veal that early afternoon, for instance. Then, he would rest from the hard training session, followed by an afternoon run.

The psychological state of a boxer is always a point of interest. What was going on in his head? Tomasz commented that he often felt a swirl of emotions. Entering the fight, he felt strong emotion, pressing him to win the bout, as his goals have always been to either become or stay champion, and these thoughts resonate at the back of his mind throughout a match. He gave thanks to God for the ability to remain mentally strong during his bouts, which is an important factor in winning and fighting. He had a strong mental inclination to outlast his opponents and a true warrior spirit, which was evident in every one of his fights. When Tomasz entered the ring, the fans knew he would be leaving all he had; unless he was sprawled out cold, he would keep pressing forward, which was dangerous for all of his opponents.

While trading punches, his mind was always focused on the goal of winning and deceiving his opponent. On some psychological level, Tomasz knew that fans were there cheering, but in all honesty once in the heat of battle, he was disconnected from everything except winning. That was how he kept himself in the zone. Between rounds, Roger would give him two or three important words to either correct mistakes or to proceed with the given game plan. Had Roger been giving him too many instructions, it would have been too much to register and remember.

In regard to Roger Bloodworth, I wanted Tomasz to open up about the legendary trainer of world champions. First, he wanted to express his gratitude to Roger and let everyone know that he was a really good person. Second, he was an amazing coach and teacher, and the two had great synergy. Since teaming up with Roger, fans could see a difference in his fighting style and level of boxing. The magic that his trainer had conjured was plain to see. He predicted that one day people would tell stories about how this smaller boxer toppled the titans of the boxing world, due largely to Roger.

Going further into his career, which at the writing of this book was a stellar forty-nine wins and four losses, I asked about a fight famous among Polish fans: his bout with Andrew Golota. Andrew is Polish and a seasoned veteran who had fought the likes of Mike Tyson, Kevin McBride, and Michael Grant, but was best known for his low-blow disqualifications against Riddick Bowe. He had tarnished his name with illegal moves. It was a grudge match, a passing of the torch of sorts.

Tomasz revealed that it was Andrew who pressed for the fight and wanted to beat Tomasz, so Ziggy, the promoter, made the fight happen. Tomasz added nonchalantly, "We put on a good show. I am not sure if Andrew thought he would beat me; I'm not sure what he was thinking." Tomasz put on a great boxing clinic, as he technically knocked out Andrew in the fifth round to win the International Boxing Federation Heavyweight title. The tickets sold out quickly, and more than ten million people tuned into the fight to watch it live—an amazing feat.

We also spoke about his famous fight with Paul Briggs, which was referred to as one of the most brutal fights in boxing history and a real back-and-forth battle. Briggs had a massive cut above his left eye early in the fight, as Tomasz bled profusely out of his nose. Two weeks before the fight, Tomasz had broken his nose, but he took the risk of fighting anyway. This was his first fight in the U.S., and he knew that canceling would have hurt his career. He wanted to prove to everyone that this Polish guy could win even in the

U.S., no matter the odds or obstacles. Would he do it again, if given the chance? Being older and wiser, he wouldn't put himself in the same situation. Tomasz really showcased his granite chin, charismatic flair, and warrior's heart, working through a broken nose, a tough opponent, and breathing problems—all to win the fight.

His only loss at the time was to Chad Dawson, and Tomasz thought that his weight cuts had hurt him. He acknowledged that there had been rumors that he had thrown the fight; however, it was quite the opposite. He looked fatigued and weakened, as he truly was. The weight cut got the better of him. He had cut over twenty pounds to get below the 175-pound limit. He was thankful that he lost the fight, as he believed that his career would have been over a long time ago due to the beatings from weight cutting.

Tomasz also thought that he should have moved up in weight classes much earlier than he actually did. He admitted that losing a lot of weight quickly was not healthy and that many people did not realize the dangers associated with this practice. Weight cutting was one of the leading causes of deterioration in fighters. It was worse than fighting because it leads to blood clots in the brain. A reporter once asked him if he would want to avenge his loss to Dawson, and Tomasz stated that he would fight anyone in the world at the heavyweight limit.

Tomasz's homeland of Poland and his immense following of fans had a lot to do with his success. He had a way of attracting fans from all corners of North America and Europe. He averaged over 10,000 sold seats at his fights; his fight with Steve Cunningham attracted around 15,000 fans. Tomasz held his fans dear to his heart, and he always aimed to give back to them with entertaining fights and by being a good representative of the sport and an ambassador of Poland.

Tomasz also has strong faith in God and is a devote Catholic. I was impressed that his priest was part of his training camp, in order to provide spiritual guidance. His mom had raised him as a practicing Catholic, and he was raising his children in the same manner. He prayed every day and felt truly blessed by God. There was a saying in Polish: "*Bez Boga ani do proga.*" It means that you cannot get far without God. The saying is something he believes in unswervingly. Knowing God was definitely a source of strength in life and in his boxing career.

His success as a champion in the light heavyweight, cruiserweight, and heavyweight divisions has done little to change Tomasz. He was still the same humble guy he had been in his youth. Everyone I had an opportunity to chat with at the Team Adamek camp reiterated this sentiment. Even after all the interviews concluded, he sat with us in the hotel dining area surrounded by his team, including the priest, and we chatted about everyday life and his strong bond to God. He even bought food for all of us. Initially, I thought that he was being clever, bribing me with food in exchange for writing kind words. It took only minutes in his presence to see that he was a great person who cared for others.

I asked Tomasz what he thought of being depicted in the *Fight Night* boxing video game. He said it humbled him but that it was also interesting. He hadn't actually played the game much—he viewed video games as having almost a narcotic-like quality, sucking many hours from life. But his face lit up with pride when he stated, "It will be a great keepsake for my kids or grandkids to know that their granddad or dad was a champion boxer and that they will be able to play a video game as my character."

When asked what it took to become the best in the world, he didn't have to think twice. He mentioned that having a God-given talent was important, coupled with a cheerful predisposition and strong work ethic. He added, "Not everyone can be a champion. You can practically count the amount of champions on your fingers. I would not be here without hard work. Everyone in life has a mission to fulfill, and I hope that I am on the right path in my life."

I asked how his training camp was coming along for the mammoth Kevin McBride, who was best-known for defeating Mike Tyson. Tomasz was ready and mentally strong, especially because the intense training was all but behind him at that point. He was always learning and transforming to become better; and being in an eight-week training camp with Roger Bloodworth made it easier. He knew that his speed would be a factor, coupled with the way that smaller fighters are usually tricky for the bigger fighters to unravel. He seemed confident and ready as he spoke about the upcoming fight. He chuckled and noted, "I will win because I have no other option. I want to be the world champion!"

We ended with a quick round of questions and concluded the interview with a firm handshake. In the following days, I watched him spar with some big training partners, in order to simulate his upcoming opponent. Tomasz had a charisma and speed in the ring that was truly mesmerizing. He popped off quick combinations to the body and then circled out of punching range for just long enough to do it again. I noticed that, as his training partners tired, he would start smashing them in the head; and a light bulb went off for me. The game plan for Kevin was to attack his torso, tire him, and then knock him out or at least punish him with violent head strikes, as his opponent's guard would undoubtedly be lowered from fatigue.

Tomasz and Roger invited us back to their cabin—an invitation we couldn't refuse. I had learned that Roger liked red wine, so we stopped at a store for wine, and happened to stock up on a bottle or two for ourselves as well. I also bought every box of Count Chocula cereal in the place, as I hadn't seen any in Canadian stores since I was young. The cashier looked at me like I had just broken out of a mental hospital.

We chatted about everything boxing with both Tomasz and Roger. Their dynamic together was also great outside of the ring, as Roger took care of Tomasz like a father would. Tomasz spoke about his family and clearly missed them after being away for so long. I asked Tomasz if MMA had been as popular when he started training, and whether he would have attempted the sport. He was clear that boxing was his element and that he would never stray away.

I also noted that Roger had a deep passion for boxing; we must have chatted for hours about the "sweet science" of it all. He stated that the sport was constantly changing. His example was that in the 1980s and 1990s, a good trainer would take an Olympic gold medalist and make them a world boxing champion within two and a half years. These days, the average was about five to six years.

I took a liking to Roger; he was complex and astute, from all the years of being deeply rooted in the sport. Having trained champions such as Tomasz Adamek, David Tua, Evander Holyfield, and Andrew Golota, Roger was a legendary boxing trainer to say the least. His love of the sport was evident, and his boxing IQ was off the charts.

Tomasz had taken me into Team Adamek. He gave me his life story, as did Roger, allowing Greg and I to stay much longer than the other media representatives. I even had access to his famous sparring sessions, where no one outside of Team Adamek was allowed to step foot. Tomasz treated us to ice cream, drinks and round-table chats with his entourage. We felt like part of the team from day one.

A man of his worth is not easily found in other professions, yet in a sport such as boxing, in which the key to defeating your opponent was pulverizing his face with punches, we found humility, kindness, and humanity. This self-made man from a humble background had journeyed over 6,000 miles (nearly 10,000 km) to chase his dreams and attain greatness. He secluded himself in the mountains, uprooting himself from his family to become the best, as he crossed off fighters' names from his list, one-by-one, inching closer to his goals. Through sheer hard work and quick thinking, as well as by surrounding himself with the right people, he was a veritable David fighting the Goliaths of the world. His perspective was something from which we can all learn.

QUICK ROUND
Favorite junk food?
Bananas. For meat, it is steak.

What would we find on your music playlist?
Hip-hop.

Favorite city to fight in the world?
New York.

Favorite drink?
Mineral water.

In your view, what was your favorite fight?
All of the ones I won.

What is your favorite punch combination?
Left, right combination.

What is your best strength?
Being dynamic.

What is your biggest weakness?
Fast driving.

Had you not gotten into boxing, what profession would you choose?
I always thought that I would be a priest.

What is your favorite movie?
Braveheart, with Mel Gibson.

Chapter Fourteen

WELCOME TO THE WAT

"The teacher who is indeed wise does not bid you to enter the house of his wisdom but rather leads you to the threshold of your mind." **—Khalil Gibran**

The Thai word, *wat*, is translated as "temple." I found a particular "temple," known as "The WAT," in New York that housed many of the best fighters in the world, including Georges St-Pierre, Jon Jones and Frankie Edgar. The Muay Thai school is world-renowned, and the man behind some of the most devastating strikers is simply known as Ajarn Phil Nurse.

Recently, The WAT moved to a larger location to accommodate the demands of its 250 students. It is quite an accomplishment given that no investment was ever made into advertising, but instead the focus was on word-of-mouth and world-class instruction to bring students into the facility. Through sheer determination and the strong work ethic of Ajarn Phil, The WAT has become a world-class facility.

The prowess of the head instructor, gained through life experiences and teachings from his Thai instructor, Master Sken, cannot be found at your local gym. Phil brings numerous world titles and the will of a lion, along with his experiences, into The WAT, which he then passes on to his students, from beginners to world champions. His classes not only teach the most devastating martial art in the world, but also a healthy way of living, physically and spiritually improving more aspects of life than just fighting.

Ajarn Phil is the man behind Georges St-Pierre's superman punch as well as his disabling rear leg kick, which was used against Matt Hughes during UFC 65. His arsenal is extensive, with wisdom and knowledge that seems limitless—a bad thing for his student competitors when the endless barrage of attacks just keeps on coming. He embodies the Thai culture with a kind heart and gentle smile, but has bamboo-like shins and steel fists. The Thai style he brings into his teachings is devastating and has been proven for hundreds of years, a style he too has incorporated into all of his championship bouts.

He may have started out playing alongside Beckham on the soccer pitch in England, but life brought him to the martial arts world in the end. Ajarn Phil is the type of guy that would survive in the Amazon with only matches and a bottle of water, and eventually build a small city while swinging from branch to branch like Tarzan, all because of his spectacular resourcefulness and his primary weapon: his mind.

He is a man of preparation; self-discipline and countless hours spent training are aspects that the average fan does not get to see. What makes him tick? How does he incorporate creativity and mind games into this brutal sport—a sport that takes no prisoners? I wanted to know how family life and early struggles helped mold him into the person he is today. Having had the privilege to interview (then) Kru Phil once at Tristar gym and then twice in his New York gym, I needed to know as much as possible about this amazing individual.

Phil's mom and dad hailed from Barbados, the people of which are known as "Bajans." In contrast, Phil grew up in northern England, in Boulder, a small town in Greater Manchester. He vividly remembered coming home when he was around four or five years old, crying and complaining to his dad that another kid had hit him. Kru Phil cracked a large smile as he remembered his dad's reaction: "I remember my dad just saying, "Don't come in here crying. Go sort it out!'"

Phil went out and did just that, then strolled into the house smiling, as his dad asked him if it was straightened out. Phil commented on this: "Hence, that is maybe when my fighting career started out; I don't know."

Phil looked up to his dad, and until this day he feels strong emotion for him. He always observed his dad working very hard, which had clearly influenced Phil's work ethic. His dad's attitude was that if he needed something done, he did it himself. Phil considered his father to be a "Jack of all trades."

Phil was known as a quiet kid who was picked on and bullied. During his early years, he fought a lot with his bullies. It was something he learned to deal with.

Jumping to his teenage years, I learned that Phil had a strong sense of himself by that point in life; he knew that he was a fighter, through thick and thin, regardless of what life threw at him. Phil has never been a quitter or a depressed guy. He would dig deep and do what needed to be done, which sounded like the story of my life. I listened intently to every one of Kru's words.

He went on to state that it was always up to him, he would get things done regardless of the obstacles in the way. There was no version of a procrastinating Phil Nurse that would sit around for years saying, "I should have, would have, could have."

His parents weren't wealthy, and there were many things Phil wanted, including clothes! He took advantage of his creativity to create his own clothes, and they were pretty good. He recounted one story that his wife always laughed about when his parents got him a pair of soccer shoes that were plastic, but he wanted leather shoes like all his friends had. His shoes had a lightning flash down the side; Phil somehow decided that since he was the fastest runner in his peer group, he would convince everyone that his shoes were better than theirs!

Phil always placed first in sprints among his peers, and, funnily enough, everyone wanted his plastic shoes. They all asked where they could get a pair. Phil added "… and somehow, by not having stuff, I made whatever I *did* have into something special." Clearly, it wasn't about the shoes; it was about the development of a strong attribute; creativity. Phil's creativity was put to good use in the fight world just a few years later.

Phil attended a Muay Thai show when he was around seventeen years old. He vividly remembered being mesmerized by one particular fighter, Vinny McGrath. That day, Phil knew he wanted to be like Vinny, but the problem with the plan was that Phil was a really good soccer player and that's the only thing he could focus on.

He was nearly drafted to play for a large professional soccer team in England. The day the scouts came to recruit for their teams, Phil was injured. He was running down the wing, which he had done many times before, when his knee snapped back. At the hospital, they told him he would need surgery, but he decided to get a second opinion. Another doctor told him to start training with strength and conditioning exercises to strengthen the muscles around the knee. That's when he remembered the Thai boxing and thought that it might be a good way to strengthen his knee. He had no idea that thirty-odd years later, he would still be immersed in the art. Sometimes, the stars align themselves for a reason, and we should just go with the flow.

Phil then began training with Thai Master Sken, who at the time only had ten students, including Phil. Phil was about eighteen years old when he started his Muay Thai training, which was considered late. Master Sken pointed out with confidence that all of his students would become champions in their art, a prophecy that became reality. Phil knew that he was very fortunate to get so much attention from Master Sken and have such high-caliber teammates with whom to train. All were champions, and even more of an incredible feat was that they all held onto their titles until retirement.

Phil only had the highest praise for Master Sken. He was always awake before any of the fighters, with breakfast freshly made and a smile on his face, even if it was the middle of the night. Of all the time spent with Master Sken, there were only a few times that Phil could remember when he actually lost his temper. As Phil put it, "It was scary!"

Recounting the story, a gentleman who wanted to beat everyone up came into the gym during a time when the school had more students. Master Sken always tried to diffuse a situation, yet this time it was impossible. The hot shot was paired with one of the original ten, a guy named Humphrey, who was a hard-hitter. Humphrey slammed him with a shot, to get him to chill out.

Master Sken paired him with another beginner again, and he would go berserk wailing on the beginner. Master Sken warned him again and paired him with Phil, who was a tricky fighter who was impossible to hit. The guy did not touch Phil once throughout the round, but Phil tagged him numerous times. He still did not get the message.

The cycle repeated with the hotshot pouncing a beginner. Master Sken paired him with Oliver, who had great knees. After some clinch work, he ate some nasty knees, and that seemed to settle him down. Master Sken had a talk with him, trying to teach him a lesson that as a beginner, he had to start slow and mind his sparring partners.

He took the opportunity to challenge Master Sken, who immediately declined. But the hotshot was challenging the teacher in front of forty students; he would not budge in his pressing of the matter. Master Sken decided to give in and spar with him. Phil exclaimed "He must have beat him up in literally seconds. Sken was humoring him, but the guy did this spinning back kick; boom, he went after him, and demolished him, knees and elbows. He eventually stopped. At the end of class, everyone was silent."

Master Sken did what he had to do, and I am sure no one dared disrespect him a second time. Mr. Sken holds the title of Master in the Muay Thai culture, a very prestigious rank, for good reason. In order to become a Master, the Kru, which means teacher, must be knowledgeable and have perseverance. Masters practice high moral standards in life, always fulfill their commitments to their students, and commit to longevity. There was no doubt in my mind as I sat across from Kru Phil that he would one day be bestowed the rank himself for all of his work in the Muay Thai realm.

Kru Phil had an illustrious career, winning coveted titles such as the European Light Welterweight Championship, double British championships, all-style super-light championship, and retiring with all of them still to his name.

Phil confided that he did not become involved in the sport to fight another human being, but for the sheer challenge. He loved the head game challenge, the strategy part of it. He used his tactical talents and wits to out-maneuver and out-class his opponents.

Phil was never knocked out in a fight. He would always play head games with his opponents. If he got hit with a decent punch, he sometimes went down to the mat so that he could arch his back and spring back up like a gymnast. His opponents would get psyched out; they couldn't believe that he had catapulted right back and was in their face again. He was a trickster and master tactician in all of his fights. He added, "It worked for me in fights where I popped up and saw guys just drained, and I knew I had them."

Phil was also very fond of Muhammad Ali's fighting style, so he would collect techniques that worked for Ali into his own arsenal. Kru Phil was known to break out the Ali shuffle during his fights, which brought a vital entertainment aspect to all of his matches.

Growing up, Phil heard people talk about fighters staying in the game for too long or that they should have retired when on top, something that he never understood. However, after a vast career of his own, he knew what they meant. He retired on top, as he did not want to be the guy that was good in the day but grew too old, all washed up. He didn't want to be the used and worn fighter that shouldn't have taken that last fight because he got demolished.

After retirement, Phil organically became busier with the business of teaching. Phil was ready for challengers and challenges, yet they just stopped coming. He started focusing more on his students rather than searching out opponents.

While training one of the best pound-for-pound fighters in the world, Georges St-Pierre, their relationship became strong. Georges came to train with Kru Phil at The WAT through a student of his, Cordel, who was training with Georges at Renzo Gracie's gym. Phil did not know GSP at the time, which was amazing. Cordel clued him in that he was a hot prospect in the UFC, an up-and-comer who was going to fight Matt Hughes for the welterweight title, an opponent who GSP had previously lost to. Cordel was adamant that Kru Phil was the perfect coach for GSP, but there was a problem; Phil was fully booked the next day and GSP was soon leaving for his hometown of Montreal.

Later in the afternoon, one of Phil's clients canceled, so Phil called Cordel to let him know of the unexpected opening on short notice. By the time GSP arrived, only forty-five minutes remained for practice. GSP learned that Kru Phil did not give orders to hit a bag, but he was all about independent action. He would fight him and bounce around the ring holding pads for GSP. They sparred and moved around for the entire forty-five minutes. GSP did not test Kru Phil in the sense of kicking him too hard or giving him a dig with a punch; there was respect between the two men.

After the training session, they sat down in Phil's office and Georges started the conversation. "I need a Muay Thai coach for my next fight, and I want you to be my Muay Thai coach." GSP also opened up about his history and his future plans in the sport. Phil graciously accepted, GSP canceled his flight back to Montreal, and he attended sessions every day for the next three days. They immediately began to form a firm friendship.

Kru Phil explained how GSP innately absorbed knowledge like a sponge. He recalled a day when Georges was sparring with one of the other students—an accomplished fighter—and the student was dropped flat on his ass. The practitioner got up and inquired, "Where the fuck did you get that from?" referring to the high-level technique that put him on the canvas. Georges politely pointed and uttered, "I get it from Phil." Kru Phil added, "I've been showing you that for years. Georges did it yesterday, and now you are flat on your ass!"

Before GSP's fight with Matt Hughes, he approached Phil and said, "I'm not sure if you're interested in my fighting career or not, but if you want to come to the fight, obviously I cannot get you in the corner since I already have my corner people, but I'd be glad to have you in the audience, you and your wife. I got you tickets.'"

Phil had never been to a live UFC event, and he was eager to see one, so he flew out with his wife to Sacramento to watch the fight. Phil's wife kept telling him that he was like a kid in a candy store. Typically, a fighter would pull off one or two things in a fight that a trainer had taught him, but GSP was pulling off five or six things that they had specifically worked on.

One of the game plans was to kick Matt in the leg. That way, the seed would be planted for Matt Hughes to focus on stopping any additional leg kicks. Kicking the leg while looking at the leg was all part of Phil's master plan; the seed was slowly germinating. The timing was right, Matt was complaining about his groin at one kick, but in fact he was hit in his leg. He did not want to eat any more kicks. When the referee paused the fight to let Matt recover and give Georges a warning about low-blows, Kru Phil was adamant for him to sell the leg kick. He could not be distracted from the game plan. Kru Phil yelled to "Kick him in the leg right away! Keep his mind occupied on his legs!"

Matt was eventually going to want to put an end to the kicks, with a high probability of Matt dropping his hands, opening the window to high kick for a potential knockout. Just like a wizard looking into a magic fortune-telling globe, that was exactly what happened.

Kru Phil beamed with excitement, "I was amazed! It was amazing to see someone absorb knowledge like a sponge. You knew he worked on everything. He won the title, and he made it look easy! That's what I wanted to show him—that he can make it look easy. If he could see it in his mind and do the right things at the right time, you could win this fight easy. Matt Hughes went to look at the leg, looking to stop the kick to his own leg, which Georges kept hitting. He looked low, Georges went high and knocked him out! We worked specifically on that, and to see it live, I was bouncing off the walls! When he did win, he came into the audience for me, and I was running around the octagon with him and people were asking, 'Who's that guy, who's that black guy that got dragged out of the audience?'"

Kru Phil was in the press conference after the fight, where Matt Hughes admitted to everyone that Georges did not kick him in the groin but that the inner leg kicks were killing him and he wanted to play it off as a groin shot.

Another specific combination Kru Phil worked on with GSP was his patented left superman to right kick, just one of his fancy combinations that evolved from others that were tailor-made for GSP's opponent, Josh Koscheck. Kru Phil noticed that Josh Koscheck would throw punches and move around. He would circle the ring to get out of harm's way. "So I remember saying, 'Georges, listen; you got to throw a superman punch. It might miss. When it misses, you are going to throw a kick. So when the punch misses and he is running, you are going to catch him with a kick, because your reach is longer on a kick… that's when you are going to catch him with a kick and that's when you start to see it with the kick, and that's where that came from.'"

Kru Phil has managed to take his magic number of holding three championship belts at once to coaching three UFC champions at once, both feats practically unattainable. He not only coached UFC Welterweight Champion GSP, but also was simultaneously training UFC Lightweight Champion Frankie Edgar and UFC Light

Heavyweight Champion Jon Jones.

He met Jon Jones at a UFC show before one of Georges fights, and they struck up a conversation. Jon mentioned that he was working on his superman punch, and, being the godfather of the perfect superman punch, Phil was certain that Jon would do it improperly. Jon countered that he had watched tapes and perfected it. After a quick demonstration, Phil revealed to Jon that he indeed had it wrong, but he offered to show him his mistakes and train him if he was interested.

A few months later, Greg Jackson—based out of New Mexico and part of the network of coaches at Tristar, The WAT and Jackson's—called Phil and asked if Jon Jones could join their large team. Phil thought that Jon would complement his own style because of his creativity.

In the very first session, Kru Phil perfected Jon's superman punch and slowly began to show Jon when to apply the techniques. Phil always encouraged Jon to also use his creativity to the fullest.

Jon Jones confided in Kru Phil that although he did have the building blocks down before they met, he did not always know when to use them until he began working with Phil. After training with Phil, Jon went on to win the Light Heavyweight UFC title in devastating fashion and reached the pound-for-pound list at a very early age.

As for reaching great heights in such a demanding sport, Kru Phil reiterated that the sky was the limit. No one could know everything, and thinking that you know everything will not get you far; you have to be open. "Being receptive to peoples' wisdom, if you know someone older than you, they've learned things…. You do not get older and learn nothing, right?" Hopefully, the things they pass on are coming from the right place.

A loss should be accepted and used to drive forward.

Kru Phil said that there may be people out there working in an office who were talented at MMA or Muay Thai, but never realized their true potential. There have always been people who went through their entire lives without acknowledging or realizing their true talent, and we all have one. However, the talent would have to be coupled with tireless development of those attributes to create magic. Fighters would reach the pinnacle of success only when both variables were present. Life's successes manifest that equation.

Phil Nurse also mentioned relaxation as an important variable in the mix. Importantly, one must learn to relax under the pressure.

Once relaxed, a fighter can begin to observe more. At this point, a fighter can start planting the seeds, as Kru Phil put it eloquently when he described playing games with one's opponent and getting into his head. He said that it was similar to chess; in chess, a player would have five attacks and fives defenses on the go at any given time.

The brain would be at a 1,000 places at once, thinking of five attacks in a fight while trying to stay relaxed. A fighter would then devise a strategy for which attack to use, along with ways to counter the anticipated retaliation from his opponent. By deducing how the opponent would counter, the fighter could catch his opponent. Kru Phil confessed that this was what got him to a higher level in his career.

To make things even trickier, just like in other aspects of life, there is always a gray area. If a fighter thought for too long, he might eat a shot and not have time to react to his opponent's attack. At that point, the chess game could easily be abandoned and the fighter could go out swinging. So, as Kru Phil gently put it, the trick was to be in the middle section, thinking a bit, not too much, and not too little for optimum performance.

Kru Phil's multitasking mind helped him tremendously as a coach, as he fought even when holding pads for his fighters in some part of his brain. Thus, his pad-holding has always resembled a fight; he would dance the squared ring, punch, and kick back, simulating the real workings of a fight. Kru Phil remembered Frankie Edgar telling him after one of their sessions: "That was really good because the fight is moving; it's not kick, punch. It's active!"

As for what Kru Phil believed was in store for Muay Thai in MMA, he believed that there would be more tricky and flashy striking with a lot more jumping. The fighters would take more risks with spins, such as spinning elbows, flying elbows, jumping knees, and flying roundhouse kicks. Overall, a more ballistic approach and less of the basic jab, cross, but more fighters mimicking a Jon Jones-style, which Kru Phil taught. He was ahead of the game, teaching the takedown to elbow, variations of the superman punch, and more, as that was his love, and he looked to inspire his fighters to take those calculated risks.

Kru Phil wanted his take-home message regarding martial arts to be that there would always be hiccups, but striving to be the best is extremely important and can make all of the difference. "If in your life you can find what your talent is, it might not be martial arts, it might be something else… find it. A lot of people miss what their talent is in life."

I thanked Phil for everything I had learned from him. He recalled walking down the street many years back when he dropped something important without noticing. Another person ran up to him to give it back. Phil attempted to thank the kind stranger, but instead, the individual simply asked that he pass on the goodness. If more people did good deeds for each other, "Things will have a greater outlook for us all!" as he gave me a bright smile in typical Kru Phil fashion.

Being in the world-class gym in New York City with the beautiful bamboo/wooden floors and highly maintained equipment, I was most at awe of the mastermind behind The WAT. Having the opportunity to train with Kru Phil was something that I could not pass up on or ever forget.

As I changed into my gear, Kru Phil was still in the ring with a seasoned student of his and a friend of mine, Phoenix Carnevale. Phoenix was a journalist, freelance writer, and fitness expert who had won many fights with Kru Phil in her corner.

She was blasting the pads as Kru Phil pushed the tempo while the minutes passed. He varied his punches, knees, elbows, and kicks, as the whopping pops resonated throughout the spacious gym. He cut corners in the ring, making Phoenix work hard to square up to him in order to release proper strikes, mimicking a real fight.

After a few rounds, it was my turn to enter the professional-sized Thai ring. I entered, completely towering over Kru Phil at my 6' 3" to his 5' 7". Size definitely did not help me in this regard. We started off nice and slowly, throwing some jabs, straight rights, and a few kicks to his pads as he dictated the combinations and pace in a stern manner. Wanting to impress Kru Phil, I put some heat on the strikes, which depleted my stamina quickly. As the round progressed, Kru Phil began doing what he did best; he started applying pressure to my training, he tried to motivate me to strike faster.

Kru Phil was known to have a fancy trick that he used while holding Thai pads; similarly to Wild West gunslingers, he would twirl the Thai pad around his wrist after it was hit. I had to admit that seeing it on television when the likes of GSP or Jon Jones hit the pads was great, but in person it was absolutely amazing. (I admit to trying to spin the Thai pad at home in front of the mirror for countless hours, and I could never get it right.)

As he swarmed me while I hit the pads, it honestly felt like I was in a fight. I was doggin' it, throwing hard kicks and punches while getting pressed back. I quickly understood why people lined up for personal sessions with Kru Phil, including famous individuals such as actor and ex-amateur boxer Mickey Rourke. I smashed quick combinations, then found myself ducking and blocking the pads being thrown at my face, while using my footwork to maneuver intelligently around the ring—or at least I hoped it was an intelligent way to move around. After throwing a jab, I saw a leg kick coming out of nowhere toward my leg then midway shifting to a teep/push kick to my abdomen that put me against the ropes.

My lungs started burning as he kept picking up the pace. We had passed the threshold of having a fun time showing off technique to gasping for air and blocking my head for dear life. Kru Phil had pushed me to the extreme. I did not have time to think, similarly to a fight. I was just trying to focus on technique and to get enough air into my lungs. Although Kru Phil did not hit me hard, his strikes felt like he had titanium bones.

On more than one occasion when speaking with his students, we would talk about the fact that all parts of his body felt like baseball bats when hit. Nearly all of the students told me about the surgery on Phil's elbow/forearm and the way that the surgeon broke his scalpel trying to cut into his forearm. That bolstered my suspicions that Phil was bionic, or at least it made me feel better to tell myself that after he put me to shame at twice my age.

It was a complete pleasure and honor to have worked with Kru Phil. I even got some instruction on the famous left superman punch to right low kick. I had no idea how to even approach the move at the time and it was amazing to learn that I had to put all my weight on my lead left foot, then throw my left leg back just like yanking a leg of a table for it to topple. Then, when my body was falling forward, I would use the momentum to propel myself forward while extending a jab at my opponent's face. Once the jab connected, I would put my left foot diagonally on the mat and throw my right kick, all with one full use of momentum. Kru Phil used the same method that, several other trainers had; he would break down the moves in a way that was easy to remember, regardless of the skill level required for the technique. I have kept this move in my repertoire ever since.

I gained a plethora of skills at The WAT. Going back home to a hard manual labor job did not seem as bad anymore. I was heading back with a game plan to better myself and find a profession in which I could use my skills. I understood why Kru Phil held three current UFC champions under his banner. As Master Sken elaborated about Kru Phil, "He is a brilliant student, excellent fighter, and one of the best instructors." I could not put it any better.

As a postscript, I was ecstatic to learn that in 2015 Kru Phil Nurse was promoted from the title of Kru to Ajarn by Grand Master Chai of the U.S. Thai Boxing Association. There was no one more deserving of the rank promotion than Ajarn Phil Nurse, and this honor will be forever etched into the record books.

QUICK ROUND

What's your favorite junk food?
Gummy bears.

In your view, who is your favorite and most notable win?
Vinny McGrath.

If you had a dream match, who would your opponent be? It could be anyone in the world.
[Laughs] It would be very interesting. Anderson Silva.

One of your favorite standup techniques?
I honestly like them all, such as kicks and elbows, but if just one, I would like to use the superman on the left side with the one-two low kick.

If you had to name your biggest strength?
My mind; I think that's my biggest strength.

Your biggest weakness in life?
My biggest weakness in life now is my son, a good weakness.

Your favorite thing to do with friends and family?
I would definitely choose the comedy club.

What is one of your all-time favorite movies?
I'm Gonna Get You Sucka, a spoof comedy movie.

Chapter Fifteen

"ACE," THE DEFINITION OF WILLPOWER

"There is always somebody else, and if you get that into your head, you can never be secure in the position that you attained." —**Rich "Ace" Franklin**

Before ever considering becoming an author, I had the opportunity to meet an icon of the sport, Rich "Ace" Franklin. Rich reigned supreme in the middleweight division for over a year and half as the champion. We packed ourselves into a restaurant for food, UFC fights, and the chance to meet Rich himself. The overcrowded establishment did not mind breaking fire codes to pack in as many fans as possible for the meet & greet.

I finally reached the end of the line to be greeted with a firm handshake and a warm smile from the Jim Carrey look-alike, thus his nickname "Ace" from the acclaimed *Ace Ventura* movies. As we chatted, what struck me right away was that he was very welcoming and intelligent.

The second time I had the privilege of being in Rich's vicinity was even more memorable: UFC 83 at the Bell Centre in Montreal, Quebec. It was an electrifying bout that pitted Rich against the jiu-jitsu phenom Travis Lutter. My wife and I were lucky enough to get floor seats as the sold-out crowd bellowed in pandemonium every time the fighters exchanged blows or attempted grappling holds. Travis needed the win to get a shot at the title, and throughout the fight he was inching closer to that goal, but not if Rich could prevent it....

Years later, I received inside knowledge from Rich himself about that memorable night. "I was so close. I had to reality check (myself). 'Hey Rich, you're going to lose this fight and you need to get moving here if you want the win!' So I fed him the arm, he went for the arm bar, great escape, and from then on it was all downhill."

At 3:01 in the second round, Rich was declared the victor due to TKO punches. Once again, Rich had overcome extreme adversity to have his hand raised in complete bliss. Rich is highly respected and loved by his fans and fellow fighters, partially because his fights are always entertaining and he displays the heart of a lion.

Rich's manager, J.T. Stewart, was magical when they held seminars nearby. After a lot of back and forth phone calls with J.T., my wife and I packed our car and drove 120 miles (200 km) to the Greater Toronto Area. As we didn't know what time to arrive—J.T. and Rich were traveling heavily the following weeks, hitting Calgary, Aspen, etc.—we decided to leave first thing in the morning so as not to miss this once-in-a-lifetime opportunity.

We were close to our destination when we received a text to be there at 2:00 p.m. That meant we had five hours to kill, so I did what any loving husband would do that has been dragging his wife around to these "manly" events (for the sake of the book, of course!): I went shopping! We navigated from one mall to the next as my punishment for all those MMA trips. I got to help my wife pick out shoes, dresses, and everything frilly.

After finally arriving at the gym, I had the opportunity to see Rich coach live, which was fascinating. He perfected and tweaked the movements of the participants and had a way with relaying the information in a sensible way that was easy to remember. His teaching style reminded me of Jeff Joslin's. I respected Rich; he actually cared if someone had proper technique, and his love of teaching reached everyone on a deep level.

In my one-on-one with Rich, he was just as I remembered, very personable and funny. His intellectual manner of speaking made him even more likable; I knew I had little time to waste, so I dove right into his past.

Rich's parents divorced when he was only five years old. They lived on opposite sides of town, so Rich had the conventional upbringing in that sense. My own parents divorced when I was in my teens, which unfortunately seems to be the norm these days. Children of divorced parents learn a lot at an early age, and the old saying that what doesn't kill you makes you stronger was definitely true under those circumstances.

Rich lived with his mom until he was a junior in high school. He later moved in with his dad, but there was some tension between him and his father. In the end, Rich explained that it was for the best, as he ended up taking a better path in life and kept himself out of trouble.

He graduated from high school in 1993 and went on to graduate from a five-year program at the University of Cincinnati in 1998. The five-year program earned him a dual bachelor's degree and some credits toward a master's degree. Once he started teaching, he went back and finished the master's degree. Overall, he ended up with a BA in mathematical sciences, a BS in secondary education, and a master's in secondary education.

Rich was a high school teacher from 1998–2002, and he taught everything math-related, except for calculus. His students ranged from freshmen to seniors.

I asked him if he enjoyed teaching, and he beamed as he acknowledged his love for the profession. He also correlated his past experiences to his current teaching of MMA practitioners, "…but I am really about teaching. I am not up here doing a presentation; I want people to go home as better martial artists or pick up tricks to add to their bag, better than they were when they got here."

As a math teacher, he was one of the last teachers out of the building everyday, but also one of the last ones in everyday, as he chuckled reminiscing about the past. Great minds must think alike, as I have the same personality trait. I seem to be fashionably late to almost everything, including work, but I tend to stay longer and put in more effort than most. I am very fond of my high school years, and I was late every day. A pink slip from the office specifying the reason for lateness was required for entry into class. The secretary was attractive, so I would always try to be smooth with her. She saw through my bullshit and began to take a liking to me. Her husband was a big bodybuilder who worked out at the same gym as I did, so we usually talked about bodybuilding in the office. Eventually, I could give her any excuse for being late or missing class and I would get a pink slip, no questions asked. Other students had a hard time getting even one pink slip with parent signatures! I still did well in school, but I seemed to always be running a few minutes late wherever I went!

Rich worked really hard as a teacher. An opportunity came up to help out with an at-risk program at his school. The director of the program constantly came to ask Rich for help when he stayed after hours. They formed a relationship, and Rich decided to help with the program, as they did not have a certified math teacher working with the at-risk students. Once Rich quit teaching full-time, he took part-time hours helping the kids, primarily with math and science. The kids worked on computers and would save up all of their math and science questions for the couple of days that Rich was there each week.

"I got to the point where I had re-learned how to do chemistry, like electron configurations. It was fun doing that and working with the kids. It's crazy because you take these at-risk kids and put them in this program, and they were highly motivated to graduate. They could see the light at the end of the tunnel, job, money, and all that kind of stuff!"

Rich's eyes were glowing with pride, not in himself but for the kids that he helped so many years ago. He had a sincere tone in his voice, the pride and satisfaction that come only from helping a fellow human being. Teaching was a very positive experience for him. He continued helping the kids up until he beat Ken Shamrock in UFC, two or three weeks before his title fight against Evan Tanner. The school year was winding down in May, and his title fight was slotted for June. Rich had to reorganize things in his life; he went to his friend, the director of the at-risk program, to let him know he would no longer be able to come back for summer school or for the following school year, for that matter. "I said my life is going to change after this, so that's when I quit my job."

Things definitely changed for Rich after he beat Evan in the fourth round to win the UFC Middleweight Championship. All the sacrifices and hard work had paid off, including the gamble to quit his teaching career and pursue his dreams.

I transitioned to broader questions, asking for a funny story from his experiences in the UFC. He started to tell me about a Canada-based story but decided to pass on it and told me instead about his fight with Jason McDonald. Rich Franklin was battling Jason McDonald at the Nationwide Arena in Columbus, Ohio.

"We're scrapping in the middle of the octagon, and as you look around the octagon you could see... like in the UFC, there is that platform that goes around where the octagon girls walk. At the proper angle, you could see between the mat and that ring what is underneath, like all the light boxes, you know what I'm talking about? If I was too low I would not be able to see it, if I was too high I would not be able to see it. So I'm right in the middle of the fight and I took Jason down to the ground and I am kind of half guard on him and I look over and my head is at the perfect angle to see underneath the apron outside, the catwalk, and I thought I saw an American flag on the ground. So Jason bumps me, and I'm off center and I'm thinking to myself 'what the heck is an American flag doing stuffed under the apron of this cage?' It bothered me so bad that I took my opponent and wiggled him back into position just so I could make sure I saw what I thought I saw. It ended up being this blue box, a blue electrical box and it had red cables coming out of it, so in that brief moment I saw that and my mind registered it as an American flag. But here I am in the middle of this fight completely not paying attention to the fight, and I'm worried about this flag being on the ground. In Canada, I'm sure it's the same, you know? If your flag is on the ground, that's about the most disrespectful thing that could happen to it. So, in the middle of the fight, that's what I was more worried about!"

I shifted gears and dove into the psychological realm of fighting, more specifically, Rich's work with Brian Cain, who notably worked with some of the world's best athletes, from the PGA, NHL, NBA, NFL and MLB, along with seven world champions in MMA, including GSP and Franklin. Rich explained the importance of working with a sports psychologist. Brian and Rich were rarely in the same geographic area, so they ended up spending a lot of time on the phone. "Brian did a lot for my fight career, whether he realizes it or not. Some of the things that stick with me most are the visualization exercises that we did."

They conducted many variations of visualization exercises, and Rich spoke about how he still uses them. Rich has always been a fighter who accepts instruction and applies it; it was as easy and simple as that. He didn't need constant reinforcements, and gave the example of his Saturday sparring sessions in which he would mimic fight day or do some visualization exercises before sparring. He would then walk out to the octagon, and from the time he got into the octagon to spar, he felt like it was fight day. That way, when fight day came, it was as if he had been there a dozen times already.

On the actual fight day, he would get to the arena and do some visualization exercises, including playing some audio stuff that he got from Brian on his iPod. Aside from that, Rich also did some relaxation exercises to calm his nerves, which were helpful, but they did not have the same impact as the visualization work that they did together. "My boxing coach Rob Radford always said 'You don't want to fight the fight before the fight.' That was a big saying of his. The visualization really helped me with that."

I asked what it was like being king of the hill. Rich dominated the middleweight division for over a year and a half. "I think once I got to the top, it wasn't what I expected." Rich spent most of his life training for it. As he was a senior, he had been intensively training, even though a part of him never dreamt of being a professional fighter. He then reached another crossroads, where hype was involved. "'Rich Franklin is the next big thing.' I was livid, I got to the point where I thought 'Am I living up to the hype? Am I as good as people say I am?' It took believing in myself… I had to have faith in myself that I can do these things."

The path was not easy. He mentioned being in the gym, hitting the grind every day, thinking "Gosh, man, this just stinks." But Rich astutely correlated that to being in college. His entire college experience could be summed up as staying up until three a.m. cramming for tests, saying the same thing: "Gosh, man, this just stinks." But once the tests and papers were over, he was sitting around with buddies reminiscing about his hardships. "Dude, remember when we were taking that Modern Lit. class and we went in for that test?…' And you start telling all these stories, like college was the best time of your life, you know what I mean?" The worthwhile things are not easy, but sometimes going uphill brings the most fulfilling experiences and results.

Then, Rich touched on something that rang true to my ears, probably true for most of the population on Earth: "People don't realize that you get so… [pausing to find the right words] it's so much a heavy search for results in life that you forget that the journey is most important. I think with me, that's what happened. Suddenly, I had the title and the world was moving so fast all of a sudden, and I did not realize that what was the most important was the journey to get there!"

I have been guilty of putting my nose to the grindstone and just pushing for the goal, the light at the end of the tunnel. This has had two counter-productive results in my life. I have sacrificed a lot of things, including time, and I became emotionally, physically, and spiritually burnt out. Keeping the pendulum from swinging too much either way is key, but it's definitely a difficult thing to perfect.

Rich changed his focus from his life philosophy to the fight game. I asked him for his formula to success. "You know what? In order to be the best in the world, you have to be willing to do what anyone else who wants to be the best in the world is not willing to do."

He continued, saying that if someone was willing to train six hours a day but eight hours were actually necessary, then it had to be done. He explained that too much training could be counter-productive, but just to get the point across he used the example. "If you are willing to do the training, you need to do it. But if you do not like the conditioning, somebody else is willing to do the conditioning, for instance. But if all else is equal and you both are willing to do it, are you willing to take it a step further with your nutrition?"

Dedication and work ethic played key roles. "How much hard work and dedication are you willing to put into something is what it really boils down to. However dedicated you think you are, there is somebody out there who is more dedicated than you trying to take your spot, trying to take it away from you, you just have to remember that. There is always somebody else, and if you get that into your head, you can never be secure in the position that you attained. The hard work that it took to get you there is the same work that will keep you there. That's your equation right there."

I knew Rich to be a solid Christian, so I also asked how his faith played into the formula. "Oh, faith goes without saying. There's my equation for success, which is the hard work and then the faith, you know faith in God. God has a hand in the things I cannot control. I believe that I am on a directed path."

But he did explain that he did not believe that God wanted him to be champion, but that he is on this Earth as a soldier for Christ. He thought that if he could be a good witness for the Lord as a fighter, then God could direct him in his path to be successful. On fighting on the world stage and God, he added "It will only amplify the witness that I can be for him, so in that sense those are the things that work out. Faith is a funny thing because people often say if you have that much faith, then you don't have to be nervous about a fight. 'God's got your back; why get nervous? You're gonna win.' I don't know what God's plan is for me; I could lose this fight because for God it could perhaps bring more glory to him, I don't know. My objective is not to bring glory to me, as a human. As a person, you often tend to get those gray areas mixed, you know what I am saying? What's important to me becomes number one all the time. That's when I have to check myself and say, 'this is not the life I should be living.'"

Since my time slot with Rich was very limited, I hopped right to his training routine. He told me that he would typically taper off a bit when he was not preparing for a fight. His typical training regime would consist of a twenty-to-twenty-five hour work week while preparing for a fight. He was kind enough to break down each day.

On Mondays, he started off the day with some road work (running) and then proceeded to the gym for strength and conditioning training. Later in the day, he did some drilling exercises or pad work with his coach. On Tuesdays, he did drill work in the morning and live grappling in the evening. Wednesdays would follow with a morning run; in the evening he did auxiliary training, maybe rock climbing for strength and conditioning. Rich loves physical activity, and by switching up his auxiliary training, he'd never get stuck doing the same things over again, keeping his workouts fresh. Thursday mornings he did situational-type drilling, depending on what he needed to work on for a particular fight, and he sparred in the evening. As there were two sparring days, one would be mixed martial arts sparring, and the other would be boxing/kickboxing. On Fridays, he would go for a morning run, and then strength and conditioning at the gym followed by more drilling or pad work in the afternoon. But if he had a heavy week, he might let his body rest and cut out the drilling or pad work on Friday afternoon. Saturdays involved fight simulations centered on sparring; he would typically warm up for about half an hour, do drill work to get his blood flowing, and possibly work on specific techniques for the fight. What followed was hard sparring. Rich wrapped up with some running or auxiliary workouts and then would call it a day.

"It's a full-time job, you know, you talk to people. Like I said, I train somewhere between twenty to twenty-five hours and people are like wow, only twenty to twenty-five hours a week? You have to realize that some of my workouts, they are the type of workouts that when they are done you just want to go home and go to bed, period. It's so crazy now that I'm thirty-seven because when I was twenty-two years old I would go work out to the point where you are ready to vomit and all that stuff, then I would run here, run there, do the errands, then back to the gym. Now I do that workout and I am driving home from the gym [Rich made a sleepy face]. I just have to get home and get to bed for an hour. I go home and crash, and come back and do it to myself all over again. It's awesome."

I had to jump into my quick round of wacky and interesting questions to get more info, but more importantly, to understand Rich Franklin's character. I asked about his favorite junk food and was pleasantly surprised that he had similar food cravings as the rest of us. What followed made me feel much better.

"It depends, okay? This is very serious subject matter. You are smiling; don't smile about this because I am dead serious. So I only get to eat junk once a week. I mean when I eat I am strict on my nutrition. I had one of these [he shows me a nutrition store protein shake], and this is not part of my nutrition. This is bad for me. I do drink protein—just not that kind, so typically what I do Saturday is wake up, have my breakfast, go train, have my lunch, and when it is time to eat again, the rest of the day is whatever I want to eat. My junk food comes in phases, I have my fattening and salty junk foods, then I have my sugars.

I would say that a good go-to sugar for me would be, man, I go in phases, and right now I am in a tiramisu phase, it's killing me. But in a basic form, one thing I never get sick of is a nice cooked brownie that's a little moist on the inside, topped with some ice cream, the hot and cold, yeah!"

I got hungry just listening to Rich describe his once-weekly delights. My stomach actually made a rattling noise to notify my brain that it was time to eat some brownies with ice cream!

I then asked what he currently had in his music playlist. He stated that he listens to all types of music and that he is a mood music kind of guy. He could easily go from listening to Korn to Frank Sinatra all in the same car ride.

As far as his favorite city to fight in, Rich didn't have strong preferences, but just stated that whatever was easiest for him was great. If he had to choose one, it would probably be Columbus, as Ohio was his home state and he had a great home crowd, but was far enough from his house. The nice thing about Columbus was that he drove there, had a car, and could easily get around. He knew where everything was, such as grocery stores for food. All of the prep work was easy to take care of and for him, that fight week is important. Why not make it easier then? But in a place like Germany, which Rich added was a great place to fight, the time zones really messed things up.

I had to know which fight was his favorite and what he considered to be his most notable win. Rich did not even have to think about the answer, as he quickly remarked, "Travis Lutter in Montreal. I will tell you why; when we drilled for that fight, training for that fight, my coach said here's what going to happen, 'Travis is going to cut the ring off. Travis is going to go for a head inside single. Travis is going to try to drag you to the ground. Once he gets you there, he's going to try to mount you.' So what did we do, we drilled not getting the ring cut off, we drilled takedown defense on the head inside single, we drilled not being mounted. What happened in the fight?"

That is exactly what happened in the fight; Travis cut off the fence, got the head inside single, and took Rich to the ground and mounted him. But thanks to his training camp, none of those actions were surprising, and they had answers for everything Travis was dishing out.

Rich continued, "It wasn't like I got hit with something and I was like, 'Oh, I never saw this coming!'

As Rich was a legend in the sport, I wanted to know what he considered to be his biggest strength in life. The answer was true to expectations: his strong faith. He explained that on his bad days, his faith is something he can always fall back on. As for personal strength, he chose his work ethic. "If I talk about working hard, it is one thing that I do. I'm not the most gifted athlete. I was a third-string football high school player. The reality of my situation was I was playing high school football; if you have ever seen the movie *Rudy*, I was that guy! I had this, like, falsified notion that I was going to get a scholarship to play ball, and I ended up getting involved in mixed martial arts. God had me on a path. Fortunately, I won a world title, things turned out great for me. Basically, that is one of those deals where God is like, 'I can take you here but you are going to have to put in the leg work.' That's exactly what I did, and that is what separates me from everybody in this world."

As we concluded the interview, I was thinking about how lucky I was to have just picked apart Rich's thoughts and experiences. He is an unbelievable fighter, but more importantly, an amazing human being. Rich had to fully place his belief in himself and his abilities before he could break through in the sport. Just as in life, we all need to take a breath and see what we are truly capable of. Tallying my responses from all of the greats, I could see a similar pattern unfolding. I was blessed with their expressiveness, forthrightness, and willingness to reveal their genuine selves.

Chapter Sixteen

THE LAST EMPEROR

"An action committed in anger is an action doomed to failure."

—Genghis Khan

In a battle involving a struggle of wills, an emotional tug of war ensues in a split-second, and quicker than an exhalation or the time it takes a bead of sweat to hit the ground, a moment presents itself where one can claim victory in a devastating and vicious fashion. There are a few men in history who could systematically find that sweet spot with precision for many years. One of these was Genghis Khan—a ruler and conqueror who claimed land the size of Africa, and who was a force to be reckoned with. Some call him cruel, but most people know his name nearly 800 years after his rule in Mongolia because he was a powerful leader who was strong and effective. The image he projects is one of a warrior in combat gear brandishing a battered sword—a powerful image.

Similarly, there is a modern-day warrior who I would call the best pound-for-pound fighter to have ever graced the cage or ring. This man is Fedor Emelianenko, "The Last Emperor." With mystique and an exotic aura, coupled with his devastating power, speed and accuracy, he has seen the best heavyweights in the world hit the bloody canvas due to his incapacitating technique; or, he pressured their undefended limbs to near break-age, forcing their hand to tap the canvas, making him the better combatant, time and time again.

This is a man who lives isolated from the rest of the world, adding more intrigue to his legend. He trains caveman style, utilizing nature, used tires and welded sledgeham-mers, without fancy and expensive equipment. His diet consists of food harvested from the land, back to the basics, without the harsh additives and chemicals of processed food, as is so common nowadays. His humble and kind ways outside the ring add a completely different and complex layer to the deadly machine. His stoic attitude shows his immense emotional intelligence, necessary for any fighter or business person. As

Genghis Khan stated better than anyone, "An action committed in anger is an action doomed to failure."

During a subsequent video shoot with Fedor (a year after the first one in Calgary, described below), with the help of Greg and Hector Quintero, Fedor further elaborated; "I never had any emotion or anger because I was trying to compete and not to project anger onto my opponent. I tried to push emotions away as far as possible and just get into that competitive mindset."

This fighter's stare was cold and lifeless, as if he had no nerves, and he knows exactly what he would unleash in mere seconds after the bell rang, thus had no need for stare-downs or gimmicks. My words cannot do justice to his legend—Fedor will be talked about for years in the annals of MMA. He is a man whose image and legend already have his opponents beaten long before entering into a physical fight with him.

Emelianenko burst onto most people's radar when he dominated the now four-time K-1 World Grand Prix Champion (three times in a row)—Semmy Schilt, who stood at a whopping 6' 11" and weighed 290 pounds. Semmy is and has been regarded as one of the best heavyweight kickboxers in the world. Many took quick notice that someone very special had arrived to the sport after Fedor dismantled him. Emelianenko also dominated the well-rounded Heath Herring in the Pride Fighting Championship and then was awarded the title shot against the champion, Antonio Rodrigo Nogueira. He was not supposed to win, yet delivered a one-sided attack to win the Pride Heavyweight belt, a title he never lost.

I jumped at the opportunity to meet one of my favorite fighters, a man for whom my idol, Bas Rutten, has immense respect. Bas has personally related to me his awe for Fedor's skills. Mike Tyson at one point called Fedor the best fighter, and the list goes on…. Fedor put the entire MMA community on notice through his devastating reign in the Pride Fighting Championships, when it was arguably the largest promotion in the business. At the drop of a hat, Greg and I had our bags packed and this time ventured west to Calgary and Edmonton, Alberta, to meet the legend.

Fedor traveled from his hometown of Stary Oskol in Russia to Canada, to meet his fans and perform a seminar. He clearly still had the fighting spark when he hit pads, as everyone stood in awe, he looked in shape and faster than ever, sending the pad holder stumbling a few feet backward during his seminar. But there was a bigger reason for this grand visit: he was an ambassador for amateur MMA as an honorary president for the World Mixed Martial Arts Association. He stated, "My reason for my trip is to promote the development of MMA and to join with the World MMA Association. I am here to help select the best Canadian amateurs to attend Minsk (world championships 2014)."

Even after his illustrious career, he still wanted to give back to the MMA community and grow the sport, even after defeating the heavyweight giants of his day, such as Mirko Cro Cop Filipovic, Antonio Nogueira, and Mark Hunt, before retiring. And who could forget the David-versus-Goliath fight with the giant Choi Hong-man, weighing 353 pounds and standing at a skyscraping height of 7'2". There was a bit of a difference, given Fedor stood six feet tall and weighed 230 pounds. But his record speaks for itself, as he amassed a streak of thirty-two wins with only one loss, even though that loss was due to a rule that stated that if a fighter is cut, he loses; thus, in my eyes it was not a loss. I have him at thirty-three straight wins spanning nine years of consecutive fighting—a record that is truly fit only for a legend and not something we will probably see again when it comes to fighting top-level opponents.

We asked Fedor at a press conference whether he would make a comeback, as he looked to be in better shape than ever, and he chuckled at the thought. He had made a promise to his wife to retire, and it was one he would not break. He mentioned that he actually enjoyed watching amateurs more than professional MMA bouts, as the pros would calculate their moves, while amateurs left it all in the cage, as they had something to prove. So he would stick to analyzing fights and sharing his knowledge with the growing youth in MMA. He chuckled again and again, and I have never seen Fedor smile so much or crack jokes, but he was in great spirits in Calgary. He smiled and added that he needed to stay in shape to prove to the younger generation in the gym that he still has it.

Something many fans did not know about young Fedor's beginnings was that he initially trained in the art of judo at the age of eleven and that his biggest and most memorable achievement in the sport was winning the Euro cup, while he was in the Russian national cup, and only then did he transition to Sambo and MMA. As for his favorite places to compete, he enjoyed competing in the U.S., and he felt very welcomed there. He also enjoyed competing in and visiting Japan, but he stated that he was always happy to come back home to Russia in the end.

At one point, I had the opportunity to sit down with Fedor for a chat, accompanied by Ioulia Reynolds of *Real Housewives of Vancouver* fame as our translator. Fedor had this aura, some kind of powerful presence that literally slouched me in my chair; it was intimidating and he was doing nothing more than simply sitting next to me. When his eyes pierced through me, it was the first time I had felt such strong energy; this guy had fire in his eyes that pushed past his big smile and friendly demeanor. I could understand his opponents' losing mindset when they fought him, as there was more than just his legend and stories to chase you from the ring—he had this energy that I cannot describe in words. He was very kind and listened to my stories before revealing some of his, and he embodied the true essence of the kindness found in martial arts.

At the press conference, I asked him what he felt or thought of, both before a fight and during a fight, as he was the most tranquil fighter I have ever witnessed, and this seemed to make him resilient, feared, and mysterious. Yet, coupled with his destructive ground & pound, sledgehammer punches, spine-busting throws, and bone-snapping submissions, he was a beast in the cage. It did not seem human to walk into a cage against a trained combatant and have no show of emotion, before, during, or after a fight. He pondered a question that many fans have wondered about and stated that right before the fight there is stress, just like any other fighter might feel. He was human! He felt the jitters too, but masked them better than anyone in the game.

He went on to state that when he started the warmup and when the sweating started, his confidence would rise, as his nerves subsided. Once in the ring or cage, he simply felt ready to fight, to get the show on the road. He also stated that he did not believe in staredowns, as it was more done for the show, and he simply wanted to fight—that is, after all, what he was there to do. While trading blows in a fight, Fedor revealed that it was all about maximum concentration, closing everything off except the fight at hand. He added "…Working at your maximum psychological and physiological strength; you need to go there and be fully ready to perform at the highest level of your being."

In a subsequent sit-down with Fedor in New York I burrowed a little deeper about his thought process within a fight, Fedor eloquently responded, "Obviously I am thinking while I fight. At the time of the training I would train so that the reflexes would become automatic. That way you can do it without thinking. At the time of the fight in the ring, when you see your opponent made a mistake, you have a split second to make your decision and capitalize on his mistake. But before that you must provoke your opponent to create that mistake, and then you can capitalize. It is similar to a chess game, you have to think faster than your opponent, you must be one step ahead of your opponent, that is success."

Another component to preparation for Fedor was doing everything long before the fight, as two weeks prior to the fight was not the time to think about strategy or let nerves consume the soul. He stated that before the fight, it would be trivial to think about what he has to do, question himself, etc., for that would mean that the fighter would have battled within himself even before the physical confrontation began within the cage or ring. That way a piece of himself would be missing during the actual fight and the much needed focus and concentration would be compromised.

So, when he teaches the younger generation of fighters, he stresses that they need to think hard about those variables during training—but not just prior to the event. The team has to support the fighter to take his or her mind to a more relaxed state, to talk to the fighter and be a steadfast supporter as well as make sure the fighter does not see his opponent before the fight.

The question also arose about which attributes Emelianenko liked about Cain Velasquez, the current reigning UFC champion. He mentioned that he took a liking to Cain's style and enjoyed watching his fights the most. He stated that he liked his never-say-die attitude in the cage and the fact that he was so focused solely on the goal to win, regardless of the work it entailed. There was the impression that if Fedor ever decided to return to MMA, fans would be in for an epic match.

As for his favorite bout from the past, he quickly chose his match with Antonio Rodrigo Nogueira. The Pride Fighting era was invigorating to fans while it existed, as it was a spectacle of the best fighters in the world, thus many questions directed at Fedor were about his days with the Japanese organization. He was asked if he had been hurt when he fought all-American wrestler Kevin Randleman, when he'd been slammed viciously on his neck with all of his weight falling on his head. Most fans held their breath when that occurred—anyone else would have been unconscious. Fedor casually stated that he was not hurt, thus he could continue and win the bout. Watching the fight replay and listening to the casual demeanor that Fedor presented was and always will be unbelievable. How he was not seriously injured and went on to win the fight is beyond me.

At the press conference during the second day in Edmonton, Alberta, someone asked Fedor about his favorite ice cream flavor, and he immediately laughed and stated that he could not eat ice cream because he had to watch his weight.

On a personal level, I did see that Fedor was close to his wife, as they were inseparable. He even took her to the largest mall in Canada, The West Edmonton Mall, for some shopping. I figured that regardless of culture, our "better halves" love to shop! They came back for the dinner, where fans could purchase a spot at the table to eat with "The Last Emperor," and he took the initiative to speak to everyone, even taking his interpreter with him to sit with his fans, which just exemplified his caring nature.

Fedor and his wife Oksana met when they were young—eighteen years old—while Oksana was studying to be a teacher. Oksana was a worker at a summer camp where Fedor was training and they instantly became friends. They would listen to music and shared similar hobbies. Two years passed and Fedor surprised Oksana by looking her up. At this reunion, a kiss catapulted their relationship into boyfriend and girlfriend status. They soon fell in love and got married.

On that note, I had to explore Fedor's softer side some more and I asked Oksana whether Fedor was romantic. She smiled and stated that he is very romantic. He liked to give Oksana gifts, although he also liked to receive gifts as well, but don't we all? She mentioned that he needed his family's attention, it was very important for him. Oksana did admit that this was probably the single largest detail that his fans did not know about him; the man needs attention and craves it.

On the third day, he taught lucky practitioners at Canuckles gym in Calgary the techniques that made him the best in the world. As he was teaching a Sambo variation to a wrestling takedown, he stated something that resonated with me ever since. He said, "You have to create your own style. To get that clinch you have to feel the opponent, feel the technique. In any type of sport, if you work at it, it will come naturally. If you use your head and if you use the right technique, you are going to be able to gain more, which is the same for striking. Everything starts from your base, the basics."

It resonated with me, not because it was some new revelation, but because it was sound advice for everything, including business and life. Regardless of how you were taught to do something, you must create the pieces and movements that form your own style, because we are all unique creatures. Through persistence, repetition, and work, the outcomes will occur naturally. Further, you must feel what you are doing, whether it is the clinch, the proper looping punch, or a negotiation tactic, you must fully be immersed in your craft and your approach to it, in order for it to be perfect. Use your head to make smart approaches, as this will definitely save you energy and time. Build on your base—those basics that will propel you toward your goals. Knowing a flying superman to spinning elbow does little for you if you cannot gauge distance or use proper defense. Fedor used basic punches better than anyone in the game, and that was enough to make him the best in the world.

Fedor's illustrious career and dominance in MMA finds a correlation in Genghis Khan's reign over Asia. They both ruled with an iron fist, and such special circumstances exist in business where it is deemed appropriate to dominate with an iron fist. Sometimes striking some fear into your competition or opponent is enough to cause them to misstep, pause, or rethink their approach, which will open up a prime opportunity for you to strike advantageously.

As for what other variables set Fedor apart from everyone else in the world, I once again turned to the person closest to him, his wife Oksana, for the details. Without any hesitation she responded, "It is very important; Fedor cannot rest—never. Maybe he can rest three to five days but after that he must work, must work a lot. If he doesn't have work, what to do? He becomes crazy. He must work, I think that this is what is very important for his career. If he works, he works very well, perfect." Work ethic, the old cliché, but I do believe that it, coupled with extreme focus, down-to-earth training and diet and a strong support system, gave Fedor just the edge to best his opponents. Fedor's work ethic was beyond vigorous.

Bas Rutten appeared on Denis Shkuratov's Submission Radio in the summer of 2015 and spoke about Fedor's first loss which was against Fabricio Werdum. "But we don't know what was going on with Fedor when they fought the first time. Maybe there was something going on, maybe… we don't know. Fedor is not the kind of guy who says that, like 'I was injured or was this,' he doesn't look for excuses."

Thus, I knew that, while composing my question regarding what Fedor thought of his three consecutive losses towards the end of his career, I would have to press him about whether there was anything out of the ordinary occurring in his life. Given that Fedor would never publicly state such a thing, the stars must have aligned for me as I was blessed to have Fedor divulge the details in an exclusive conversation.

After three losses, he stated that he thanked God for his entire career—wins and losses—and that he had to go through the losses to understand this. During the time of his losses, he stated that there is a saying in Russia that he had "too much on his head," as he broke a smile. "I had too much stress in my family, I was too worried about my child, too much emotions. I also had to be in the hospital a few times, I was definitely on the side of family more than fighting."

He did state firmly that he was not making any excuses for his losses, he was training and going wholeheartedly into the fights to win. He opened up to the fact that during this time, many people that were around him showed their true face. He gave off a menacing smirk as he collected his thoughts and replied, "I do not see them anymore."

In regards to the way that many champions and athletes in Western culture that reach success would embrace the publicity and media exposure, while he was always known to shy away from the spotlight, he gave a laugh as he bellowed, "I do not understand how you could like that!" He went on to explain that the quieter life was better for him. He enjoyed being out with his family and not being noticed. It suited him overall.

After speaking to many of Fedor's friends, they all confirmed that he was the same in his personal life as he was in the public eye, but that he added humor to his personal interaction. Fedor himself admitted, "I always try to be myself. With closer people I joke more, but I am the same in public as with family and friends."

But the final and closest witness, his wife, confirmed my research; "He is a very funny person, he is not very serious. When he comes home, he jokes every minute. Even here in New York, he came here for work (purposes), he did not feel like work because we are here. So in the plane he was very glad, smiled, joked and so on. He is very comfortable for me, but of course every man is very difficult...." She laughed playfully. I immediately knew that my wife would be good friends with Oksana; they had the male gender well figured out.

That was not something I was prepared for; Fedor was not the machine we MMA fans were used to seeing in the ring while in the company of his family—he let loose. I did notice that by the third time I had the honor of interviewing him (in St. Louis), after getting to know me, he definitely cracked more jokes.

I had to ask the baddest man on the planet what scares him, and he revealed that it was not another human or the boogeyman that he feared, but something more introspective: "I am afraid to do the wrong things in my life so that I can be cleared before God." Fedor is widely known as a devoted believer, and he has harnessed the power of his faith to reach excellence and keep his life in order and dedicated to following God's will.

Psychological warfare as mastered by Fedor has long been used in war, business, and the fight game. It doesn't have to entail verbal warfare, as Fedor has always conducted himself in a professional manner. He is always soft-spoken and picks his words carefully, so how come he was so psychologically imposing? The legends, myths, and tales surrounding Fedor had the greatest champions thinking twice about signing the contract to fight him, as the fight-or-flight impulse in their minds begged not to step into the ring with him. His stoic attitude, concentration, lack of emotion, and the trail of devastated opponents gave him a sense of mystery and danger throughout his total domination in MMA.

Taking it into a business context, there is no way a business can take on every competitor, nor can a fighter take on every opponent in the division—it is an impossible task. Thus, when you choose your fight, let news of your conquest ripple to the rest of your potential competition, and serve the fear of your capabilities up on a silver platter. Genghis would destroy villages overnight, but presented the option for his foes to surrender. He could not take on all battles at once, and seeing the opportunity to grow and not have to fight was an astute observation and something that occurs today in the business sector. Fedor put the world on notice through sheer power, yet he has a religious and gentle side that's evident in his personal life. It was outstanding seeing him care for his wife, connect with fans, and go out of his way for others, even though he had been dragged from event to event after a long flight.

Create an aura around yourself, and your reputation will precede you. Genghis Khan strategically exaggerated the tales of his mass destruction, and the brutal killings and death tolls instilled fear and fostered obedience around the world. Similarly, the media, the fans, and the fighters spread the fear and message of Fedors' destruction around the world within the MMA realm and beyond. Shape public opinion to cater to your goals and be larger than life, my friends!

In my opinion, there will never again be someone like Fedor in the MMA game. Many will aspire but fall short. He ruled the ring with an iron fist, but found faith in God and presented humility in his everyday life. He is an introverted soul who keeps to himself. He doesn't create a spectacle for entertainment, but when this lone wolf enters the ring, he unleashes his true power and breaks his opponents in half. Sometimes, we too must become that lone wolf, detach from fast-paced life, the electronics, and the modern-day items that encumber us, and conjure our inner power and strengths to do the talking for us—from our creativity to keeping strong throughout our battles—all to be the best at what we do and reach our given goals. If you take a lesson from "The Last Emperor," let it be this one.

I knew our paths would cross again, especially after the great Fedor Emelianenko announced to the world that he was coming out of retirement....

QUICK ROUND

What is your favorite junk food?
Borscht and pierogis but I try not to eat the pierogis because you get a big belly after that.

If we opened your fridge, what would we find?
I eat normally, fish, meat, milk, sour cream, no problem.

Name you favorite movie.
It is hard to say, but on the way to New York I watched a film called *Brother*. It was a very interesting Russian movie.

Is it true you can bench press 400 lbs?
A little bit less than that.

What is your favorite stand up technique or combination?
I would not divide it into categories because it depends on the moment in the fight.

What was your favorite city to fight in the world?
I was in many cities around the world obviously and liked to explore and discover all of them. The only one city I prefer more that I would like to go back (aside from Russia) is Belgrade in Serbia.

In your household, who gets possession of the television remote?
[big smile] It is collecting dust, I have tried to be more with the family than with the TV.

Chapter Seventeen

THE GOD OF WAR IS THE RED KING

"The art of war teaches us to rely not on the likelihood of the enemy not coming, but on our own readiness to receive him; not on the chance of his not attacking, but rather on the fact that we have made our position unassailable." **—Sun Tzu**

Rory MacDonald has taken the mixed martial arts world by storm, his deathly piercing stare forcing his opponents to take him seriously. His gripping body slams, whipping strikes, and vicious ground & pound brings chills to his opponent's spines. At the age of twenty-five, his soft-spoken nature coupled with a no-bullshit attitude and an air of mystery surrounding him has made him an instant star with the fans.

By dismantling world-class opponents, the Tristar prodigy was awarded with the nickname "Aries," but some have dubbed him the "American Psycho" on the underground and Sherdog forums, and even in the media outlets. During preparation for his 2015 title fight, he changed his nickname to "Red King" as suggested by his Irish/Gaelic name. He has always had a warm, inviting personality, but with the rise in his stardom, he has retreated into a more of an introverted destroyer, similar to the lead character in the American Psycho movie. He reminded me of Fedor Emelianenko, a legendary heavyweight in the sport, stern and focused when entering a fight and someone who would dispassionately take care of business in devastating fashion.

Joe Ferraro, the famous MMA analyst and host of Sportsnet's *UFC Central*, gave his insights on Rory MacDonald as a fighter and a person. "In his DNA, he is designed to fight. I think his only self-satisfaction is to compete and to fight. That is how he is wired. He is not just one of these guys that does it for fun or does it just for the business. It's almost like he has to do it in order to survive. As a person, he is very reserved, very conservative, you do not get much out of him in interviews, even if you are just hanging out with him. He is a man of a few words. He is a good guy, but I would not mess with Rory MacDonald, that's for sure."

When Rory was fourteen years old, he was given the nickname "The Waterboy" by his friends because his personality reflected Adam Sandler in the comedy movie of the same name. He couldn't imagine using this as his official fighting nickname. It didn't represent how he fought or his mindset during a fight. One day, he thought of "Aries," the Greek god of war. As he had decided against being called "The Water Boy," he picked his own new nickname, a new moniker suiting him much better. Now, "Red King" may indeed suit him best as he assumes his rightful place as the king of his division.

Rory's parents divorced when he was only five years old. He bounced around, spending a significant amount of time with both parents. His parents both married other people, and his mom and step-dad moved to Langley, British Columbia. As law dictated, Rory lived with his mother, but his brother—who was of legal age could choose who he wanted to live with; and he went to live with their father. At the age of twelve, Rory joined his brother and his father in Kelowna, which was a change for Rory, as his mother and step-father were wealthier. His father was a firefighter who worked hard to provide for his family.

Rory torched his way through smaller shows to get to the big show in the UFC with an impressive 9-0 record. Rory attributed his success to having a great coach and training partners, not to mention a lot of hard work and focus.

Rory was in high school for most of the nine fights, and at the same time held down a myriad of jobs, all of which he passionately hated. After graduating, he gained different experience working as a waiter and a framer or carpenter on construction jobs. Rory's choice of words when describing these jobs very clearly expressed his dislike for them, and I can relate from my own experiences in the field. The final job he had before transitioning to a full-time pro fighter was at a grocery store stocking shelves.

These employment "opportunities" motivated Rory to train harder and focus his energy on the mixed martial arts. His dedication on a daily basis was revealed through his performances as well as by the UFC brass. He was more than ready to enter MMA shows, even if he was only twenty years old at the time.

Rory was never a kid who would do anything half-assed and was never content being second place in anything. The innate drive and ambition has just always been deeply rooted within him, which has undoubtedly helped him achieve success. All he had to do was feed it.

I asked Rory for his philosophy on fighting, and he responded without a pause: "I am ready to fight at any moment, and I train all the time, so I am prepared for anything, as long as I'm healthy." Tomasz Adamek and others have given the same answer, demonstrating the importance of consistently adding the building blocks of new skills in order to reach the highest level possible.

Along with his quickly increasing fanbase in the UFC, Rory also gained respect from fellow fighters with his spectacular performances. Was it hard to stay grounded and focused? "At the end of the day, the cameras and tension are all second to what I really enjoy, which is training and competing. So, I mean, I just keep the same friends around me and my family close, so it's not really a big deal."

Having family close by was definitely an advantage when he fought in Canada, but his preference for fighting in Canada was also because his fans would go crazy for him. Another reason to stay local, one that I had never thought about, was taxes! A Canadian fighter was taxed heavily for earnings in the U.S., so fighting north of the border let Rory keep a bigger piece of the pie.

Rory was known for training hard and putting in long hours at the gym. Rory explained that each day looked a little different but that he would go to his first training session for a couple of hours, then go back home to eat and maybe play video games or hang out with friends. He would then go back to the gym for a few more hours before leaving to eat, relax, hang out, and get plenty of sleep, and then repeat this process the next day.

A nutritionist, George Lockhart, planned Rory's meals. It was a complicated system, and Rory wanted to spare me the details. "It's complicated as shit!" A chef prepared his food according to the plan, making things easier on Rory. He considered his nutritionist to be like a scientist whose precision and formulas help his performance.

Rory also used the diet to lose weight, in order to hit the welterweight mark of 170 pounds the day before his fights. He would hover around 195 pounds while preparing for his bouts, and then he would diet down to 170 pounds.

My friend and world-class trainer Kru Mel Bellissimo brought in four UFC fighters for a super-seminar at Lanna MMA in Toronto, which included Marcus Brimage, Walel Watson, Brendan Schaub, and Rory MacDonald. After attending the session with the UFC standouts and chatting with all of them, I could definitely say that they are all great human beings as well. Brendan discussed his key strategy, which was similar to Rory's when it came to preparation—he did not focus on his opponents' skills, but on his own.

I brought this up with Rory, and he reiterated that he had to understand what his opponent was going to do, but he also left a lot in his trainer's hands. Firas Zahabi could look at a situation and figure out what type of training was needed. He didn't tell Rory what B.J. was going to do, but instead told him how to train; thus, Rory could react to the situations as they arose without having to delve too deeply into his opponent's game plan. So, in a sense, Firas was preparing him for what Rory's opponent would be bringing to the table, but it was on a subconscious level, which I thought was genius.

Actor and martial artist Alain Moussi described his thoughts on fellow Canadian Rory MacDonald during my sit-down with him in his gym in Ottawa. "Rory is very methodical. He comes in and doesn't go nuts, he takes his time and he is very analytical. He goes in there, he is waiting for the right time and then, bam! I like that, it shows he has a lot of smarts. The fact that he trains with Firas, and Firas is a genius of a coach, he is a strategist. Rory is extremely analytical, that is how he operates. You can tell that

Rory takes that from him (Firas) and then applies it." He also added that Rory would have the UFC belt around his waist one day, a sentiment I completely agreed with.

Rory was always trying to improve himself, working on both his weaknesses and strengths. Rory, Brendan, and Firas seemed to have mastered the time-tested strategies set forth by the famed Sun Tzu. "*The Art of War* teaches us to rely not on the likelihood of the enemy not coming, but on our own readiness to receive him; not on the chance of his not attacking, but rather on the fact that we have made our position unassailable."

On fight day, the key factor for getting into the zone was focus. While being in the cage with another man, trying to hurt him, he had no choice but to focus on the task at hand. Getting himself into a deep focus was easy; coupled with his adrenaline pumping, it definitely helped get him into the right state of mind.

Joe Ferraro shared his thoughts with me on how and where the mental discipline came from that made Rory such a devastating force. "One thing that I learned from Rory is that he doesn't know where that comes from, whether he was bullied or not; it is just something that he fell in love with. If you notice before he fights, before the cameras focus in on him, whether it's Bruce Buffer announcing him or him getting ready to take on an opponent, you see a certain blank look in his eyes. He tells me all the time, it is clarity. It's got to be clear, he cannot be thinking about anything but what he is programmed to do. He looks at his opponent across the cage and he doesn't want to think about anything else. He doesn't want to think about something like girls. He has a job to do, and the job is to hurt his opponent as quickly and efficiently as possible. It is actually scary. It reminds me of a *Dexter* sort of thing, but that is just the way he is. He doesn't know where it comes from. I don't know where it comes from, but it is definitely a caveman-barbaric-DNA thing."

I wanted to know what emotions Rory felt before a fight, while he was in the locker room, what was he feeling before venturing out in front of 20,000-plus screaming fans into a cage to do battle. Rory answered "Well, I get anxious, a feeling of anxiousness is definitely an emotion, you know? Obviously, fear can come into it if you let it, but if you can learn how to control it and to be realistic about your situation and to put all the other big stuff out of your head, like people's judgments, the show and all that stuff … just think about fighting. Like once you are in there, that's it. Basically your outlook has to be like, this is the last day of your life, nothing else matters, but if you think about what people are going to think of you, think about if you lose, you won't get that money, or you don't get that title shot, then you are going to start freaking out, getting nervous and scared, you know?"

Controlling these variables is what set Rory apart from the rest. I was beginning to realize that at the elite level, it wasn't enough to just be a well-rounded fighter; there were outside pressures and variables that each world-class athlete had to learn to juggle in order to find success and calm the nerves.

To prevent these outside pressures from creeping into his mind, Rory always approached fights with the attitude that when going to battle, he would be ready to die and just went with the flow, or, as his trainer Firas Zahabi put it, "Flow with the go." He approached each fight with an attitude of readiness and would not over-analyze things, which definitely worked in the UFC superstar's favor.

Thought processes occurring during the fight were not as complex as one might guess. Rory didn't talk to himself; he would just flow and react. There wasn't time for analyzing different aspects of the fight, but knowing that he had completed grueling workouts in preparation eased his mind and allowed him to react to encounters as they occurred. That brought me back to a lot of the same answers I had received from other great athletes in the course of conducting interviews; I noticed a pattern. A free mind was a dangerous mind.

Being dangerous led to my next question regarding his opinion of a fighter vs. a mixed martial artist. He said that it was the same thing; fighting was fighting. Whether one looked at the traditional arts or the newer hybrid forms, they all stemmed from a system to "be able to kill and survive—to annihilate your opponent, and have you alive at the end of the day. That's why it started at the very beginning. That's why people started training."

This was the first time I had heard a response from this perspective, but Rory's words were true. Martial arts were a physical form of attacking and defending. Maybe Rory was on to something. He had a "kill or be killed" attitude, with the self-defined goal to "annihilate" his opponents—that's what let him win in devastating fashion and that's what cemented him as a fan favorite in the sport.

We had discussed preparing for a fight, along with his mindset before and during a fight. On finishing fights, in a blood sport, fans liked decisive endings. The president of the UFC, Dana White, had been vocal not only about creating exciting fights but also about not leaving fights to decisions, as some of the judges had made awful decisions in the past. Rory was an advocate of finishing fights. His view was that if a fighter did not finish a fight, the win reflected the opinion of the judges, but it was never really definitive.

I asked Rory about a question that was lighting up underground forums, and, unless these two already met in the cage before you read this, this is something that fans are likely still wondering about. What would he do if he kept eliminating the top fighters in the welterweight division, eventually leading to a fight with his training partner and friend, the champion in his division, Georges St-Pierre. He wouldn't answer the question, and replied that he always likes to live in the present moment. Rory was looking at his next contender, which was the legendary B.J. Penn. He had successfully dodged my question.

Rory's fight with B.J. Penn, who was coming out of retirement to fight the young gun, was quickly approaching. Although a lot of trash talking occurred leading up to the fight, Rory had only nice things to say about the "Prodigy." He had been watching the very talented fighter for years; he respected him because he was a real fighter. But Rory was also adamant that he himself was the best in the world and that B.J. Penn was going to be in for a rude awaking, and that the fans and promoters would be in awe after the match.

Rory's boast was not just bluster—he dismantled the legend only weeks later. Rory used the tools of MMA to prove that he was the better fighter. When I interviewed Rory for mmacanada.net long before my book interview, he talked about the importance of displaying his full arsenal of skills. Rory stayed true to his commitment. In every fight, he showed off different techniques and skills, which is remarkable for a fighter his age.

Everyone who works so hard also needs time to recover and relax. Rory liked going to the spa, getting massages, being in the sauna, and taking cold baths for physical recovery. For mental recovery, he spent time with his friends, including his good friend and fellow UFC fighter, Mike Ricci. Rory could be found regularly at Ricci's family's house; they were his second, extended family. Rory was also an avid gamer, and between *Call of Duty* and *Battlefield*, he was able to fill his downtime.

Rory was confident that he would become a world champion, possibly the greatest fighter in history. He added that happiness played a key role in his formula for success, as well as to be financially secure, have a family, be healthy, and to give back to the community in the best way he could.

As with most fighters, Rory was not immune to hardship. His discomfort at addressing the difficult times was clear, but he said that maybe at the end of his career he would disclose the details to the public. What he could tell me was that he struggled while growing up, but learning martial arts saved him. It was MMA and his coach at the time, David Lea, that helped him get his life back on track. David Lea remains a close friend.

His new coach, Firas Zahabi, was hands-down the best coach in MMA, according to Rory. He stated that Firas did not receive the credit he deserved, but that the world was slowly beginning to see this, as the gym's popularity grew each day.

Looking back on his career, which was still in its infancy, he had earned his way into the top echelon of the UFC by steamrolling some very talented opponents. Rory wouldn't have changed a thing and stated that he felt really blessed by God. His life experiences had made him the person he is. He clearly thought that the suffering had been worth it.

Rory personified the yin-yang phenomenon; he was a genuinely nice guy, especially once you peeled back the layers. However, when he flipped the "warrior" switch, he was easily one of the scariest individuals to face off against in an eight-sided cage. Between his athleticism, well-rounded capabilities, and aggressive attacks, he really was "The God of War." He stayed true to himself and never gave in to media or fan pressure. He really knew himself on all levels, which helped him stay composed and calm, not just in the ring but in all aspects of his life.

As a warrior, athlete, and fighter, Rory brandished a stare that not many possessed; cold and lifeless, cognizant of the destruction he was about to unleash. His self-assured attitude should not be mistaken for arrogance; his belief in himself and all the hours training were all helping to carve out his legacy in one of the most demanding sports in the world. According to Firas Zahabi, Rory has not yet reached his peak. There was still much to see from the cerebral fighter, and the world is waiting to discover just how far the "Red King's" path of destruction will reach

QUICK ROUND
What's your favorite junk food?
Ice cream or cheesecake.

In your eyes, who is your favorite and most notable win?
Probably Nate Diaz.

If you had a dream match, who would your opponent be? It doesn't have to be someone from MMA.
Carlos Condit.

What is your favorite jiu-jitsu technique?
Any kind of choke.

What's your biggest strength?
Being balanced.

What would we find in your music playlist?
Anything from rock & roll, hip-hop, dance music, punchy music, R&B … everything.

In your eyes, who are the three best fighters in the world today?
Me, Anderson Silva, and Jose Aldo.

What's your favorite video game?
Probably all of the *Call of Duty* games.

What would we find in your fridge?
Healthy food. I try not to bring junk food into my house, because I don't eat it all.

Who do you look up to in MMA or in life?
Georges St-Pierre, Vitor Belfort, and Wanderlei Silva.

Chapter Eighteen

THE CEREBRAL LION TAMER

"A teacher is never a giver of truth; he is a guide, a pointer to the truth that each student must find for himself."
—Bruce Lee

One of the best gyms that produce some of the highest-skilled fighters coupled with an admirable win ratio is located in my favorite city in the world: Montreal. The cerebral lion tamer, Firas Zahabi, leads his lions, the kings of the jungle, to war every day so that their battles in the cage seem easier as they devour their prey.

I was lucky to call Firas my friend. He is a self-made man who had nothing given to him in life. He had to create his own circumstances and opportunities. Like other great coaches the world over, Firas exhibits a true sense of self, high intelligence, and a calculated approach when mentoring his fighters, and applies this to life in general.

Joe Ferraro, a seasoned MMA analyst, weighed in on the extraordinary individual. "I have known Firas for a very long time. He is finally getting the respect he deserves, but I still maintain that he is one of the most underrated coaches in all of mixed martial arts. Firas took Georges St-Pierre from the first Matt Serra fight to where he is right now. He has done a fantastic job. Whenever we have lunch or dinner together, anywhere in the world, it always starts off with mixed martial arts and always ends up talking about our kids!"

Like most immigrants, Firas' parents were not highly educated when they came to Canada in search of a better life. They also had only a modest amount of cash in their bank accounts. Firas fell behind in school on a regular basis. He never had anyone to teach him or help him with his homework; he was failing. Aside from struggles at school, he had a normal childhood with a lot of television time, but he never had anyone to teach him extracurricular activities, such as hockey, wrestling, golf or a trade. Firas has always been a strong believer that "You really want what you never had; there is a void there."

After completing high school, Firas became obsessed with acquiring knowledge. He wanted to know everything—anything he could comprehend. He eventually came to the conclusion that he could learn and actually teach himself something, which was very liberating. When he was younger, he believed that knowledge had to come from other people, that he was too simple to learn things. But that epiphany of self-instruction was empowering for him. Since then, he rarely listens to music on the go, but instead has opted for thousands of audio books. His search for knowledge led him to read books on a daily basis. His focus shifted to a love of philosophy, as he immersed himself in the teachings of Socrates and stumbled upon a physical form of chess called Brazilian jiu-jitsu at the age of twenty. Another new world opened up to him. The powerful grip of martial arts grasped Firas' soul and has never let go.

Craving, almost yearning for that knowledge, Firas saved up his money and traveled around the world to participate in seminars, hitting the U.S., Thailand, and other places, to become better in all forms of martial arts. He followed his dreams, but his funds were depleted after returning from a trip. He would then save up the minimum amount needed to go on another trip, and off he'd go again. In that sense, Firas' story was similar to mine; it would always be scary coming back home with ambition to spare and new knowledge but with empty pockets. Yet when it was time to travel again, we would both make the conscious decision to gamble, common sense be damned. At least we were following our dreams and living on the edge.

Firas' interest in martial arts occurred in a fashion similar to most. After watching a commercial for UFC 2, Firas noticed a small guy hoisted up on his coach's shoulders after beating monsters in an octagon cage. Royce Gracie has been and always will be an inspiration to most in the martial arts field.

Firas was obsessed with the smallest details. Given how much money, time, and effort went into learning all disciplines, he wanted to be the best student and pay attention to the hundreds of minuscule details that produced the final technique. To this day, Firas retains that trait, an obsession and penchant for detail matched by very few.

When it came to the "gentle art" of jiu-jitsu, he recalled how he was blessed to work with Angelo Exarhakos, who was a purple belt under Renzo Gracie back in the day, as there were no true BJJ clubs around, just a lot of karate guys trying to capitalize on the wave, teaching their diluted forms of BJJ.

Within six months of training, Firas was winning tournaments because other BJJ practitioners were not learning the true form from Gracie's. Knowing a handful of moves was putting Firas ahead of the pack. Flashing forward to the present day, things have definitely changed, as information has become more widely available. There are jiu-jitsu and MMA gyms popping up like mushrooms in every city, with good instructors to boot.

When his travels took him to Thailand, Firas trained under Sagat Petchyindee, a famous eleven-time world champion. Sagat was the inspiration for the Muay Thai character boss in the classic *Street Fighter* games, who was also named "Sagat." Firas also trained with Sagat's brother, to whom he gave only the highest praise. Firas' Muay Thai coach in Canada, Master

Peter Sisomphou, was also a student and fighter of Sagat's in Thailand. Similarly to the BJJ lineage, the lineage in Muay Thai was very important, and Firas had learned from the best.

Firas mentioned how they groomed him well, showing him the formulas that worked. He would return each summer, soaking up the knowledge and traditions that the land of smiles offered. He would live with them, eat with them, and become part of their daily lives, like a member of the family.

He was training pro but fighting amateur; he had an edge. There was no such thing as pro mixed martial arts in Quebec, as it was illegal. Firas, a humble man, told me that he fought amateur, but the level was actually pro, just cloaked under the classification of amateur. As he started practicing MMA late in life, he went to the gym every day. Missing a day of training would drive him crazy. Back in the day, they paid $500 or $1,000 to fight, so he wasn't doing it to earn a living. Firas was doing it for the love of the sport, while going to school, hoping to become a lawyer. During this time, Georges St-Pierre asked him to take over coaching duties as his main trainer. David Loiseau's fights were getting bigger, and Firas had to tend to his growing skills. There was a vacuum pulling Firas away from fighting and into a life of coaching; fate had its way of putting Firas where he was supposed to be.

The fighters needed a trainer; they kept asking him for favors. Firas would put his own training on hold to attend a camp with one of the fighters. He got pulled in from one fighter to the next, and as fate would have it, he didn't fight again but traveled further down the coaching path.

The day we were at Tristar gym with Greg, there were thirty pros training at once. Firas decided to go with the flow, or "flow with the go," as he put it best, and it was beneficial for him as well as the fighters.

On molding his teachings to different fighters, the universal Firas was a good match for nearly any type of fighter out there. Daily, he would tutor and train in all disciplines, including wrestling, jiu-jitsu, and striking. Firas added that if a world champion boxer came to him, he also trained him in a field outside of boxing, as he was not very useful in the boxing realm. It was impossible for a fighter to be an expert in all positions; Firas could always find a gap that needed bridging. The best fighters in the world require tweaking, even if on the most microscopic level. "My job is to find that one thing I can help you with that is going to make the biggest difference. Once you absorb that, I will show you the next-most important thing. I think that is the key."

One of Firas' main philosophies in fighting was taken from Bruce Lee: daily decrease, not daily increase. Firas had always been a huge fan of Bruce Lee's, not necessarily for being the best martial artist, but more for being the best philosopher in martial arts. It was not about always adding to a fighter's arsenal, but removing inefficiencies.

While Greg and I visited Montreal for a third time, we were sitting in the famed Tristar gym watching David Loiseau outscore his sparring partner, which was a dream for us. A who's who of MMA covered the mats; the sparring sessions were intense, fully padded meant hard shots were exchanged.

The next day, Greg and I had unlimited access to another closed session of Tristar's best. We watched GSP circle the ring as Firas held pads for him in dynamic fashion. Only a short time after GSP received the green light to train following his knee surgery, he looked hungry and in top form. His leg kicks snapped the pads as his punches popped loudly across the gym; other fighters stopped to watch the session. One of those fighters was my bro, Chris Horodecki, from London, Ontario. He was shell-shocked to see me across the room. He came over right away to greet me kindly as we marveled at what a small world it was.

Watching Georges St-Pierre go head-to-head with Rory MacDonald was something that few MMA fans could ever hope to experience, yet I had a front-row seat as the two sparred. Rory landed a light overhand, and Georges grabbed Rory's leg deep enough to show him a possible takedown. As they reset, Georges landed a jab, and Rory bobbed the right hand and landed a three-hit combo of his own. The back-and-forth game lasted for the entire round, and both men looked sharp, even landing on each other almost at will.

The dynamic was intense as my mind raced. Who would win had there been a referee? We'll never know. They pumped fists and smiled as they concluded a few hard rounds of sparring and tested each other, brushing up on their skills.

Firas Zahabi was holding pads for Rory "Aries" (now "Red King") MacDonald at the far end of the Tristar gym, which had a long chain-link cage separating the area, in order to simulate the UFC cage. Firas was dictating the furious pace as Rory MacDonald slammed the pads. He ducked and weaved anytime Firas swung the pads at him; Rory retaliated, not giving Firas time to swing again. In a fight, when missing a punch, not only would it tax the attacker, but also it would leave him open for a counter, which was exactly what these quick combinations were drilling into Rory's psyche.

Rory looked quick, relaxed, and in his element. After kicking, his lead foot would land too close to Firas, meaning in a fight, he would be close enough to his opponent to get hit. Firas approached this problem by using one of Bruce Lee's principles. The principle of daily decrease, not increase, as Firas showed his young student the problem with his current stance. He only needed to say it once for Rory to make the proper adjustment.

Firas put it into perspective as he broke down his approach, "I was working today with Rory. He would kick with his left leg and drop it back in the wrong place. I tweaked it a bit so that he puts his foot back in the correct spot so that it creates a type of space between his opponent, so that he does not get countered. That one step was a problem. It was less efficient; it was slowing him down and getting him countered every so often. We took away something that was problematic. It's not always about adding new moves and bells and whistles, it's also breaking down moves and finding out what the problem is, and this is one of the most important coaching aspects to success. It's called "reductionism." You reduce the problem to the most important detail and fix that one issue."

It was clearer than ever why Firas was one of the most sought-after trainers in the world. He was meticulous with his approach and was astute at considering history to piece together the best strategies—something that would work in all aspects of life. I wanted to know his broader approach to honing his fighters' dynamic and seemingly unstoppable wrestling skills—skills not acquired in a collegiate setting.

One of Firas' epiphanies in the wrestling realm had helped his fighters exponentially. He explained that the takedown/takedown defense was the most important aspect of the fight because if a fighter was looking to keep a fight standing, he would use his takedown defense, or, for a better grappler, he would take the fight down to his world. By dictating where the fight would take place, Firas could control the fight by dictating the pace, commanding which martial art would be utilized, and thus stacking the deck in the superior wrestler's favor.

Firas further detailed his approach to wrestling, stating that if he were to double-leg me (wrestle me to the ground by snatching both of my legs), he would have to take a step to get my legs. If I never allowed him that step, he wouldn't get the takedown, but if he got the step on me deeply enough, it was universally accepted that with a good grip he would be able to take me down with ease. That one step was of vital importance; thus, Firas spent a lot of time training his pupils on that initial step, how to avoid it, and how to create it.

He found that his students' wrestling improved exponentially. Everyone began winning on the wrestling front. They were dictating the fight, staying within their strengths, which translated into more overall wins. Firas demonstrated how he thoroughly and ingeniously broke the chain of teaching philosophy from little details to bigger details to reach the backbone, or "nucleus," as Firas dubbed it, of the issue at hand.

This approach was not only important in MMA, but in any life situation. Firas exclaimed with a warm smile, "What is the smallest factor that I can change, what is the root factor, the nucleus of this problem that we're having that will create the chain reaction to make you become the best, so that you are the one with the advantage? That's one of the most important principles, finding the nucleus of the issue. What is the root of the problem?"

In order to find the root of the problem, one would have to follow the chain back to the smallest component. The analogy he presented was of a bicycle. If Firas was sitting on a bike, putting his weight on the pedals, the pedal would pull the chain, turning the little wheel. That little wheel is attached to a bigger wheel, would make the bike propel forward. The entire mechanism was predicated on one action, so the right question would be how to stop the bike from rolling? He could outperform the strongest cyclist in the world, Lance Armstrong himself, just by breaking one link of the chain and making his opponent's process inoperative.

The correlation made sense to me on many levels: hard work coupled with the due diligence of putting that work ethic in the right directions would foster an advantage to anyone. Firas enlightened me with a business analogy on a greater scale as he told me about the story of Dell Computers.

Dell's creator, who took on IBM in sales of personal computers when he was starting out making computers in his dorm room, was a prime example of David versus Goliath. Dell built computers with specs chosen by their clients. IBM, on the other hand, could not tailor their computers, as their service was not built for that, which ended up being their Achilles' heel. Dell found the chink in their armor, that little detail that he could exploit, helping Dell bring IBM down in the end.

After watching Tristar's pro workout, GSP sparring Rory MacDonald, and Rory hitting pads with Firas, he welcomed me into his home and introduced me to his wonderful family. Words could not express my appreciation for all he had done for me, and it dawned on me why so many of his fighters not only respected him but looked up to him as a father figure.

As we sat at his dinner table recounting the finer details of the fight game, I asked him about the strengths of his star pupils. Firas said that GSP mixed his striking with his wrestling better than anyone else. He out-wrestled a wrestler because his set-ups were based on his strikes, not his wrestling tie-ups, which were not feasible in MMA. He struck out a striker because strikers were deathly afraid of his takedowns. They would be so preoccupied with his takedowns that their attention would be divided between defending the takedown and defending the strikes. They could pay only half of their attention to his strikes, so it made GSP's striking look even better against an opponent who had been striking for longer than him. Firas enthusiastically added that GSP's strengths lay in the correct space between a striker and wrestler; they were exactly in the spot they needed to be.

I had to ask whether it was true that GSP, the man that looked like a Greek god chiseled from stone, had a weakness for McDonald's fast food. Firas smirked and corroborated the story. I also asked whether GSP would ever go down to 155 pounds from his current reign in the 170-pound welterweight division. Firas mentioned that GSP is not a big welterweight; he worked hard to stay around 185 pounds. Firas knows several lightweights who would walk around at 185 pounds. "It's not impossible. Would Georges actually buckle down and do it? No, he likes eating too much. One day, if he finds the motivation, he could do it. I know guys who have dropped a weight class that were farther away than Georges is now. Kenny Florian did it. He used to walk around at 185. I've worked with George Lockhart (nutrition consultant) and seen what he could do with a diet. GSP has an incredible metabolism, so it's not impossible, and if you ask George Lockhart he will say the same thing. 'It's not impossible.'"

I was blown away; the welterweight kingpin had a weakness for fast food. Maybe these guys really weren't that different from the rest of us, and my notion was corroborated again.

As for Rory MacDonald, his strengths were completely different from the welterweight champion's. Firas Zahabi designed his style differently because when Rory came to him, he did not have a wrestling pedigree; he had a different set of skills. Firas designed the sixty-second guard for when Rory got taken down. Rory had sixty seconds after being taken down to do something drastic, as seen when he fought Mike Pyle. When Mike Pyle took Rory down, Rory popped back up almost immediately. Firas spoke about jiu-jitsu guys pulling into guard when being taken down, looking for sweeps and attack limbs, but after they had spent the vast majority of the round on their back, the judges would give the round to their opponent.

Firas beamed, "I say, how do you turn the tables on this guy? He just took me down; well, if he took me down, he had to spend some energy to explode. I did not just fall over." So, by falling over because the opponent took out his legs, there was little energy expended by the recipient of the takedown. "So if I get back up and use your takedown to get me back up to my feet, who needs a rest now, me or you? The guy who took the takedown, so now is the time for me to jump on you."

For Rory's sixty-second guard against Pyle, Rory got up right away for the first two takedowns. Mike was expending a lot of energy. The third takedown attempt was his downfall, as the rate of takedowns in a short period was too high. That was when mistakes were most probable, and Rory caught him in a choke. Mike had to dive onto his back. Rory got on top of him and released an onslaught of ground & pound to obtain the win.

There did not seem to be a loophole in the equation that I could find, and, more importantly, no one in the UFC did either; thus Rory's incredible breakthrough. Firas found a way to turn the tables on Rory's opponents, regardless of their game plans. They stayed true to the principles, and Firas mentioned that he encouraged all young martial artists to find the style that would work for them. Not everyone would fight like GSP, nor did Firas train everyone like GSP. It was a true science.

On a personal level, Firas' mentoring and father-like qualities surfaced. He respected Rory and GSP tremendously. He spoke about how close they were, and he felt like he helped bring up both of them. All of the hours spent in the gym and outside the gym definitely created strong bonds of brotherhood. During my time at Tristar, it was evident that they were all more than just practitioners at a gym—they were one big family.

Rory made exponential gains, and Firas spoke about the scary fact that he would not hit his peak for another five to seven years. "When he is twenty-eight or thirty, he will have a tear that will be pretty terrifying. It's going to be something special. Am I putting it that far away? Yes, I am. Yes, he does have that much to learn, and the game has changed. Look at all the best guys, they all started young and have a lot of years. Rory did not start training at Tristar until three or four years ago, full-time. He is still gaining a lot of knowledge. Not to say he won't peak sooner, but I think he will go very far, very fast, and I am always expecting more from him every time."

The big question as to whether the two close friends, GSP and Rory, would fight each other was hard to answer. Firas would never want to see it, and I generally agreed with his view, although the president of the UFC, Dana White, was an advocate of training partners fighting each other for the sake of the sport and for fans. But here I was getting the opposite perspective from Firas. "I feel like I'm the connection between the both of them. It may very well be that they both will be ready to take the same spot at the same time but I don't want them to fight. It has a lot to do with their personal relationship and my personal relationship with them. I feel that it would put me in a position that would be impossible for me. I wouldn't be able to train both guys, and I wouldn't want them to fight without me or against one another. No win for me there." Only time will tell if the fans will see a fight between GSP and Rory MacDonald.

Firas ran a strict camp, very militant, and his students were obedient. When they were not, they did many burpees. During a typical training camp, as each camp was tailored to a specific fighter, everything was done in isolation. Wrestle on one day, box on another, and jiu-jitsu on a separate day, etc. Then, when a fighter was gravitating to one style more than others by picking it up faster, Firas tailored the program to bring the pupil's strengths to bear against the opponent's advantages. By tailoring his pupils' proficiencies to counter his opponent's strengths, he was giving his pupil the advantage.

Firas was kind enough to give me an example in light heavyweight champion Jon Jones. Jones had an incredible gift for striking and used his wrestling in reverse, but when he did take opponents down, he used the ground & pound. He would not mess around with jiu-jitsu by passing the guard or trying fancy chokes. He would choke his opponents once they were beat up and hanging on by a thread, to finish the fight. He always played to his strengths, gravitating to what he did best. "He forces everyone to play his game, that's the bottom line. If you figure out what *your* game is, and try to funnel everyone into that game (you will find success). It's impossible to learn every game out there," Firas pointed out.

I asked Firas how to prevent fighters from overtraining. Firas was brutally honest and told me to give him the formula if I found it. He pointed out that it was one of the hardest things in the trade, determining the right amount of training. Over the years, he was able to eyeball it. He confessed that it took years of experience and no one had come up with an exact science; Firas had definitely done extensive research.

When it came to exercising the secret weapon, the brain, I asked Firas if he had his students practice visualization. He said that among other things, he had his guys write down ten reasons why they would win their next fight. They carried their lists around, looking at it every so often. It would be a compass for the fighters. Examples would include having better takedowns than their opponents, having a better jab, better cardio, and so forth. Whenever his fighters had doubts creep in, they could reaffirm that there was no reason to doubt and brought in "green light" thoughts, as famous sports psychologist Brian Cain introduced to this author. Firas believed it to be a simple but powerful tool, and who could argue with his pupils' track records over the years? Firas exclaimed, "If I look at the paper every time I am nervous or stressed, see why I will win and truly believe it, it will comfort me. I don't want to go through negative thoughts but positive ones. I believe in redirecting the mind to something positive."

Firas clearly had a passion for learning, for MMA, and, most importantly, for his family, which included his students. He truly cared about his fighters' careers and even more so about their thoughts and feelings. His face lit up with pride as his fatherly side started shining through. All of his actions were driven by one question: 'Is it good for my fighter?' If the answer was yes, he would do it; as simple as that. His fighters trusted him, and their needs were his highest priority.

Many trainers did what was good for themselves but not necessarily for their fighters, but Firas knew that in the long run that this attitude would bite them in the ass. Firas believed in building strong relationships with his fighters, although there were times when a fighter would accept his help and then screw him over. He nonchalantly stated that "You raise a snake, he is going to bite you. You just accept the fact that you will get bit. That's life."

We transitioned to another one of Firas' philosophies: the use of pain and consequence. Simply put, "If doing something wrong doesn't hurt, you will keep doing it wrong. I find a way to teach that will lead you to fucking misery and pain if you do it wrong. You will start doing it right all of a sudden, and you will take the time to not cut those corners!"

He gave the example of very obese individuals who do not work at losing the weight, even though being obese is not healthy. However, when their doctor tells them they have six months to live and they have to lose weight immediately to prolong their lives, they suddenly do not touch sugar, they eat healthy, and they exercise because they are scared of pain, scared to die, to take it to the bottom line. They are scared of the negative consequences.

Firas cranks out negative consequences for his fighters, each one tailor-made to each student after identifying their ambitions. Losing a fight would sometimes propel a student a new level. Losing was painful for a number of reasons: prestige, ego, money, position in their division, or internal promises that got broken, all due to one loss.

If Firas wanted to motivate a fighter, he would suggest what might happen in case of poor training that would lead to a loss. He asked them a simple question: "Can you live with it?" The beauty of it was that it worked brilliantly. Firas took advantage of his students' innate ambitions to help them reach their full potential.

The Tristar gym had some of the most strategic fighters in the fight realm; a lot of work went into research and formulating game plans. Firas didn't have a lot of blood & guts fighters, by design. They did not go out and swing for the fences and take a pounding in the process. Firas didn't recommend that style of fighting, but did admit that someone could become a world champion with some level of efficiency, heart, will, and chin, which were all important factors in a fight. Firas believed fighting in a blood & guts manner took away from the science of martial arts. Although blood & guts fighters are some of the most exciting to watch, these fighters have shorter successful careers due to their absorption of a lot more punishment.

I asked Firas to explain the difference between a martial artist and a fighter. When Firas thought of the MMA culture, he didn't really like it; he loves MMA but not the culture. He compared it to an NBA- or NFL-type of culture. "I'm good and you suck. It's got a type of arrogance, trash talking, flaunting of pride with no traditional respect for what you are learning. It is harmful to other people. You have to have respect for knowledge and power. You have to respect that these techniques that we are teaching you are lethal and that you should not use them for the wrong reasons—only for self-defense. That's why we do MMA. We see what really works, and it's a learning experience."

Firas was cognizant of the "wrong reasons" for training. Doing it for glory or to make money moved it away from traditional martial arts culture and toward mainstream sports culture. Firas expressed his fascination with seeing a guy win with an amazing move or superior technique, but not with seeing a guy get messed up in the cage. Firas would find it awe-inspiring when a fighter was efficient; it was admirable to see a fighter with skills and techniques polished to the point where he leveraged his force to a new level of excellence.

Firas was hooked on the science of it, the development of the person achieving new heights of excellence. That's what it should be about. There should be a tremendous respect, and I agreed wholeheartedly with the master sitting across the table from me. He added that "It should be an unwanted side affect that someone got hurt, and if you want to hurt this person, that to me is wrong. It's malicious, it's a vice, it's not a pure heart, it's an evil. Don't get me wrong; if I have a chance to hurt my opponent and finish him, I will, but I would try not hurt him more than I have to."

Before Firas described a new world of fighting and life philosophies for me, I wanted to know what the master strategist, the "Cerebral Lion Tamer," wanted to be remembered for when his era passed. He spoke honestly about wanting to one day develop an innovation, something unique, something so precise it would be a noticeable advancement in martial arts. "Like a scientist discovering something new, like a new algorithm, a new breakthrough, something that has never been done before. I am looking for something … for a break-through that only we do and that I can innovate to the point where I can go around the world teaching it."

The million-dollar question was one that Firas had been asked many times: how did he build his fighters? What was the secret? He always responded that he had to build fighters from within. Firas thoroughly explained it: if a fighter was a pyramid, the first level was motivation.

Firas has known people who tried to reach their goals with all of the necessary know-how. He returned to the example of losing weight; people hired dietitians, had special programs, personal training costing $500 an hour, the priciest machines, and it was all convenient and smart. The problem? They didn't lose weight. On the other side of the spectrum, there were individuals who did not have the know-how, the fancy equipment, yet they possessed motivation. They exercised a little more, ate less, put in the extra hours, and eventually got more out of their workouts than the people who had all the tools. "If you do not have the motivation to do something, even though you have the best method, you won't get it done because you did not do it."

Firas could teach guys some good moves, but they would never become proficient at them if they didn't have the motivation to drill it, to put the game together, which took a fire inside the person that led them to believe that they knew something special but still had to work on it to reach perfection.

Firas enjoyed studying philosophy, and there was one particular story about Aristotle that he shared with me. A child approached Aristotle and said "I want to know the truth. What is the truth?" Aristotle, amused with the child, dunked the child's head into the river and nearly drowned him. He let him live and gave him a chance to catch his breath. Aristotle then told him, "If you want the answer to the question as bad as you wanted air a second ago, come back and I will teach you." The kid just wanted a quick fix, but you have to want it badly. You have to possess a deep-seated desire in order to reach the next level.

As Firas shared this story with me, my mind flashed to prior interviews that had eloquently related similar messages. Firas told the seminar crowd in New York that his teachings were never free, in the sense that he had traveled the world. He put in the blood and sweat to learn these lessons; thus, they were not to be taken lightly, but that students must absorb them and train in the techniques. John Danaher talked about not simply dipping a toe in the art, but becoming fully immersed, in order to be the best. Rashad, Rory, Tomasz, Phil, and Bruno, as well as others, relayed the tremendous work ethic and immeasurable time practicing, necessary to reach the top. Aristotle knew this in the 300s BCE. It wasn't news by any means, but by human nature we must be reminded periodically. The question arises: how badly do you want to know the truth?

To motivate his fighters, Firas would try to give them the opposite of what they already had. If a fighter had a soft life, if his parents paid for everything, and maybe he didn't have to go to school because his parents were wealthy, then Firas would give him hell. He would state how lazy the fighter was and that he had to move and do something positive with his life. If he got a kid who was poor, from a broken home, he would be positive. He would encourage the kids with the fact that he could come out of this, be successful in life, and that the tools given were all he needed. Firas added that "Everyone needs what they do not have, and they do not need what they already have. If a fighter has a lot of yes-men around him, he did not need another one around him, but needed a guy that would cut to the chase and tell the truth."

It all boiled down to Firas' philosophies of training. He really believed that people respond to what they did not have, which was a Socratic idea. Why do people eat that piece of cake instead of staying on the diet? The bottom line is that they want sugar more than they want to look good and be healthy, so Firas followed what students crave the most. He found ways to manipulate it, turning the tables around on their motivation.

The sheer penchant for detail and the hunger for developing knowledge was just the tip of the iceberg that made Firas such a revered world-class trainer. He was a genuine person that embodied that Thai spirit, as he looked to help others not just in the fight realm but spiritually in all aspects of their lives. He understood human nature. In a sport that attracted individuals of all walks of life, backgrounds and thought processes, he could precisely mold them to reach success, starting with the fighter within.

QUICK ROUND
What's your favorite junk food?
Cookies.

If you had a dream match, who would your opponent be in MMA?
Sakuraba, as I respect him and admire him; not for any personal reasons.

If you had a dream match, who would your opponent be in life?
I'd like to get my hands on Hitler.

What's your favorite standup technique?
The jab.

What's your favorite BJJ technique?
The crucifix.

What's your biggest strength?
Being well-rounded.

What would we find in your music playlist?
A lot of audio books, and Pearl Jam.

Who are the three best fighters in the world today?
GSP, Jose Aldo, and Lyoto Machida.

What's your favorite thing to do with your friends and family?
Outdoor activities with my family.

What's one of your favorite movies of all time?
Limitless.

What would we find in your fridge?
Fruit.

Chapter Nineteen

JIU-JITSU PRINCIPLES
By Firas Zahabi

"That which does not kill us makes us stronger."　　　**—Friedrich Nietzsche**

Jiu-jitsu is a philosophy. The guys who invented jiu-jitsu, the first practitioners, were samurai. Capitalizing on specialized tactics and techniques to use their strength more efficiently was the only way they believed that they could beat larger invaders. So if I have X amount of strength, I need to multiply it, gaining the necessary leverage to beat you. If you have X-plus strength, you will beat me every time. The mother principle of jiu-jitsu is maximum efficiency. If I could apply X amount of force to you, how can I get the most out of it? Whenever I teach a class or formulate my curriculum at Tristar, I always try to find the most efficient way to create a change in my fighters' game. What's the most efficient way to achieve our end game?

This is where we differ from good or bad. A lot of people ask is "jumping rope good or bad?" But it's better to think of activities as good, better, and best. I consider jumping rope to be good, but there are many other drills that are better. I don't just settle for what's "good."

I don't want to train in a good way, but in the best way. Training with a purple belt is good, black belt is better, and a world champion black belt is the best. If you hold yourself to their standards, you will get a lot farther than training with lower belts.

Additionally, maximum efficiency is crucial; one must be very critical and ruthless when it comes to eliminating inefficiencies.

The next principle is what the Japanese call *kazushi*, which is a disruption in an opponent's balance. There is a counter to every attack. Theoretically, every time I attack you, you should have a counter. However, if I create *kazushi*, then and only then can I execute a technique that has no counter, because if you are off balance, you cannot counter.

You must recover your balance before reacting. If I pull the rug out from under you, at that moment you are not in contact with the ground anymore, so if I push you in any which way, you are going to fall. This is another guiding principle of jiu-jitsu.

People always come to me with comments such as "I tried this move and it did not work" or "I tried the arm bar and it did not work; I followed it step-by-step." None of the moves "work" in isolation; it's only a combination of moves that gets results. If my opponent blocks the arm bar, I'll attempt a triangle; if the triangle is blocked, I'll attempt an omaplata. After that, I'll go to a sweep, followed by an attempt at a clamp, then a leg lock, and I will keep attacking until you are unable to defend one of these moves. This is the principle of *kazushi*, combining the moves to place your opponent in an off-balance situation.

Kazushi always works. If it doesn't work, it is because you were not able to find the *kazushi*, but it was there. This philosophy must be adopted to achieve the highest level of excellence. Believe the answer is out there, because if you don't believe, you stopped looking.

The next principle is to go with the flow, or "flow with the go," as Rickson Gracie says, a very famous saying. You don't want to go head-to-head, in any situation. If my opponent pushes me and I push him back, I am not using jiu-jitsu. I'm using athleticism or strength. If my opponent pushes me and I pull him, I am using his force to my advantage because I am redirecting his force in the direction that he is already going. It is not going to cost me any energy; in fact, it will be the easiest direction to go in. But of course, I don't want to push his force in the direction he wants it to go. I want to redirect it slightly in a manner that is harmful to him, in order to turn the tables. You can name this philosophy "turning the tables."

This principle is applicable to everyday life. I might want to ask my boss for a raise, but I know he wants to keep his money. We're butting heads; we don't like each other because our interests are not aligned. If I flow with the go, I put my interests in line with those of my boss. I might say something along the lines of "if I reach these quotas, will you agree to fairly increase my pay?" In turn, he will consider that "This guy will bring in a lot more money, but he only wants a little of it. I like that. Now we're best friends, I don't want to fire you, and you are not secretly considering leaving and starting your own business." We are working together, creating a bond and a relationship. One day my boss may ask me to open up another branch somewhere else because he likes and trusts me. That's the type of jiu-jitsu that one can use in the real world.

Go with the flow. You don't want to hit the brakes and push in the other direction. Only the biggest and strongest guy in your field can use this philosophy. It will work if you are Brock Lesnar. If you are not Brock Lesnar, learn jiu-jitsu, and "flow with the go."

The next principle is the principle of leverage. In jiu-jitsu, if you do an arm lock, you isolate the guy's arm from the rest of his body. Think about it, when you do a submission, it is never general; it is specific to a limb. Your whole body is around a limb. If I get my opponent in an arm lock, it's my body against his arm and he will try to desperately bring the rest of his limbs into action, but I have put him into a position where now he can't. His legs are useless, his other arm is useless, and his head and upper body are in a position that doesn't allow him to put his weight on me. He's completely useless; it comes down to me and just his one arm. And that's a type of body chess, just like a great chess player moving in for checkmate; he has used several pieces against the king. The king now is trying to defend against all of these pieces. If there was another piece that came into play to block the checkmate, he doesn't have the checkmate. So, the principle of leverage is multiplying the influence of whatever force I have, and one of the ways I can do that is by isolating a limb, finding the opponent's weak point. Using all of your body and all of yourself on that one point—once you defeat that point, the whole house of cards comes down. If I break my opponent's arm, there is no way he is winning this fight, even if he doesn't tap. We're going to continue fighting and he's missing one arm; the odds sway in my favor so heavily now that the ref will most likely stop the fight.

Another principle is structure versus force. Never use force; use structure. I'm sitting on the chair right now. How much strength and how much muscle does it have? It has no muscle, so how is it holding me up? Why am I not crushing this chair and falling right through it? It is using structure to hold me up, because of its shape.

Whenever I am under my opponent, if I try to push him back, I am violating this rule of jiu-jitsu. Now, I would be using my chest muscles, my ab muscles to hold him up, and that is going to be very taxing on my muscles and not so taxing on him since he is just letting gravity do the work, lying on top trying to smother me. So what I do is make a frame. I put my body in the type of shape so that he is pushing against the strength of my bones, not my muscles. A horse sleeps standing up. How does he get any rest standing up? He actually locks out his knees; he's not using his muscles, his muscles are carrying no specific weight to put his body into a shape. In jiu-jitsu, I am not using force, but another means: structure. My structure can withstand any amount of weight that a human can put on me.

The next principle is to always use the stronger versus the weaker. Whenever I attack, I always use a stronger body part of mine against my opponent's weaker body part. I want to create an unfair advantage. My jiu-jitsu instructor John Danaher always said, "Jiu-jitsu is the art of creating an unfair advantage." If I am in the mount on top, I am in such a strong position and my opponent is in such a weak position that I will make sure that the rest of the battle stays there. If both of us are standing, we are in equal position; I am not using anything stronger against his weaker. If I am fighting, then I am not using jiu-jitsu. I'm fighting from a place that's fair. If I take my opponent's back, I am fighting from a place where I can do so many bad things and my opponent can do nothing but try to improve his position by escaping. That's where jiu-jitsu really takes place, and where it is really powerful. Where I can do so many bad things and my opponent can only do one thing or nothing to me.

In real life, you can think about it, if you're competing with somebody for a position, it might sound devious, but I will be cautious not to show my hand until I become the boss. Then I can show people my ulterior motives. I do not want to give someone the head's up because I want to secure the position. It's about struggling for position; when you get these dominant positions, then and only then can you start to engage in a battle.

Here's a real-life situation: Shooto was a rival grappling art to jiu-jitsu. It was very famous in Japan; their philosophy was submissions, submissions, submissions. Jiu-jitsu's philosophy is to stabilize for a good position and then look for submission. Submission was on the back burner, not the main goal of the art. It was to get to a proper position, a position of leverage and strength, and *then* execute a submission.

Shooto guys were marvelous to watch because every fight would end with a spectacular submission. In the blink of an eye, a submission would occur. However, whenever they would wrestle a submission guy, they would lose consistently until the sport died out because everyone was doing jiu-jitsu. And it wasn't that the moves were different, but that they were organized differently.

It is important to always get leverage first. If I'm competing for the same position as a competitor in the business world, I may need to get outside help and outsource. I am going to get four or five people, maybe even pay them out of my pocket, just to get my work done better than the other guy. Then, when my work is recognized and I become the boss, my former competitor will answer to me and it will probably be like that for the rest of our careers. But I will do what it takes to get that control first.

Chapter Twenty

THE PARADOXICAL LIFE NEEDS THE FIGHTER WITHIN

"The two most important days in your life are the day you are born and the day you find out why."
—Mark Twain

The fighters described in this tome have had to use their emotional and intellectual prowess to beat their opponents and find success. They did so by facing themselves, by not looking to outlast their foes in the ring, but to continuously bring their best qualities to the surface while shoring up their vulnerabilities and limitations. Thus, they created advantageous circumstances when they need it most, making their work seem like art.

That uphill struggle to prepare mentally and physically boils down to a fight that lasts mere minutes, and when your star shines, it is an unsurpassed feeling in life, a flurry of emotions and a state of happiness that can only be achieved when one pushes himself or herself past the red line.

Martial arts are like a jigsaw puzzle; every time you test yourself in the gym and in a match, you uncover another piece of who you are. The feel of the crowd as you throw a strike that lands perfectly, get that takedown slam, or put your opponent in a submission literally leaves the hairs on the back of your neck standing up. Receiving the gold or that championship belt gives you a feeling of accomplishment and shoots confidence straight into your being.

Competition is invigorating, something that has been practiced since the beginning of time, and something that is instilled in us from birth, spurring us forward in the early grades at school, through sports, and beyond. As human beings, we are programmed with many different skills, and if we can capitalize on those skills to increase our potential, we are one step closer to being complete and happy.

Some people gain a toehold in business and go on to own multi-billion dollar companies at an early age, while others have an athletic edge and pursue martial arts on the world stage, bringing us some of most awe-inspiring matches we could ever dream of. Mixed martial arts are not biased in race, gender, age, or wealth. We all have a fight in life, a cross to bear, and how you approach this can result in a great outcome for your life and for your happiness.

All of the champions described in this book learned to surround themselves with the right individuals who would foster a positive atmosphere and be there for them. The right coaches, nutritionist, massage therapist, lawyer, doctor, family, friends, and even sponsors all contribute to their success. Sponsors such as LIUNA are invaluable as they support fighters and their careers with a network of over 500,000 members in North America. I asked why such a large labor union would sponsor fighters, and business manager Jim MacKinnon replied, "We fight for the well-being of our members, as they also generally watch MMA and are fans. We are simply responding to their desires and wishes, we like supporting winners who acknowledge and support our union."

It was only during the conclusion of my journey for this book that I had an epiphany. Many thanks to Firas Zahabi, who brought this initial thought to the surface and who beat me over the head with it. The thought had been present in the back of my mind for a long time, but required excavation. The life stories and paths to success of the fighters could be emulated in the business world, which mirrored the fighters' success. There is something to be said about the strength that comes through a struggle with an overabundance of adversity, which can give the upper hand. There are many underdog movies produced for a reason; there is nothing exciting about traveling a short distance with little effort and with predetermined advantages in life. The opposite is quite thrilling. Many individuals strive toward their goals only to fumble and give up, so those that become triumphant after having to endure trials and tribulations are revered, and rightfully so.

Most fighters that reached the epitome of success did not have broken homes; they had not been beaten or neglected during their childhoods, contrary to what the stereotypes suggest. The commonality was that they had obstacles to overcome and they yearned for what they did not have. They had a black hole that only grew bigger when they fed it. They had a deeply rooted inclination to succeed and win. That is desire that others may not have. Creativity is not just for fighting, but it's for life in general. When he was younger, Ajarn Phil Nurse psychologically bested his peers by making them believe his plastic shoes were better because he easily outran them and manipulated them into buying the cheaper sneakers he wore; he could not afford the expensive shoes. These sparks of greatness had been instilled by the classic variables of nature and nurture. It was the environment and experiences as well as hereditary gifts that produced these legends.

In its simplest form, they all embarked on the journey of life to reach their goals and find happiness. They pressed forward even when facing obstacles. They were not perfect and made mistakes, but were astute enough to learn from them. They made thousands of mistakes in the gym so that they would not make them in the cage. They assessed the best route and passed those obstacles by going under them, over them, around them, or through them. They did not have leverage or any significant advantages. However, they took chances when opportunities presented themselves and created openings through hard work and smart approaches. What I slowly came to realize was that they are all like you and I. We all have the same opportunities for success, and if we capitalize on them, we, too, will reach our goals, whatever they may be.

Fighting could be construed as one of the most metaphorical experiences out there, and is relatable to all of life. A fighter has to face theirself during their most powerful and most vulnerable times, constantly working on peculiarities while striving for perfection. Fighting speaks to the human experience, as every day is a new journey filled with a spiral of emotions, such as pride, fear of the unknown, relief, disappointment, growth, and the use of a creativity that bring us closer to our goals. The experience in itself is a mix of rewards that leave the practitioner filled with a sense of accomplishment at the end of a hard work day. Just like in any high-stress job, taking chances and fear are regular feelings that creep up on the best of us; what is important is how we approach those feelings.

Any successful businessman or world champion described in this book has had to not only surpass those feelings, but also use them to their advantage. Rashad Evans was astute enough to bring his concerns before seasoned veteran Randy Couture right before his epic fight against Chuck Liddell. After their talk, Rashad changed his approach for the biggest fight of his career. He stopped worrying about all the "what ifs," and used his fear to produce one of the nastiest knockouts in UFC history and claim his right to be counted among the best in the world. A range of emotions usually swirl in the pit of my stomach before something great is about to happen because only important events cause those butterflies. And by the time I get those emotions, I am at the point where I know that I have done everything in my power to produce such a magic moment.

The same character traits and dexterity necessary to be successful in martial arts are also needed in one's professional life. How could a world champion Thai boxer run such a successful gym in New York as Ajarn Phil did? How could a UFC champion help create a revolutionary training mask, at one point operate a successful flooring business and write articles in his spare time as Sean Sherk did? The answer is simple: they used the teachings passed on to them by their coaches, parents, and even opponents to create greatness. They had strong will and the endless fire of ambition, which were used effectively in the most difficult of moments, but they learned from their own mistakes and, more importantly, from the mistakes of others, as they transcended in all fields pursued. Importantly, their successes did not come without effort.

Sean Sherk was in the same position as mine in life, in the sense that the harder he tried, the more he found himself descending rather than ascending to success. Rashad

Evans asked himself what he had done to deserve such a hard path in life when he was younger. I, too, was in a dark place in my paradoxical existence. Like Ajarn Phil Nurse, I decided that my spiritual and life journey would be devoted to finding success in the fighting world.

One night, while struggling to find direction, I sat alone before being consoled by my wife. I prayed to our maker, humbled by his power to intervene, as my path in life was completely skewed. I was a shell of a man, my soul was tainted, and my mind was burned out. I asked God, "There is more for me to do in this life to positively affect others, right? When will this nightmare end?" It was the second time in my life that I hosted a personal pity party, looking for an end to the struggles.

Shortly after beginning my tenure at the factory, I was enrolled in night school with hopes of one day getting more out of life. I enjoyed the complexities of my studies, learning about the various areas of psychology and business. Once the factory closed its doors, however, another struggle rose to the fore following my certification from Athletic Performance Inc. It was a tough market in Southwestern Ontario, and it was difficult to get a job paying as much as the factory, but I kept my chin up.

I began working for a large banking institution in the city, besting 800 others to win a spot on the team. I had won customer care awards and other managers asked me to sit with their teams so that others could emulate my skills. The trick was that I had compassion, which wasn't a marketing tactic, but it was the same character trait that allowed me to be part of the company. However, selling products that people didn't need was not for me, especially during a recession. For the first time since I was a newcomer to the labor market at twelve years of age, I decided to carve my own path elsewhere. I followed my heart and I quit.

Yet again, I was looking for work in a market that was saturated with minimum pay and openings that paid even half of what I used to make at the factory were scarce. I bounced around to different housing construction jobs that were heavy in the labor department, without a lot of opportunity for cognitive functioning. It was the story of my life: it was hard to find the balance or the happy medium, yet I pushed forward.

When work with one builder slowed because of declining sales, I would find myself laid off again, and then again. The prospect of sitting at home with no income, bills piling up, and a severe need to do something great led to my decline. It was hard on both the ego and the soul to constantly give 100% while getting very little back. It was tough living from paycheck to paycheck; my wife and I couldn't go out to do anything fun. Half the time, I was too tired to peel myself off the couch after days lasting more than twelve hours.

I had a thick skin; I could handle many things in life. The problem was that I had been living on the edge for too long. It was an accumulation of years of not knowing my place in life; I progressed through my life, I was unable to strike out in a new direction to pursue the balance I desperately needed. I came to understand the feeling of putting all the loose change in the house together to buy our groceries. After many years, things finally began to change.

I managed to step into the executive director role for a few months for a non-profit organization that I volunteered for, as I had free time. This opportunity turned out to be a godsend. This was an opportunity to put my skills on display. I rocked the role with ambition, creativity, and hard work. Within a very short time, I was rubbing elbows with city councilors, the mayor, members of provincial parliament, and members of national parliament. My hard work was my business card, and the entire city would see my abilities. Due to our bylaws regarding volunteer board members, I was unable to stay in the role full-time, but midway through my tenure another tragedy struck my family.

My proudest day was when my wife was beaming with excitement, telling me that I was going to be a father. Things seemed to finally be falling into place, but the dark clouds were still around us. We were trying to get caught up with the bills as quickly as possible, but the transition period between the labor job and office occupation hurt. We also found ourselves being taken advantage of for our good intentions. It pained me to watch my wife go through this while pregnant, able to do nothing to alleviate the situation. A month later, we went through a crisis when my wife miscarried; a massive pall of devastation covered us.

Shortly after my eight-month tenure, I found myself working for a local city councilor. Within a few months, I worked for a member of Provincial Parliament, which was the big league of politics. The clouds had parted and the beam of light I had dreamed about was finally shining, life was good. I had a bigger podium at which to stand, while helping others going through tough times. I came from a blue-collar background and earned two college diplomas while working full-time. I did not have a university degree, I did not come from money, and I did not have a shred of political experience. But I fought and crawled my way up, I used my wits, I read and upgraded myself continuously, I devoted a lot of time volunteering to help others, and I had formed city-wide connections. All of this was accomplished by staying true to myself and maneuvering at a continuous pace while pushing forward, knowing it would take us somewhere good.

My fight instincts had pushed me through a dark world, though not unscathed. I wore my warrior wounds with pride. I felt like I had climbed Mount Everest, battling through the difficult conditions and all that could be thrown at me, short of a falling piano. Truth be told, I had scaled a medium-size peak; there is always more fight left, more mountains to traverse. My appetite for success had only grown more insatiable. This was not attained quickly. While others camped at the base of the mountain, I carved my own path, chasing the legends through sleet and snow. I made life-long friends during this journey. I grew as a fighter and as a martial artist, and gained a lifetime of experience. I can only show my appreciation by passing it on. My fuel has always been my family;

I kept the pace as others slept. I made plenty of mistakes, and I now know to smell the flower along the way, as Rich Franklin had reminded me to do. It is much too crowded at the base of the mountain; in life, the fruits are found on the mountaintop. Thus, I encourage everyone reading this to accompany me to the top. We all have a fighter within. No one said that life is a bed of roses.

Much of the wisdom found within this book is from wiser and more experienced people than I, which can and should be applied to daily life and in one's career. Some teachings may seem new, but they have been passed on for generations because they are warrior-tested and perfected. One thing is for certain: it takes the application of our gifts to be successful. Joe Ferraro, host of *UFC Central*, gave a remarkable example.

"When I first got into this business, I was working at a call center while building this career here. Surely, I stayed away from promotions while working for the cable company. I did not want to be promoted because then I would have to manage a team and would thus not focus on the career that I am doing right now. There were times that I would end a nine-to-five shift, race to be at the airport by 8:00 p.m. in order to get to Montreal by 9:30 p.m. Then, I would step into a recording booth at the studio at midnight, and start doing voiceovers and play-by-play commentary for some of the fights. Like, basically live to tape and staying in Montreal until 6:00 a.m., make it to the airport, and make it back to Toronto, drive to where I was working, step into the shower at the gym, and get right back to doing it all over again. It was basically balancing two working careers for about ten years until I was finally able to do what I wanted to do. It was a lot of work and a lot of hours. I don't want to get to deep into it, but there were times I almost lost everything I owned, my wife and family, because they gave up on it a long time ago, but it was something I really believed in and wanted to do, and now everyone is reaping the benefits."

Joe went on to host a leading UFC show, and today he is the personality for a leading MMA radio show, as well as a supporter of amateur MMA and grassroots MMA in Ontario, as this is important for the development of Canadian athletes. He is also a certified referee and judge under big John McCarthy. The most important accomplishment, though, is that he is doing what he loves to do and has a loving family that put in a lot of strategic effort to juggle life's responsibilities.

The definition of "vocation," which is derived from Latin, means "a strong desire to spend your life doing a certain kind of work," according to Webster's dictionary (http://www.merriam-webster.com/dictionary/vocation). It is of vital importance to understand this definition, even at its basic level. It is something that has been lost during this day and age when humans seem to be more detached from each other and, more importantly, themselves.

A fast-paced world is very competitive, and technology does make our lives easier, but it is important to build ourselves from within, as Firas Zahabi, the head trainer/part owner of Tristar gym, expressed. Only then will we understand what our true calling is in life, what field we are destined for—instead of swearing every time the clock inches closer to the start of our shifts at work; been there and done that. We should find enlightenment and joy in what we do for our vocation. I mean, we spend enough time geared toward our employers and our work duties. All of the fighters and coaches in this book expressed their gratitude in finding their vocation, but for most of them it took a long time and a lot of effort to get there.

First and foremost, the path to your destination must be laid out as soon as possible after identifying the destination. What are your short-term goals? What are your medium-range goals and what do you imagine is your grand finale of goals? Dream big, be bold, but remember that reaching higher means that there will be more goals between your start line and your final goal. Each will be difficult, but attainable, and will propel you closer to the next.

Create a flip chart, and re-examine it when you need motivation. Firas asked his fighters to write down why they would win their match; do the same for every one of your goals and keep it in your wallet. Look at it for inspiration when necessary. Keep a how-to bible just like one of my coaches, Jeff Joslin, did, which reached over 700 pages. Your page count may not be as high as his was, but keep it for refreshment in your business tasks as well.

The importance of preparation cannot be overstated. Whether at school or sitting in an office, there is a certain amount of work required to be the best. Matt Hughes spoke about the importance of outworking others. That means preparing for a meeting or going the extra mile for an exam; as hard as it is, suck it up and follow through.

Balance in life is another key ingredient to success and happiness, as demonstrated by Professor Fernandes. He is a busy man, but always makes time for his family and for doing what he loves while detaching from the rat race, by taking surf trips around the world. He is definitely onto something; find a hobby such as martial arts or do something with your family to detach from the "real world." Walt Disney once stated, "A man should never neglect his family for business."

A good work ethic coupled with sacrifice is the next step to success. All of the fighters and coaches described have an excellent work ethic. Sean Sherk was known to practically live in the gym as he outworked his peers to reach success in a very competitive field. With this slow economy, as I search for employment, any job that pays more than minimum wage seems to be dreadfully competitive; thus, the work ethic is important for getting to the front of the pack. Everyone has been in a situation that could result in an improved situation only to get thrown curve balls. Whether you start a business or complete a job that doesn't go right, things can get tougher before getting better; remember this and keep trudging forward.

World-famous Muay Thai master and mentor of Ajarn Phil Nurse, Master Sken, said that "All people have within them the seeds of immense greatness. All you need to do is water them regularly."

Making sacrifices along the way goes hand-in-hand with success. Tomasz Adamek uprooted himself from his comfortable life, from a world he grew up in, to move thousands of miles away for training. Rashad Evans spoke about crucial time sacrifices, like missing his baby's first steps while attempting to reach his success. Sometimes, getting out of that comfort zone and sacrificing is dependent upon the prize, but it is something that comes with the territory.

The loophole to hard work is smart work, as Firas kindly mentioned in Chapter 19, "Jiu-Jitsu Principles." Do not be scared to use all resources and connections at your disposal. This is related to preparation; be smart with your game plans in life, business, and finances. Planning work in the preliminary stages only makes it easier to execute in the action stages. Fighters go through hell in the cage in training sessions so that they do not have to go through it during a bout. If you are looking to move up the corporate ladder and have some stiff competition, do not be afraid to outsource items, use your contacts, or pay now to perfect your work so that you do not have to pay later as your career suffers. Use your mind and psychology to work in your favor, as famous sports psychologist Brian Cain stated, "It's the six inches between the ears that control the six feet below them."

Find time to take care of yourself and keep healthy. You can easily maximize your productivity and alertness by working out on a regular basis. Just as inevitable as taxes are, stress will creep up on you when you least expect it. Working out some of that aggression by going for a run or hitting the punching bag while envisioning your boss's face plastered square in the middle of the bag will make a world of difference. Whatever floats your boat, just keep physically fit with proper exercise, adequate sleep patterns, and a healthy, balanced diet.

Never give up when you get knocked down. Tomasz Adamek is a real-life version of Rocky Balboa, who had the heart of a lion. No matter how many punches he absorbed, he rolled with them and kept coming back to succeed and win. Many people have lost their businesses since the recession began, and even more have been laid off from work. Using a can-do attitude and being creative with a well-thought out approach is key. Over the past ten years, I have personally endured the closure of my family business and tasted the bitterness of long layoffs six times. At the beginning, I took it personally. But I learned to use the layoffs as opportunities to gain momentum that could be used to my advantage. Do not turn back because you never know how close you really are to reaching your goals; keep at it. Richard Branson, the founder of Virgin Group, eloquently stated that "Business opportunities are like buses; there's always another one coming."

You will go much further by listening to the experience of individuals wiser than yourself, rather than going it alone. Having a mentor, especially when starting out in any given field, will only bring positivity to your working career. Rory MacDonald understood that he needed to join a world-class facility with the best coaches available, including Firas Zahabi and John Danaher, to take him to the next level. Find a mentor in your field and see if that person can take you under his or her wing, as learning from your mistakes could be a life-long journey. However, having someone show you how to do something right the first time is invaluable. Keep growing your network to include good positive people.

Martial artist, businessman, stuntman, and actor Alain Moussi (who plays the lead role in the 2015 *Kickboxer* remake and has done stunt work on feature films such as *Immortals, White House Down, Pacific Rim, Warcraft* and many more) personally detailed his thoughts of mentorship to this author, "I think that mentorship is something that many people forget. I think in martial arts you are always with a mentor, you are always working with a teacher so you get into that mode, that lifestyle of having someone show you the ropes. If you want to get into marketing and you want to open a business, well, you find the best marketer ever, which should open your eyes to what the possibilities are. Maybe you talk to individuals you believe are successful. When I was looking to open up a dojo (NX Martial Arts in Ottawa), I knew a lot of individuals who had very successful dojos, so I talked to them. Tons to know, not to reinvent the wheel but to try to avoid the mistakes that they made and to move forward faster."

MMA analyst Joe Ferraro also added, "I'm a firm believer that the wheel is already invented and that there is no point in reinventing the wheel. I got to where I am by looking at the best people in the industry and creating my own mixed martial arts persona in terms of being an analyst and television & radio host. People that have had success are perfect examples for you to follow and emulate, and then carve your own niche. A model is there for anyone to be successful, but it is up to you to choose which path you desire." Sound familiar?

The way you approach life is very important, as negative thoughts or "red light" thoughts, as famous sports psychologist Brian Cain calls them, will only hold you back. Because our minds typically adhere to one line of thought, make it positive. Alain Moussi strongly believes in keeping the focus on positivity as much as possible as well; there is not much use for negativity, it is a poison.

Remember that you are as powerful as you want to be, and do not let others walk over you unless it is part of your strategy. Ajarn Phil would fall back as if he was hurt in a fight to plant the seed into his opponent's mind for only a second before springing up like a cat in psychological combat with his opponent. The working world is difficult; in fact, it can be tougher than a fight because at least in a fight, you know that your opponent is trying to render you unconscious or make you tap. The professional world can be more devious because you do not know the motives of your co-workers or how they may be plotting to step over you to climb the corporate ladder. All of the fighters mentioned in the book are personable, humble, and caring, but they all have that psychological switch that brings out their primal instincts; it is scary enough to let others know not to flip the nuclear switch or else all hell will break loose, then the monster within will be released. No one wants that.

Rashad Evans would release his inner beast, "Sugar" during his bouts, and we all have something similar inside. Be confident, plant your own seeds to success, and keep that fire lit in your eyes to let others know not to cross you in the wild kingdom of life. Fedor Emelianenko ruled with an iron fist, he let his display of skills strike fear into others, and had an air of mystery around him, which made others think twice. Scott and Matt from API took no bullshit from others, but at the same time helped individuals that wanted to be helped, such as family. Your edge must be displayed to cause others to think twice before considering crossing you, even if it is to just steal your pen. It can be a dog-eat-dog world, and pens go missing all the time!

Believe in yourself and that you will indeed achieve your dreams. They wouldn't be called dreams if they were easy to attain. Rashad Evans discussed the importance of believing in yourself to the point of almost being delusional. Do not get caught up in what others have to say, just stay focused on what you have to do. In the end, that is what you have control over. Napolean Hill, one of the greatest writers on the genre of personal success, was quoted as saying, "Whatever the mind of man can conceive and believe, it can achieve. Thoughts are things! And powerful things at that. When mixed with certainty of purpose, and burning desire, thoughts can be translated into riches."

There is an easy transition to integrate BJJ's strategy into the business world as Firas pointed out. Alain Moussi expressed his love of the line of attack and tactics. "Brazilian Jiu Jitsu…. [grinning] I love the strategy, I love the idea that you can beat somebody by suckering them into something. You lead them into what they think is good and bam, you got them and that's it, they are tapping out." Use your brain power and strategize your line of attack well, just as Fedor also pointed out.

A factor that many people seem to ignore is the importance of having an outwardly professional appearance in public. Rashad Evans was known for wearing business suits to interviews and post-fight conferences. He projected a very professional and respectable image not just for himself (each fighter is really a brand of their own), but for the company he worked for, the UFC. He showed respect for the reporters and the fans, putting his best foot forward.

In the business world, make sure your tie is properly tied, your shirt is tucked in, and, for the females, that your skirt is ironed with clean edges. Change your look in increments regardless of whether you are already working or still looking for work. Keep people guessing about your personality and depth. Create an image that is respectable, intriguing, and masterful. We are all performers on the grand stage of life.

Joe Ferraro has a lot of thoughts on public image. "I think image is the most important thing in anyone's career, especially when you have kids involved and especially if you are, like myself, in the public eye. It's not just keeping a clean image, but doing the right things. Another thing is protecting that image. You're going to get haters, but that is irrelevant. I encourage debate. I want a clean image for a purpose. I want to be a great example for my son."

As we grow older, we also tend to move farther away from our youthful inclinations, we generally become numb to our surroundings when dealing with hardships. Many people turn to drugs, alcohol, or risky activities to amplify certain aspects of our lives, even if just for a minute. I agree that, with the given poor state of the global economy and the fast-paced everyday rat race, we can put a lot of pressure on ourselves to succeed and live prosperous lives. The truth lies in balance in life, and as Rich Franklin intelligently added, by enjoying the journey in life as we progress through it, both the highs and the lows. The hardships are times that we will one day reflect on and reminisce about, remembering how great they were and how we got past those barriers, even when it seemed impossible.

I learned how to live off of a few dollars at a time and made do at parts in my life without knowing from where or when more money would be coming. Looking back, it now seems like an entertaining movie, and I am proud to say that I moved past those hard times and that Beata and I are about to welcome a small bundle of joy into our family. Today, I believe it added to my character, as I know where I came from and I know who is on my side. Through the difficult times, I found out who had my best interests at heart and who did not.

Another variable I noticed that brought a heightened sense of clarity and happiness was the power of harnessing creativity to our advantage. Ajarn Phil mastered this element, revealed through his confidence and kind approach toward others. He did not conform to societal rules nor did he imprison his creativity in exchange for conservatism by not taking chances, but instead chose to take the difficult path by unleashing his true self on the world. If we consistently cage our creativity, as I did while working in the factory, we begin to feel dead inside; a numb blanket spreads over our souls as our minds stop producing the aspects that help us thrive as humans, inside and out.

Ajarn Phil Nurse spoke about Jon Jones harnessing a strong quality of creativity and that he saw that extreme potential long before he became the most feared fighter in the UFC light heavyweight division. By using creativity and being immersed in that process, we become more alive, and our own misconceptions of ourselves get thrown away. We utilize a deeply rooted strength that we all possess. We begin to evolve as better versions of ourselves by working on creativity, like a muscle, getting stronger with each use. The creativity also detaches us from the rest of the pack, which could include co-workers or opponents during our fights, and people will definitely take positive notice.

Bruce Lee is often considered to be one of the first pioneers of MMA by not focusing on one discipline but by utilizing his strong creativity and imagination to train in many art forms, as well as creating his own style by taking the strong points from everything he had learned. All brilliant minds have utilized this creative potential to their favor, so do everything in your power to bring yourself into that open state of consciousness and tap your God-given resources to work for you. Best of all, it doesn't cost you anything in monetary terms, just some time and focus.

Seeing these artists create a powerful portrait for their adoring fans using their fight skills as "paintbrushes" was fascinating. I found the preparation even more mesmerizing, as I noticed another key quality that actually prevented their creativity from becoming rigid. They all had the drive to reach perfection, harnessing the right environment to keep their creativity in an operational state, which helped it constantly flourish. Over time and with enough practice in our given fields, we can begin to evolve these strengths to suit our spirit. Fedor spoke about feeling the punch; feel your work and creativity as it becomes one with you.

As for the fighter within, we must learn when to unleash our aggression and when to tame it. The personality we project to the world is paramount to reaching our goals and finding success in life. Each and every individual listed in this book has showed their charismatic and caring ways in multiple forms. They all have an aura that draws positivity toward them, an undeniable attraction with a life force that puts a smile on people's faces. That is strongly needed in almost any job field, as we are creatures of interaction and undoubtedly need a charismatic way to interact with people.

So how can one turn the other cheek to negativity or change negativity into something that is pure and tranquil? Experiences and life journeys help us reveal and understand ourselves. Your inner fighter comes from the basis of your deep psyche. It communicates to the outside world through creativity and uniqueness, and constantly functions subconsciously. Use your emotional intelligence as Fedor Emelianenko and Rory MacDonald did, turn the negativity into something positive. So what can you do? Stay true to yourself and let your creativity soar while playing the game; don't let others change you, as only you can give them the power to do that.

I changed throughout my journey, which was a positive indicator that I am moving in the right direction. I wholeheartedly tried to use the teachings from these wise individuals and from every interaction and interview. They helped me in my personal life, fighting life, and business life. Looking back, while I was sitting at the dirty breakroom picnic table at the factory and dreaming about MMA, I would have never believed that I would reach success or party and hang with my MMA idols. I worked hard, volunteering my time and working on my craft for years, while taking chances at any smart opportunity that I created. Notice the last sentence: I had to help create many opportunities by asking, working, and having many doors shut on me, but I continuously pressed on knowing that I would eventually get my way. Just like an investigator, I pried deep and put the formulas and teachings to the test; not surprisingly, they worked, and I hope they work for you as well.

Take a deep look inside yourself. Be honest with what you see. How strong is your fighter within? Do you see something extraordinary there? If not, look deeper, it is there simmering within you, ready to be unleashed. What legacy do you want to leave behind in this world? Now is the time to make the positive change. Get out of your comfort zone and start your unique transformation now to be the best version of yourself, and that will be more than enough to get you into the realm of greatness. Use the jiu-jitsu principles as described by Firas Zahabi, they truly work.

You must be willing to go to war, day in and day out, to be the best in your field. The fighters that we idolize all go through personal and physical battles leading up to the spectacle that we all watch. But know this: the hardest part is preparation as you juggle challenges to find your style and the system that works. There will always be a battle brewing, so become a warrior and make it a part of your daily job to demolish obstacles placed in your way.

I hope that these individual journeys inspire others. Use this inspiration to your advantage, do something positive with your life now, and go out there and show the world what you are made of. Do not wait for tomorrow, as tomorrow you have another goal to look forward to. Train hard, work hard while utilizing the power of mind, and bring yourself to your A-game, to a point that you can honestly look in the mirror and state with confidence that, "I am doing everything within my power to be the best that I can be, and that is enough because my fighter within is strong!"

As my idol, the great Bas Rutten says, "Godspeed and party on!"

Acknowledgments

This tome, just as much as my life, could not have been a success without a plethora of the most amazing individuals that have supported me, taught me valuable knowledge and bestowed the strength to persevere and reach unfathomable goals, I could not have done it without all of you. I would like to thank my mom, Elizabeth Olech, for instilling all that is good and helping build my fighter within from an early age, I miss you. My loving wife, Beata Bartnik for being by my side through thick and thin, I would not be the man I am without your love and unwavering support, I love you. My son, Christopher Olech Jr., who is an angel sent to our lives from Heaven, has only brightened our lives tenfold to perfection. Irena and Bruno Bartnik for being my second parents and giving me the opportunities to pursue my dreams, regardless how grand they may have seemed at the beginning.

My brother Greg Bartnik, none of this would have been possible without you by my side, and we would not have had all the stories to share, even though some might not have seemed funny at the time. I apologize on the record for the tight spots I put you into in the past … and the future. Also a sincere thank you to Jeff Phillips and Brydon Siberry for always having my back. Saba and Spotty, you will always be in my heart.

All of the individuals throughout my journey have showed their caring nature, unveiled their innermost secrets and dug from the recesses of their souls. They provided their valuable time, sometimes hours and hours-worth, well into the night, granting me the honor of sharing their inspiration and knowledge. It has been a true honor and responsibility I take seriously, as their raw stories are invaluable given all they had go through to learn those lessons and philosophies. They may not realize it but it has brought out the best in me during this spiritual journey.

With all the respect in the world, I would like to thank my idol, the modern day gunslinger, Bas Rutten for the support, help and inspiration long before we even met. The creation of your foreword for this book and the opportunity to meet and learn from you truly means the world to me. On a side note, I learned that you missed Dan Henderson's gym opening in order to attend my interview with you. Once again, words cannot express how much it means for a young hungry lion like myself trying to make it in the world to receive such a helping hand from "The King" himself, my sincerest thanks.

Through so many teachings, I can proudly state that I have learned from one of the greatest minds, in sport, business and spirituality. Firas Zahabi; you are an inspiration and I cannot thank you enough for all that you have done for me, even changing the course of this entire book with your amazing knowledge. Your teachings on the Jiu Jitsu Principles is something I utilize every day.

Through a few sit-downs, including one running past midnight after a long day, Rashad Evans: I cannot thank enough for your inspiration, time and friendship. Your insight into the world of fighting is raw and passionate, it has only increased my love of the game. Your kindness and generosity has made a large impact in my life, I am rooting for your second UFC title win my friend!

Thank you Fedor Emelianenko for your time, kindness and inspiration. Having watched your fights, glued to the television screen, I cannot wait for your strong run after a three year retirement. It is an honor to share your story and learn from the pound from pound best.

Everyone at Tuttle Publishing for having faith in me, my work and my stories, and for putting up with my phone calls and penchant for detail—that goes to almost everyone else, too. Amanda

Meyer who is a whiz at editing, God knows I gave you work. Also Dave Rino for the amazing promo photo work and my lawyer Rod Refcio.

All the amazing individuals that have provided their stories and inspired me on the television screen and in person including Sean Sherk, John Danaher, Matthew Olson, Scott Ramsdell, Bruno Fernandes, Rich Franklin, Rory MacDonald, Jean-Charles Skarbowsky, Jeff Joslin, Rafał Chwałek, Jorge Britto, Joe Ferraro, Kru Mel Bellissimo, Brian Cain, Mike Smith, Chris Horodecki, Chris Clements, Mark Hominick, Alain Moussi, Ajarn Phil Nurse and Tomasz Adamek, sharing your compassion and clever reflections are just two of the deeds I will pass along to others. With some of your stories planned for my second book, I am truly blessed to have been in the presence of you all.

I would like to thank Ryan Loco for the amazing photo contributions of Rashad Evans for the cover and inside of the book, I aspire to take one photo near your caliber of quality, one day with infinite practice. As well, Hector Quintero for the Fedor Emelianenko photo contributions on the back cover and inside the book, we went through a lot to capture those shots, but we did the impossible brother! As a shameless plug, I would like to thank Hector for your friendship and partnering to create a one of a kind MMA documentary together, visit www.thefighterproject.com.

With a project spanning eight years, there has truly been an army of amazing individuals I must thank. If I missed anyone, please forgive me, I was choked out in today's BJJ class and will use the lack of oxygen to my brain as an excuse. Thank you: Mookie Alexander, Jason Bechard, Alan Belcher, Fateh Belkalem, Robert Bellamy, Roger Bloodworth, Joe Botnick, Jeff Cain, Phoenix Carnevale, Elias Cepeda, Marc Cessford, Conner Cordova, Glen Cordoza, Michael Costa, Donovan Craig, Spencer Cunningham, Tom DeBlass, Chris Doucette, Brian J D'Souza, Marcelo Dunlop, Chad Elliott, Andrzej Fonfara, Lance Foreman, Bear Frazer, Yoram Gazit, Thomas Gerbasi, Michal Gladysz, James Haourt, Kirik Jenness, Jon Jones, Master Sken Kaewpadung, Rob Kaman, Jason Kelly, Mike Kogan, Kevin Leeuwestein, Sean Lennon, Dean Lister, David Loiseau, Glen Mackenzie, Natalie Madej, Demian Maia, Damon Martin, Ryan McKinnell, Lex McMahon, PNut Nalls, Val Opolinski, Stephan Quadros, Josh Rapport, Marta Rawicz, Bobby Razak, Tony Reid, Zofia and Edward Ring, Charles Ruocco of mmacanada.net, Michael Schiavello, Ane Schwanck, Mark Sementilli, Matt Serra, Ken Shamrock, Jeff Sherwood, Master Peter Sisomphou, Renato Sobral, J.T. Stewart, Mike Straka, Master Toddy, Chris Toplack, Frank Trigg, Eric Wong, Karim Zidan and Jerry Ziler.

The support from my sponsors has been absolutely special, I would not have been able to conclude this journey and project without your help. LIUNA (Laborers' International Union of North America) has been a tremendous help, special thanks to Howie Brox and all the hardworking men and women throughout all the locals. Perfect Image Studio with the best tattoo work, thank you Kfir Ohayon and Jesse Smith. The amazing Lumiere Place Hotel and Casino with a warm thank you to all the staff who helped a lot, including Johnny Lewis. Five Star Dealers in London Ontario and Les McEwen as well as Pump'd Supplements in London Ontario and Scott Milne. Thank you to Gracie Magazine as well as Ane Scwanck and Marcelo Dunlop. The beautiful Mohegan Sun with a special thank you to Cody Chapman. Thank you to Gus Dupuis and the staff at Sutherlands Furniture. Thanks to Gordy from Gordy's Brewhouse, Chad Macaulay, Stephen Marco and Jeff Kubisch of Future Freedom Group and Rick and Linda McMullin of Ricky Ratchets Auto Repair.

Christopher Olech's Corporate Sponsorship